FROM THE ELBE
TO THE RIO GRANDE

*My Jewish Family in Germany and
the United States*

April, 2020
To my dear friends,
Nancy & Steve,
Olga

FROM THE ELBE TO THE RIO GRANDE

My Jewish Family in Germany and the United States

1845–2021

BY
OLGA BORNSTEIN WISE

Austin, Texas
2021

Published by Olga Bornstein Wise.

Available on Lulu.com Bookstore.

Unless otherwise noted, any and all translations from the German language to English are by Olga Bornstein Wise.

Book and cover design by Sara Rubinett.

ISBN: 978-0-578-33975-7

Front cover: Clara Bornstein holds baby Aaron, on the bank of the Mississippi River near St. Louis, 1947.

We all come from the past, and children ought to know what it was that went into their making to know that life is a braided cord of humanity stretching up from time long gone, and that it cannot be defined by the span of a single journey from diaper to shroud.

Russell Baker, *Growing Up*, 1982

TABLE OF CONTENTS

FAMILY TREE

Clara's Löwenstein Family Tree
as of July 1979

Emmi/Emmy Hüneberg Löwenstein's Children:

Clara 1909–1988 El Paso, Texas

Hans Joachim 1911–1950 Buffalo, N.Y.

Emmi is the German spelling for Emmy. Emmy is
used most frequently in this book.

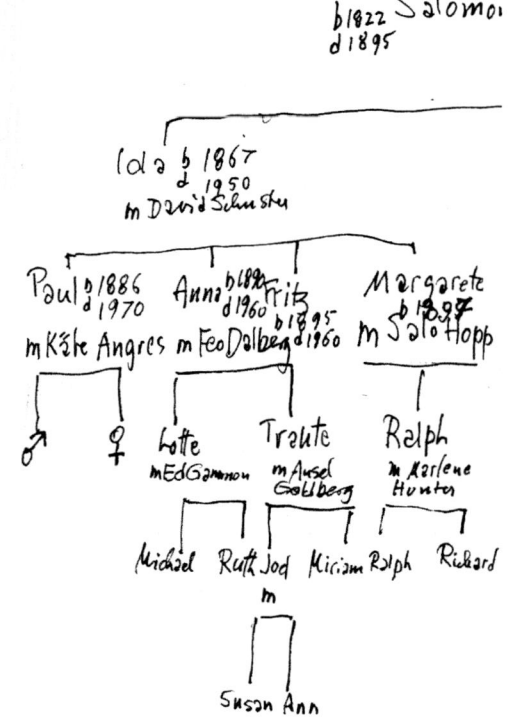

FAMILY TREE

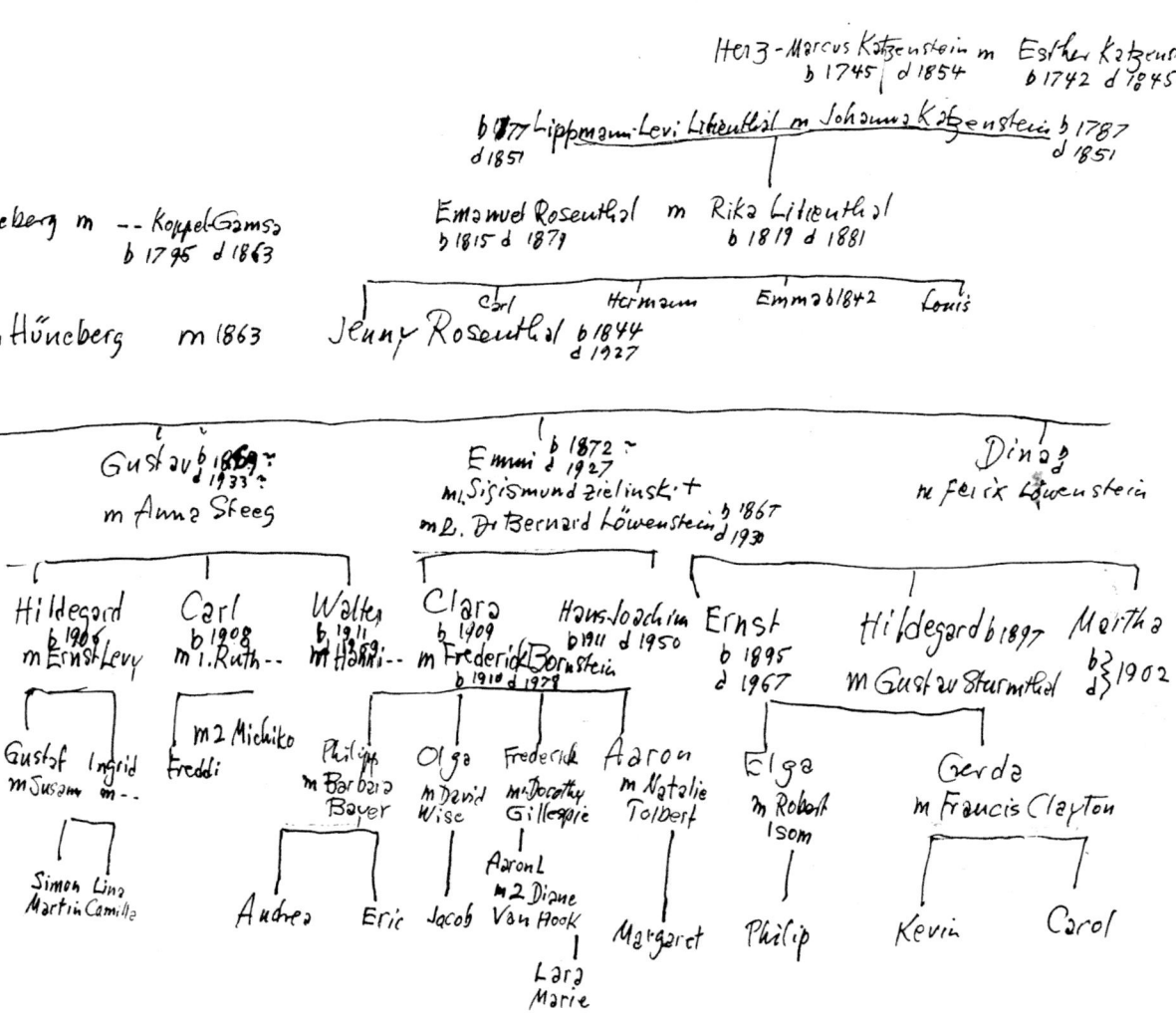

Herz-Marcus Katzenstein m Esther Katzenstein
b 1745 d 1854   b 1742 d 1845

b 1777 Lippmann-Levi Lilienthal m Johanna Katzenstein b 1787
d 1851   d 1851

eberg m -- Koppel-Gamsa   Emanuel Rosenthal m Rika Lilienthal
b 1795 d 1863   b 1815 d 1879   b 1819 d 1881

Hüneberg   m 1863   Jenny Rosenthal b 1844   Carl   Hermann   Emma b 1842   Louis
d 1927

Gustav b 1869   Emma b 1872   Dina b
d 1933   d 1927   m Felix Löwenstein
m Anna Steeg   m Sigismund Zielinski †
m 2. Dr Bernard Löwenstein b 1867
d 1930

Hildegard   Carl   Walter   Clara   Hans-Joachim   Ernst   Hildegard b 1897   Martha
b 1905   b 1908   b 1911   b 1909   b 1911 d 1950   b 1895   b 1902
m Ernst Levy   m 1. Ruth --   m Hanni --   m Frederick Bornstein   d 1967   m Gustav Sturmthal
b 1910 d 1979

Gustaf Ingrid   m 2 Michiko   Philipp   Olga   Frederick   Aaron   Elga   Gerda
m Susan m --   Freddi   m Barbara   m David   m Dorothy   m Natalie   m Robert   m Francis Clayton
Bayer   Wise   Gillespie   Tolbert   Isom

Simon Lina   Aaron L   Margaret   Philip   Kevin   Carol
Martin Camille   Andrea   Eric   Jacob   m 2 Diane
Van Hook

Lara
Marie

FAMILY TREE

Bornstein/Löwenstein Family Tree

Frederick Philipp Emmanu
Bornstein, MD

Olga Bornstein Wise

Jenny Bornstein's Children:

Arthur 1881–1932 (Hamburg) married Olga Brunstein

Therese (Röse) 1883–? Married Vladimir Brunstein.
Two Children: Ilse and Emanuel.

Susanne (Suse) 1888–1954? Jerusalem. Never married.

Clara Bornstein (Lowenste
(1909 - 1988)

Olga Bornstein Wis
Tree
Showing 26 people.
Printed on May 26, 2020.

Print and share your own family tree at www.gen

FAMILY TREE

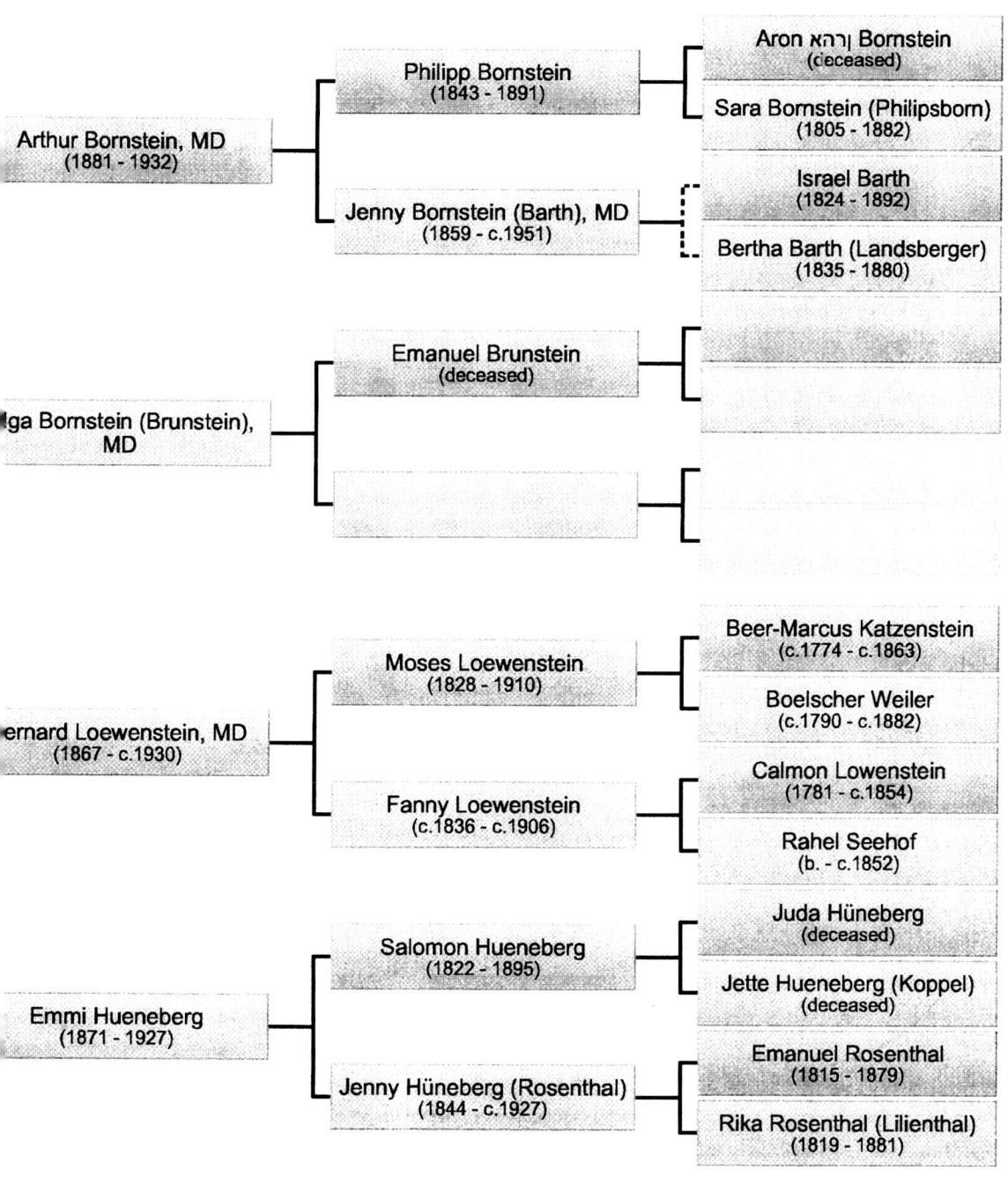

Arthur Bornstein, MD
(1881 - 1932)

Philipp Bornstein
(1843 - 1891)

Aron ןרהא Bornstein
(deceased)

Sara Bornstein (Philipsborn)
(1805 - 1882)

Jenny Bornstein (Barth), MD
(1859 - c.1951)

Israel Barth
(1824 - 1892)

Bertha Barth (Landsberger)
(1835 - 1880)

Iga Bornstein (Brunstein),
MD

Emanuel Brunstein
(deceased)

ernard Loewenstein, MD
(1867 - c.1930)

Moses Loewenstein
(1828 - 1910)

Beer-Marcus Katzenstein
(c.1774 - c.1863)

Boelscher Weiler
(c.1790 - c.1882)

Fanny Loewenstein
(c.1836 - c.1906)

Calmon Lowenstein
(1781 - c.1854)

Rahel Seehof
(b. - c.1852)

Emmi Hueneberg
(1871 - 1927)

Salomon Hueneberg
(1822 - 1895)

Juda Hüneberg
(deceased)

Jette Hueneberg (Koppel)
(deceased)

Jenny Hüneberg (Rosenthal)
(1844 - c.1927)

Emanuel Rosenthal
(1815 - 1879)

Rika Rosenthal (Lilienthal)
(1819 - 1881)

SHORT TIMELINE OF GERMAN HISTORY AND POLITICS

1848. Liberal, pro-democratic revolts break out throughout Europe and in Germany. They are suppressed, but the liberal political movement grows stronger.

1850–69. German Jews gain full civic equality throughout Germany. Germany begins an extremely rapid process of industrialization and urbanization.

1870–71. Prussia defeats France and becomes Europe's dominant military power. The German states unite in a new German Empire (Second Reich, 1871–1918) with Berlin as its capital. Berlin experiences a real estate and construction boom.

1879. Political anti-Semitism reappears and finds broad support. Anti-Jewish political parties grow ever stronger between 1879 and 1933.

1914. World War One breaks out (1914–1918). Germany is defeated, loses territory, and is saddled with huge reparation payments. Its economy collapses. The Empire dissolves and is replaced by a shaky democratic government (Weimar Republic, 1919–1933).

1929. Wall Street Crash plunges U.S. economy into the Great Depression. By 1931 the depression is world-wide; it will last for a decade. Germany's economy collapses (again). Hyperinflation wipes out German household savings.

SHORT TIMELINE OF GERMAN HISTORY AND POLITICS

1933. The Nazi party takes power in Germany and immediately enacts anti-Jewish laws. Jews are barred from civil service jobs, including university posts. They may no longer practice most professions. Jewish students may not study alongside "Aryans." Emigration of Jews from Germany begins.

1939. World War Two begins in Europe. The U.S. enters the war in 1941. Germany is defeated in 1945 and divided between West and East. Overall WWII deaths of 70-80 million include six million Jews murdered by the Nazis and their agents. Almost no Jews are left in Germany.

1945. American economic boom begins, fueled by wartime savings and pent-up demand. The U.S. will be the richest nation in the world for 25 years. The postwar "Baby Boom" begins; 76 million American babies are born between 1946 and 1964.

1946. Start of Cold War between nuclear-armed U.S. and Soviet Union, with their respective allies and satellites. Lasts until collapse of USSR in 1991.

1964–1975. The U.S. is engaged in the Vietnam War ("Second Indochina War").

1989. Communism collapses in East Germany; the Berlin Wall is torn down.

1990. Germany reunified under a democratic system of government (West absorbs East).

CHAPTER 1

Introduction

1009 Park Road, El Paso, Texas c. 1960.

OUR MOTHER, CLARA, died in El Paso, Texas in early July 1988, far away from her birthplace of Berlin, Germany. Our father, Fritz, had died ten years earlier in October 1978. I and my brothers Philipp, Fred, and Aaron, and our families, were together in El Paso to attend mother's funeral and to sort through the accumulation of over forty years of family life. It was now time to let go of the house that had been home.

Our childhood home, once bustling, was now over-quiet. We had no cousins or aunts or uncles. Suddenly we were the core of our family, left to realize that we had no close living relatives except each other.

The house itself was built in 1917 in the Spanish/Mexican style popular at that time. Located at 1009 Park Road, the house was a block away from a lovely, large city park.

The sprawling rooms at 1009 had successfully accommodated our active family of six from January 1953 forward. As our parents aged and we children grew into adulthood, certain areas of the house, in particular the outbuildings, were neglected and almost forgotten. We found old leather suitcases and boxes stored in the garage, untouched since the family moved into the house years before.

Attached to the garage was a small maid's quarters. Never occupied by a maid during all our years in the house, it accommodated Philipp's bedroom along with two other storage rooms. In the first room we found Fritz's jars of post-autopsy brains residing on several dusty metal shelves as well as an ancient Sears Roebuck refrigerator. During the years when our house was filled with visitors, the Coldspot, complete with tiny freezer compartment, served as the repository of cold beer, mother's cured beef tongue, and tins of stale cookies for the unsuspecting visitor. Of course, as we grew older, we and our friends came to appreciate the Coldspot for our access to free cold beer—usually Mexican brewed beer like Dos Equis or Nochebuena, a special Christmas beer.

We could still see fraying world maps plastered on the wall of what was Philipp's former bedroom. No wonder that Philipp became a non-stop world traveler. After Philipp finished college at Texas Western[1] in 1962 and left home to attend medical school at Washington University in St. Louis, the entire maid's quarter became neglected and forgotten. In the decaying bathroom, we found the leftovers from Philipp's teenage hobby: here is where he developed his own black and white photographs. The light cord still held a special red bulb for use during the development of film.

Garage and bedrooms at 1009 Park Road.

---

[1] Today, the University of Texas at El Paso.

Luckily for us, El Paso has a hot, dry climate. Everything we found during the work of those sad July days was covered in a fine layer of desert sand, but otherwise still in decent condition—clothing still bright, papers legible, and suitcases with contents undisturbed. Here we had a veritable time capsule of materials, many predating our parents' arrival in the United States in the mid-1930s.

Among the items in this treasure trove we found a "*Jahzeits und Trauerandachtsbuch*," bound in black silk cloth. This "anniversary of death remembrance book" was issued to Clara and her brother Hans Joachim by Berlin's Jewish Weissensee Cemetery after their mother Emmy's death. Before WWI in an undivided Berlin, Weissensee had become the largest Jewish cemetery in Europe. After WWII, the miraculously undisturbed cemetery was "relocated" to East Berlin when the Russians occupied that part of the city. Thus, for years the Weissensee Cemetery was inaccessible to visitors from the West.

Rows of gravestones at Weissensee.

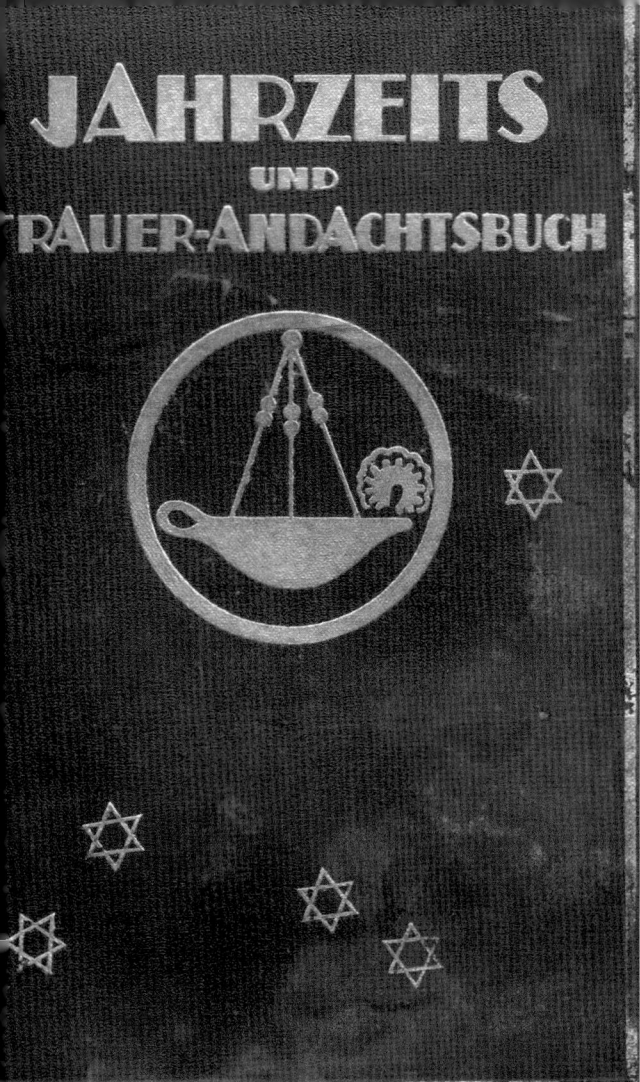

Mourning book to celebrate anniversary of a beloved's death.

Dates for future graveyard visits.

Year	Day	Date		Year	Day	Date
1927				1952	Sonnabend	9 Februar
1928	Sonnabend	4 Februar		1953	Donnerstag	29 Januar
1929	Donnerstag	24 Januar		1954		13 Januar
1930	Dienstag	11 Februar		1955	Sonnabend	Februar
1931	Sonnabend	31 Januar		1956	Donnerstag	26 Januar
1932	Donnerstag	21 Januar		1957	Dienstag	Januar
1933	Donnerstag	9 Februar		1958	Montag	3 Februar
1934	Montag	29 Januar		1959	Donnerstag	22 Januar
1935	Donnerstag	17 Januar		1960	Donnerstag	11 Februar
1936	Donnerstag	6 Februar		1961	Montag	30 Januar
1937	Montag	25 Januar		1962	Donnerstag	18 Januar
1938	Sonnabend	15 Januar		1963	Donnerstag	7 Februar
1939	Donnerstag	2 Februar		1964	Montag	27 Januar
1940	Dienstag	23 Januar		1965	Sonnabend	16 Januar
1941	Montag	10 Februar		1966	Donnerstag	3 Februar
1942	Sonnabend	31 Januar		1967	Dienstag	24 Januar
1943	Dienstag	19 Januar		1968	Montag	12 Februar
1944	Montag	7 Februar		1969	Sonnabend	1 Februar
1945	Sonnabend	27 Januar		1970	Dienstag	20 Januar
1946	Donnerstag	15 Januar		1971	Montag	8 Februar
1947	Montag	3 Februar		1972	Sonnabend	29 Januar
1948	Sonnabend	24 Januar		1973	Dienstag	16 Januar
1949	Sonnabend	12 Februar		1974	Dienstag	5 Februar
1950	Donnerstag	31 Januar		1975	Sonnabend	24 Januar
1951	Sonnabend	21 Januar		1976	Donnerstag	Januar

Gebet beim Anzünden

Ich zünde das Licht an zur Ehre und zum Heile deiner teuren heimgegangenen Seele. Möge sie eingehen in den Bund des Lebens mit den Seelen aller Frommen im Eden.

אֲנִי מַדְלִיק אֶת הַנֵּר הַזֶּה לְזֵכֶר נִשְׁמָתָךְ הַיְקָרָה תְּהֵא נַפְשָׁהּ צְרוּרָה בִּצְרוֹר הַחַיִּים

When I first visited Berlin in 1962 the city was divided. I had no idea about the existence of the cemetery, much less that I had close relatives buried there. During this visit to Berlin, I finally came to understand in person how post-war political decisions can affect individual lives. I spent an evening in East Berlin, visiting with friends of friends. We conversed, smoked many cigarettes, sipped vodka, and talked into the night. This was what was left of my mother's Berlin: no more Nazis. You were either a believer in democracy or communism.

Only much later did I learn about the Weissensee cemetery, in the former East Berlin, and the graves of Löwenstein, Bornstein, and Barth ancestors. After the German reunification in 1990, East Berlin was again open to visitors. I could visit Berlin and Weissensee almost immediately after German reunification.

The Trauerbuch[2] included information about the location of the burial plots for Clara's parents: mother Emmy Hüneberg Löwenstein, who died in 1927, and father Bernard Löwenstein, who died in 1930. According to Jewish tradition, family members were to make annual gravesite visits on Yom Kippur (Day of Atonement). The dates for visits to the Löwenstein graves were listed in the front of the book up to 1976. Can you imagine what I was thinking when I first saw that long list of dates? After 1934, certainly no family had ever visited the graves on the dates given in the Trauerbuch.

Clara never spoke to me about where her parents were buried; she certainly never mentioned the book. I was overwhelmed when I held this slim, black book in my hands for the first time on that hot day in July 1988. The neglected and forgotten book somehow encapsulated what had been lost because our parents were forced to leave Germany. The slim volume demonstrated the enormity of Hitler's campaign against the Jews. Not only had we lost relatives without graves but also family grave sites were forlorn and abandoned. Further this slim book defined the distance between me, my siblings, and our ancestors. Now that Clara was gone forever, I had my first opportunity to find the graves of ancestors whom I had never known.

Starting in 1990 (after the fall of the Berlin Wall), I began visiting family gravesites in Germany. I found headstones for Fritz Bornstein's family in cemeteries in Hamburg and Berlin. In 1994, Philipp, Aaron and I visited Clara Löwenstein Bornstein's family gravesites in Berlin and the Westphalian villages of Steinheim and Volkmarsen. In 2005, I walked the streets in Odessa, Russia, where my grandmother Olga Brunstein Bornstein grew up. With the help of my friend Uli Ness in Berlin, I located official, original birth and death certificates for members of the Bornstein/Löwenstein/Barth families.

After mother's death, my brother Philipp owned a house with the largest storage space. Thus, he inherited grandfather's antique rolltop desk. Evidently, Philipp went

---

[2] Trauerbuch can be literally translated as grieving or mourning, book.

through the contents of the desk thoroughly without telling his siblings what he found. Many of the family's most unusual documents had been hidden in the secret compartments of this ancient rolltop desk located in Fritz's study at 1009 Park Road.

Antique rolltop desk with many secret compartments which held important family documents.

Upon Philipp's death in 2006, that chaotic mishmash of diplomas, letters, report cards, photographs, and more came to me in Austin Texas. I was the only remaining family member who was fluent in written and spoken German and I had a career in information science. It seems I was the ideal person to arrange this archive and make use of the unique trove that came to us after Clara's death. Thus began the germ of an idea to produce a "short" Bornstein family history.

In September 2009, our distant cousin Naomi Wolman flew to Austin from Los Angeles, bringing with her a notebook which had been handwritten by our great-grandmother Jenny Barth Bornstein.[3] Jenny was one of the first female medical doctors in Germany. Jenny wrote the contents of the notebook in 1941, the year Philipp and I were born. At that time, Jenny was living with her nephew Erich Fraenkel in Alexandria, Virginia.

---

[3] My great-grandmother Jenny was aunt to Naomi's grandmother Lucie. Jenny inspired Lucie to become a physician.

David and I translated, edited and published Jenny's memoir as *A Jewish Girlhood in Berlin*.[4] Her memoir, written when Jenny was around 80 years old, has been my inspiration for compiling this Bornstein family history. I finally am completing my work when I, as Jenny did, turn 80.

From childhood onward I was always fascinated by my family history. My mother, Clara, was an expert storyteller as was great-grandmother Jenny. As I was growing up, Clara and Fritz would often say that I was going to become the family archivist, probably because I was the child with the greatest interest in their life before I was born. Little did I expect that the time would come when I would actually fulfill their expectations.

This family history results from efforts that began after our surprising and unexpected discoveries on that hot, dusty day in El Paso. I have drawn from old letters, documents, stories my parents told me, photographs, diplomas and readings in German and Jewish history—in short, any relevant materials that can fill out a distant and complex family history.

My wish is that future generations of our family will understand how Clara and Fritz were not deterred by the many obstacles which might have deprived them of their quest to begin their life together as strangers in a strange land. Despite the fact that nothing in their bourgeois, educated upbringing had prepared them for the huge changes they encountered, they survived and survived well. As you read these pages, I hope you appreciate their extraordinary grit and resilience as they transitioned from the familiar German world of childhood and young adulthood to their adulthood in the United States. What would await them there?

---

[4] Available on amazon.com

Our translation of Jenny Bornstein's memoir, 2010.

CHAPTER 2

German Jews

THERE PROBABLY HAVE BEEN no practicing Jews in the Bornstein family for the last 100 years. Yet our German-Jewish ancestors defined us and set the course of our family's history.

The two main ethnic groups in the Jewish world are the "Ashkenazi"[1] Jews and the "Sephardic"[2] Jews. The term "Ashkenazi" includes most Jews of European or Russian origin, while "Sephardic" refers to the descendants of Jews expelled from Spain or Portugal around 1500. Genetic testing can differentiate between the two Jewish groups.

German Jews are a subset of Ashkenazi Jews. I understand and use the term "German-Jewish" as referring to an ethnicity or a group with a shared history, not primarily as a religious affiliation or belief. In the term German-Jewish, the words German and Jewish have equal weight and are not separable.

The families of my parents, Fritz Bornstein and Clara Löwenstein, were fully aware of their Ashkenazi Jewish ancestry, but most members of the two families stopped being religious or practicing Jews by the early 20th century. Even then they carried both the baggage and the pride that came with being Jewish in Germany.

It can be difficult for American Jews today to understand the intensity of anti-Semitism and exclusionary practices of many European countries towards Jews in the 19th century. The British, for example, excluded Jews from their universities. Benjamin Disraeli,[3] Britain's prime minister from 1874 to 1880, became a paper convert to Christianity when he was young after his father had a dispute with their synagogue. This conversion also permitted Disraeli to obtain a British university education. The Russian Empire regarded Jews as aliens and confined them to the Pale of Settlement.[4]

It is easy to forget that even in the United States, and well into the 20th century, informal quotas limited the participation of Jews in public and private institutions. Famous universities, including Harvard and other Ivy League schools, had "Jewish quotas" limiting the number of Jews they accepted. Many neighborhoods across the United States excluded Jews as buyers or residents, usually by means of "restrictive covenants."

---

[1] Ashkenazi—Term for German Jews. Name of one of Noah's descendants.
[2] Sepharad—Hebrew word for Spain.
[3] Disraeli = from Israel. The family was descended from Sephardic Jews.
[4] The Pale of Settlement (from the Latin palus, meaning stake) was a western region of Imperial Russia with varying borders that existed from 1791 to 1917, outside of which residency by Jews was mostly forbidden.

German Jews

Many social institutions were also closed to Jews or restricted their membership. A prime example was the exclusion of Jews from membership in country clubs. The Young Men's Hebrew Association (YMHA), a Jewish equivalent to the YMCA, was founded in 1874 so that Jews could find a place to socialize comfortably. YMHAs also provided temporary residences for men when they arrived to work in a new town. In 1951 the YMHA was renamed the Jewish Community Center Association (JCCA). Today's JCCs are in part a remnant of those days.

The Bornstein side of the family came to Berlin from Posen, a region that is now part of Poland. The Löwenstein side originated in Westphalia. In the 19th century both Posen and Westphalia formed part of the sprawling Kingdom of Prussia. Over the course of that century, Jews—especially those who became middle-class and wealthy—became more accepted in general German society. They gained political equality under the Prussian constitution of 1850. In 1867 all restrictions for Jews on their place of residence, purchase of real estate, and choice of profession were abolished in the states of the North German Confederation. The states of southern Germany also abolished anti-Jewish restrictions at this time. These laws of equality were extended in 1871 to all the states of the German Empire.

German statesman Otto von Bismarck, chancellor of Prussia and later of the Prussian Empire (1862–1890), relied on a Jewish banker, Gerson von Bleichröder,[5] as a financial advisor for both the Prussian state and for Bismarck himself. Jews served as soldiers in the Prussian Army of the 19th century, but until shortly before WWI were still excluded from the officer class and from higher-level government posts such as university professorships.[6]

Ambitious German Jews sometimes converted to Christianity (Lutheranism in the North, Catholicism in the South) in order to enter official German society and to qualify for positions otherwise closed to them. These Jews were known as *Taufjuden*, or baptized Jews.[7] These converts were not especially numerous before 1900 and their new

---

[5] Note the "von" preceding Bleichröder's surname. Bleichröder was only the second Jew to be given noble status in Prussia (in 1872) without converting to Christianity.

[6] Amos Elon. *The Pity of it All: A Portrait of the German-Jewish Epoch 1743–1933.*

[7] My father Fritz, himself baptized into the Lutheran church at the age of four at the outbreak of WWI, once commented that conversion to Christianity held little appeal for most German Jews, because, in his words "they had already converted from Jewish to metric." I.e., they already belonged to the modern world.

religious identity was often a mere formality. But still, what irony! You could become a Christian (on paper), but everyone still knew you were a Jew and treated you as such.

In the 19th century, many German Jews internalized the bourgeois ethos of *Bildung*[8] which emphasized literacy, cultural accomplishment, a humanistic education based on the Greek and Roman classics, and, of course, German literature. Their world view was based in good part on the principles of the European Enlightenment and of the French Revolution. "Liberty, equality and fraternity" were political principles adopted by German liberals and underpinned the pro-democratic revolts that broke out in most of Europe in 1848.

The children born to this 19th century "bourgeoisie of learning," such as my grandfather Arthur Bornstein (b. 1881), learned the classics in school, but at university many of them gravitated to the pure sciences, such as physics and mathematics, to applied sciences and engineering, and to medicine in all its branches. By the outbreak of WWI in 1914, Berlin had a surplus of physicians, a large portion of them Jewish, who scrambled in a crowded market to become specialists and/or find an academic post. The Jewish cliché "my son the doctor" was certainly not invented in the United States.

German Jews were notorious for considering themselves more "European," more educated, and superior to the Jews of Eastern Europe or *Ostjuden*, most of whom lived in small villages (*shtetls*), spoke Yiddish as their main or only language, and studied Torah and Talmud.[9] Many German Jews had already broken free of these boundaries and were among the most liberated Jews in Europe. They could enter (at least in theory) all occupations and professions, could live anywhere, and were for the most part secular rather than religious Jews. Prominent figures such Albert Ballin (shipping magnate),[10] Albert Einstein, and Henry Kissinger come easily to mind.

The fact that the German Jews were less miserable and had greater opportunities for advancement than the Jews of the Russian and Austrian empires should not hide the reality that German society remained broadly and stubbornly anti-Semitic. After the Prussian victories over Austria and France (1866 and 1870) ushered in the German Empire

---

[8] Bildung = literally education but including much more than formal schooling.
[9] Torah—first five books of the Old Testament. Talmud—commentaries on the Torah.
[10] Whose ships brought most German immigrants to the United States.

on a wave of patriotism and good feeling, anti-Jewish agitation burst out anew. From 1879 until the Nazis seized power in 1933, anti-Jewish political parties grew in strength and were a permanent feature of the German political scene. The expulsion of the Jews from Germany in 1933 and after, and the destruction of those who stayed, was a catastrophe foretold.

Clara and Fritz were inheritors of a middle-class, liberal, and secular European culture. That culture molded their *Weltanschauung*—their mindset or way of seeing the world. In important ways they were and remained Prussian. The German ideals of honor, discipline, education, trustworthiness, and especially duty guided Clara and Fritz in leading their lives, raising their children, and how they related to others.

Clara and Fritz were also representatives of two different sets of German Jews: the urban and the rural. The Bornsteins (after about 1850) were urban Jews, while the Löwensteins (until about 1900) were small-town Jews in Westphalia. We will explore the two families in the upcoming chapters.

CHAPTER 3

The Barth and Bornstein Families
From Posen to Berlin

ALTHOUGH BERLIN WOULD BECOME THE CITY where Frederick Bornstein and Clara Löwenstein first met in around 1929, their meeting was preceded by the arrival in Berlin first of Israel Barth (1824–1892) and then of Philipp Bornstein (1843–1891), both from the eastern province of Posen.

Bentschen, Posen, now Zbaszyn, Poland.

Between 1772 and 1795 Poland was divided between Russia, Austria, and Prussia, and ceased to exist as a nation. Prussia annexed Polish-speaking Posen and in 1848 made it part of the Prussian kingdom. Poland would be re-created only in 1919, after the end of WWI.

Israel Barth 1824–1891.

Israel was born in 1824 in Bentschen, a small town in Posen about 130 miles east of Berlin. Today the town is in Poland and known as Zbaszyn.[1] In 1833 about 25% of the town (population around 330) were Jewish. Both Israel and his future son-in-law probably came from the area around Bentschen.

Jenny Bornstein's sister Paula Fraenkel wrote her own version of the Barth family history after she emigrated to Palestine. She tells us that Israel's father Meyer Barth was a carpenter and a pious man:

> *"At Passover my grandfather Meyer's brandy making still was sold for the duration of the holiday. There couldn't be any Chometz[2] in a Jewish business during Passover…The entire business was sold with witnesses to sign the document. Then after Passover grandfather repurchased his business."[3]*

When Meyer supposedly demanded that his son Israel become a rabbi, Israel ran away from home. We do not know, but we can easily imagine why Israel first settled in Berlin. Berlin was Prussia's capital and a thriving town rapidly growing into a city. It had already a substantial Jewish population. Because Israel went into the clothing business in Berlin, it is possible that he was trained as a tailor. We learn from Jenny's memoir that he would cut out wonderful paper dolls for his daughters.[4]

Family lore says that Israel fought on the barricades in Berlin during the revolution of 1848, which sought a democratic government and full rights for all Germans. With time, Israel was alienated from Jewish religious practice. The following story has survived: at Passover, he insisted on eating a pork roast in his study while the rest of the family celebrated the Passover meal in their large dining room. Once when Israel joined in a Passover seder meal, he shouted to his daughter Hanne: "This damn stuff the Jews were eating when they were wandering around in the desert. Just awful! Hanne, please bring in the dumplings." Of course, dumplings were made from leavened flour and not a Passover dish at all.

---

[1] Today Zbaszyn has a population of around 7300 inhabitants.
[2] Chometz are foods with leavening agents that are forbidden on the Jewish holiday of Passover. Why? To commemorate the exodus of the Jews from Egypt. Only matzos, unleavened bread, is eaten during Passover.
[3] Paula Barth Fraenkel. Unpublished memoir. In Bornstein family archive. Translated by Olga Wise.
[4] Jenny Bornstein. *A Jewish Girlhood In Berlin*. p. 41.

Israel's politics established the family's political leanings for the next two generations of this family—liberal and non-religious, only occasionally following Jewish rituals at home.

Israel first worked at and then owned the Landsberger Tailoring and Wool Shop located near the Reichstag (Parliament), in the center of Berlin. Here he and his staff tailored suits for influential members of parliament. I suspect this work made him privy to local events and gave him tips on successful business opportunities. The shop became one of the main cloth suppliers for Prussian army uniforms.[5] Israel later invested, profitably, in Berlin real estate.

Israel's first marriage was to Bertha (Bella) Landsberger (1835–1880), the sixteen-year-old daughter of the owner of the Berlin tailoring business where Israel worked. I presume this is the shop that later became Israel's profitable business, and that became known as "Barth and Bornstein." Bella and Israel had a son who died as an infant[6] and two daughters: Johanna or Hanne (1851–1922) and Jenny (1859–1951), our great-grand-mother.

Jenny was about six years old when Israel and his wife Bella divorced. She had no idea why her mother suddenly left their household, and the divorce was clearly a traumatic event for the young Jenny.

What happened? Here's the story I was told, I think by my mother, Clara: Bella and her daughters, Johanna and Jenny, were on vacation at the North Sea to avoid the blazing summer heat in Berlin. Someone later reported to Israel that Bella had been seen talking to an army officer. I've always thought that "talking to an army officer" was a euphemism implying that Bella had an affair. Of course, that was unacceptable behavior back then. I think Bella was probably quite naive. Poor Bella—married so young to a much older man, then suddenly divorced and separated from her two daughters, Jenny and Johanna (Hanne).

---

[5] Prussia fought three wars between 1864 and 1871, with Denmark, Austria, and France.
[6] Date unknown.

In the 1860s, divorce was rare in middle-class Jewish households, so Israel's decision to divorce Bella was a family catastrophe. Jenny at first had no idea why her mother disappeared so suddenly out of her life. The story of Bella's disgrace was not a story to be shared with her young daughter. Later Israel married for a second time, to Therese Simon-Meyer (1839–1881). Together they had a daughter, Paula.[7]

In Jenny's memoir of her childhood and adolescence, which only came to light in 2008, she paints an absolutely fascinating picture about her life, growing up in an affluent, urban, liberal Jewish household during the 1860s. Jenny wrote her memoir in 1941, the year I was born, when she was 82.[8] I think it is just amazing how beautifully she reconstructed her life with the hindsight of sixty years.[9] She was also writing for her first great-grandchildren Philipp and Olga Bornstein. She wrote her memoir by hand in a lively German, even though her great-grandchildren were going to be raised in the middle of the United States as potential English speakers.

In the late 1940s as our great-grandmother was approaching the age of 90, she lived down the street from us in Herrin, Illinois. When I was around eight years old, I visited with her often. She entertained me with stories from her youth. Here's one example: Jenny was once asked to sit at a table separately from the adults. Why? Because tradition held that it was unlucky to have thirteen people seated at the table. The children were "booted off the island" first!

Jenny and her sisters would play little games to amuse themselves at adult parties. They'd ball up tiny pieces of paper and flick them towards a woman's bustle, the protruding back of a Victorian lady's dress. Did the mischievous children successfully land the paper on the bustle, or did they need to try again?

When Jenny was about 20 years old, she first met her husband to be, Philipp Bornstein (1843–1891). Philipp Bornstein came from the same area of Posen as his future

---

[7] Whose husband, James Fraenkel, later became instrumental in persuading Jenny to enter medical school.
[8] As I finish up this manuscript, begun almost ten years ago, I've just turned 80 years old.
[9] Without a doubt my decision to write this family history is inspired in part by Jenny's memoir.

Hanne Barth at twenty.

Braetz, Philipp Bornstein
birthplace 1843.

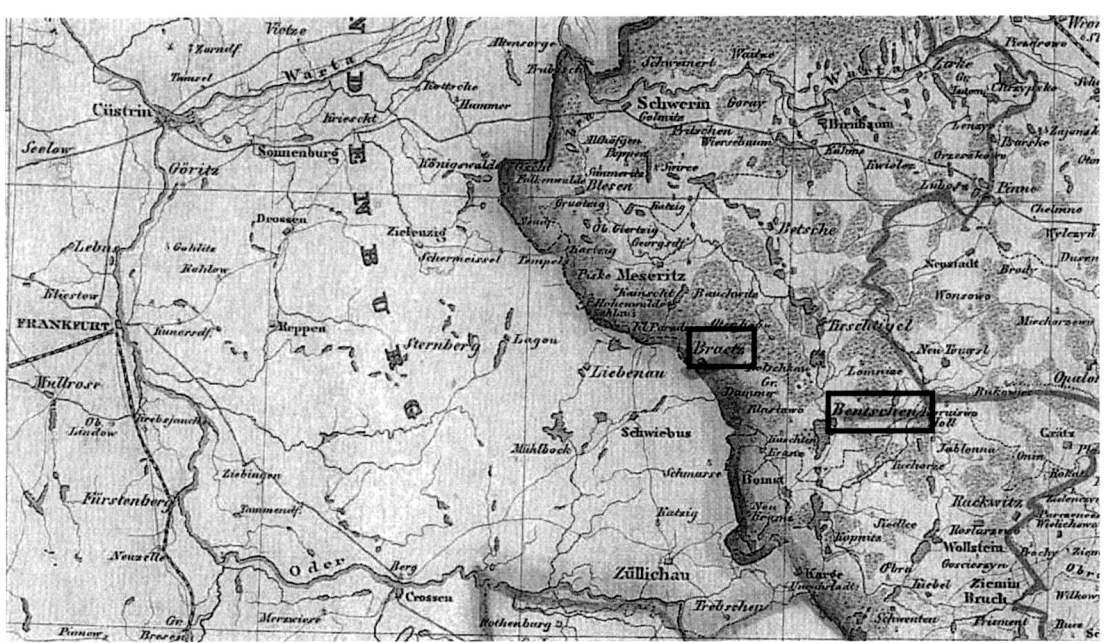

Braetz is on the west, center border. Bentschen to the southeast.

The Barth and Bornstein Families: From Posen to Berlin

partner and father-in-law Israel Barth.[10] Like Israel, he left home at a young age to work at the North Sea shipyards and serve in the Prussian army, notably during the 1866 war with Austria. Military service was obligatory in Prussia and Jews served patriotically to show their loyalty to the nation. Before she left Germany in 1935, Jenny obtained a copy of Philipp Bornstein's Prussian army record:

> **Prussia – Dept. of the Army. Record of Military Service**
>
> *Enlisted man (businessman) Philipp Bornstein, born on 27 April 1843, living in Berlin. (religion Jewish).*
>
> **General comments:** *Received several honors. Several outstanding accomplishments in battle. Was disciplined by military court, rehabilitated.[11]*
>
> **Military service:** *Served Oct. 16, 1865–Nov. 5, 1866: Campaign against Austria. Served Nov. 6, 1866–September 17, 1868 in infantry. Served July 22, 1870–July 4, 1873 in several campaigns against France.*

We do not know whether Philipp had a formal education. He may well have been self-taught and, like Jenny, had a great passion for reading. We do know that his family in Posen was Jewish and religious.

After moving to Berlin, Philipp went to work for Israel Barth who was now the owner of Landsberger Tailoring and Wool Shop. Perhaps Philipp found work with Israel because of their mutual connection to the Bentschen/Braetz area of Posen. Soon the enterprise was named Barth and Bornstein.

We have two stories of the first meeting between Jenny and her husband to be, Philipp. The first story goes as follows: Philipp Bornstein was working with Jenny's father in their clothing store Barth and Bornstein. The first time Philipp saw the blond, blue-eyed Jenny, he said: "That's the woman I'm going to marry. She has such beautiful blue eyes." In her memoir Jenny writes about meeting Philipp and falling in love with his dark

---

[10] Philipp was born in Braetz, about 120 miles from Israel's hometown of Bentschen. In her memoir, Jenny describes her engagement to Philipp (p. 148) and makes a point of saying that earlier she heard Philipp talking with Israel in Polish rather than German. She had only heard her father speak German, never Polish. We presume Philipp was asking Israel's permission to marry Jenny.

[11] We do not have information on what Philipp may have done to deserve punishment.

sad eyes.[12] We don't know much more about Philipp except that his father was named Aron[13] (thus my brother Aaron Claire Bornstein and my nephew Aaron Landon Bornstein).[14]

Jenny and Philipp married in 1879 and soon had three children: Arthur (1881–1932), Therese, known as Röse (1883–c. 1938), and Susanne (1888–c. 1952). The couple spent most

Villa on Grossbeerenstrasse 1, home to the Berlin Bornsteins and Barths.

of their marriage living with their children in the large villa belonging to Israel and his wife Therese.

Two silver objects from Jenny's household are perfect symbols of the prosperous 1860s household in which she grew up. The first is a silver egg cup that shines today as brightly as it did over 150 years ago. Great-grandmother Jenny brought the egg cup to the United States from Germany and used it when she lived near Fritz, Clara, and their children. Soft boiled eggs eaten from an egg cup were and still are a special German delicacy. In Jenny's day, she used a special carved, ivory spoon to scoop out the egg yolk and white

---

[12] A very 19th century trope: we know a person through their eyes!

[13] A spelling variant for the name Aaron.

[14] While my sister-in-law Dorothy was pregnant with Aaron, Fred was serving in Vietnam. She lived with Clara and Fritz. Aaron took her to all her medical appointments so of course everyone assumed he was her husband. We'd joke that Aaron was in place to take care of Dorothy should Fred be killed in Vietnam. That was also a time-honored Jewish tradition: brother fills in after death of brother.

because silver would tarnish upon contact with egg yolks! Little quilted egg caps would keep the eggs warm until eaten. What a breakfast ritual!

A second object passed down from Jenny's household is a huge silver soup ladle inscribed with a large B for Barth (and conveniently later for Bornstein). This sort of ladle always accompanies a porcelain soup tureen.[15] By extension, the ladle and companion soup tureen imply a large dining table where family members are seated, ready for the first course of their meal. In her memoir Jenny writes how assorted uncles and other relatives came to the house, often staying overnight or for long visits.

By 1873, Israel Barth had become wealthy by investing in real estate. The Barth and Bornstein families were nouveau riche, but with a social conscience, as later events

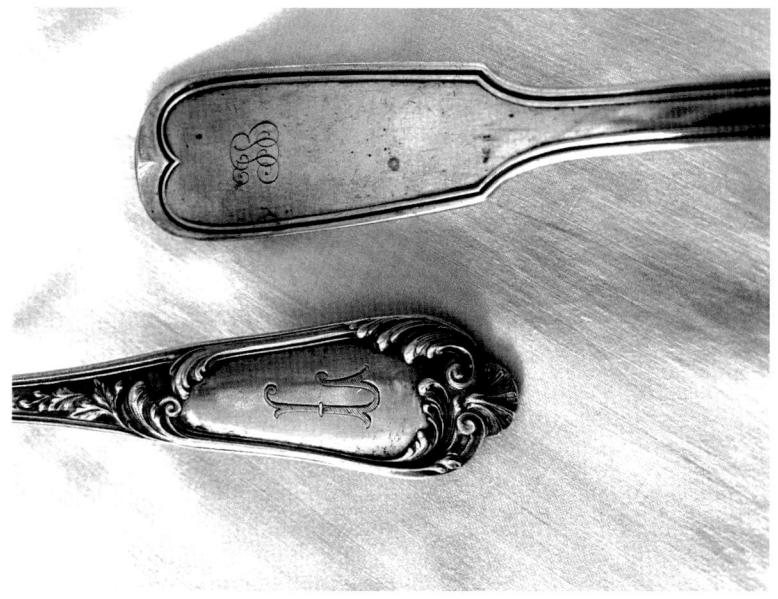

Soup ladle handles. B for Barth, L for Löwenstein.

Jenny's silver egg cup.

---

[15] The tureen did not make it to the U.S.

will show. They adapted to the demands of a city that became the capital of Germany when Germany was united in 1871.[16] After unification Germany became an industrial leader and a great European power.

Unfortunately, Jenny's memoir stops around the year 1879, the year of her marriage. The remaining information we have about the Barths and Bornsteins comes orally from my mother Clara and great-grandmother Jenny, and from a short, handwritten memoir written by Jenny's son Arthur when he was about 17.

We do not know when Philipp's health began to deteriorate, perhaps around 1889. There came a day when Philipp asked Jenny and their three children to accompany him upstairs to a large window, to join hands with him, to jump out the window together, and fly to heaven. Fortunately, the family didn't follow his orders! Thus began the next chapter in Jenny's tragedy-filled life.

After Philipp made his crazy suggestion to his family, he was diagnosed with "general paresis," a term that covers syphilis and other neurological diseases that often destroy the central nervous system. Luckily Jenny's sister Paula was by then married to a physician, Dr. James Fraenkel. James was the director of a state-of-the art sanitarium designed by his brother, a gifted architect. In those days the biological, scientific study of mental illness was in its infancy. Many of the early ideas about mental illness were developed from the treatment of patients with syphilis or schizophrenia (a term not invented until 1908). Before then mental illness and physical illness were not considered separate disease entities.

While Philipp was a patient at Dr. Fraenkel's sanitarium, Jenny spent a great deal of time and effort nursing her ill husband. Philipp died at the sanitarium in 1891. He is buried in the Weissensee Jewish Cemetery in Berlin. Jenny became interested in becoming a physician during Philipp's illness. Her physician brother-in-law, James Fraenkel, encouraged her to consider the study of medicine. Jenny's father, Israel Barth, died in 1892, the year after Philipp's death. Jenny was now 33, a widow and financially comfortable. What would she do now?

---

[16] The German Empire (1871–1918) consisted of 26 political units that ranged in size from Prussia (the largest and most populous) to the small free cities of Bremen, Lübeck and Hamburg.

ADDITIONAL MATERIALS

Until 1990, I had no idea that Israel and Philipp were buried in Berlin in Weissensee Cemetery. The only relatives about whom I had information were my grandparents, Emmy and Bernard Löwenstein (my mother Clara's parents). In 1990, after the Berlin Wall came down, I visited the cemetery with our dear family friend and Berlin resident Uli Ness. With us we carried garden shears in case we needed to clear the untended graves. Surprisingly the original cemetery records had survived and were still on file in the cemetery's main office. So Uli and I had a very fruitful day. We found the graves of Israel Barth, Therese Barth, Philipp Bornstein, and Emmy and Bernard Löwenstein, scattered from section A1 to section P. Israel was one of the early residents of the cemetery, which later became the largest Jewish cemetery in Europe.

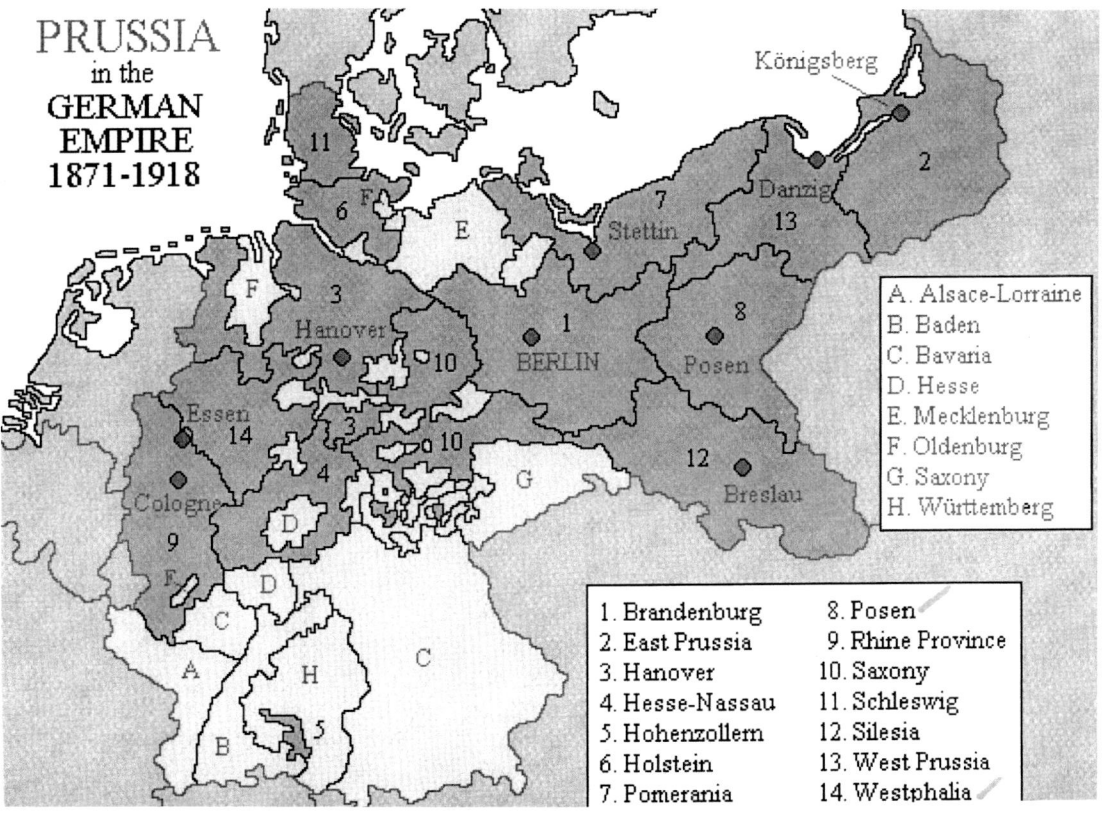

Map of Germany 1871.

Sterbe-Urkunde.

Nr. *206.*

Gross-Lichterfelde, am *26. December* 1891.

Vor dem unterzeichneten Standesbeamten erschien heute, der Persön-

lichkeit nach ———————————— _er kannt,_

der Inspector der Doctor Fränkel'schen Privat

Heilanstalt Georg Beneke ————————

wohnhaft zu _Lankwitz_ ————————

und zeigte an, daß _der Kaufmann Philipp_ ——

Bornstein ————————————————

————————————————— *48 Jahr*

7 Monat 28 Tage alt, _mosaischer_ ——Religion,

wohnhaft zu _Berlin, Regierungsstraße 7_ ———

geboren zu _Bratz bei Meseritz, verheiratet_

mit der in Berlin, Regierungsstraße 7 wohnhaften

Jenny geborenen Barth ——————

————— _Sohn des zu Zbentschen verstorbenen Gast-_

wirths Aron Bornstein und dessen ebendaselbst

verstorbenen Ehefrau Rosa geborenen Philippsohn

zu Lankwitz in der Doctor Fränkel'schen Anstalt

am fünf und zwanzig ——ten _December_ ——

des Jahres tausend acht hundert _neunzig und eins_

————— _Vor_ mittags um —_elf_—_einhalb_ ——— Uhr.

Philipp death certificate
December 26, 1891.

Philipp Bornstein (1843–1891) gravestone
with great-grandson Philipp E. Bornstein.
Weissensee Cemetery.

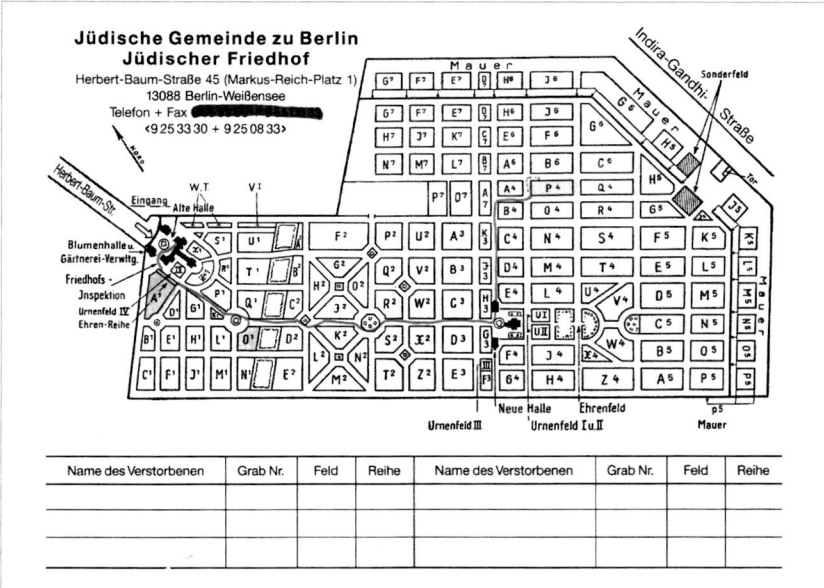

*Map of Weissensee
Cemetery. Israel
Barth Sect. A1;
Philipp Bornstein
Sect. O,
Bernard and Emmy
Löwenstein Sect. P.*

*Photocopies of original burial
records at Weissensee Cemetery.*

*Israel Barth (1824–1892) and Therese
Barth (1839–1881) gravestones
Weissensee Cemetery.*

From the Elbe to the Rio Grande

CHAPTER 4

The Hüneberg and Löwenstein Families
From Westphalia to Berlin

CLARA'S HÜNEBERG AND LÖWENSTEIN RELATIVES came from the country villages of Steinheim and Volkmarsen in the north of Westphalia. Here they lived among the few other Jewish families in the area. Today Westphalia is still a rich farming area and Westphalian ham is one of the most famous German culinary exports. The name Löwenstein comes from the German words for lion and stone: *Löwe* and *Stein*. The origin of the family name Hüneberg is a bit more difficult to ascertain. *Hüne* could have been a place name; *Berg* is the German word for mountain.[1]

According to Clara, these families regarded themselves—with irony—as the *Jüdischer Uradel Westphalens* or the "Ancient Jewish Westphalian Nobility." This term shows the influence of Clara's Berlin sense of humor since that is how the citified Löwensteins joked about their country relatives. These country relatives thought they were the best of the best without a doubt!

Greetings from Volkmarsen. Eventide. The cows return from their pasture.

---

[1] There is a hill named "Hüneberg" close to Volkmarsen.

Löwenstein is a name granted to the paternal branch of my mother's family after the end of the Thirty Years War.[2] Clara can trace her family tree back to the 1700s. The Steinheim Löwensteins and the Volkmarsen Hünebergs were not farmers as their neighbors were, but rather grain dealers and merchants. Clara's father Bernard Löwenstein was the first in his family to attend university and attain a medical degree (1893) at the University of Leipzig.

Contrary to the standard joke about "my son, the Jewish doctor," in reality the medical profession in Germany was largely closed to Jews until the last quarter of the nineteenth century. Then the study of medicine was opened to Jews, and then only to men. Women were not admitted to the study of medicine in Germany until 1908. The female doctors on the Bornstein side of the family (great-grandmother Jenny and grandmother Olga) both had to study in Switzerland.

Here's a Hüneberg anecdote about an event that may have taken place in the eighteenth century. As I and my brothers were growing up, we loved this story and could listen to Clara's spirited delivery over and over: Clara's grandparents on her mother's side, the Hünebergs, were grain dealers in the village of Volkmarsen. One day, a member of the grain dealing family was felled at work by a large bag of grain. Everyone thought he was dead. According to orthodox Jewish custom, he was buried within twenty-four hours.

The next day a farmer plowing in a field near the Jewish cemetery heard shouting and screaming coming from the new grave of the very recently departed. The farmer sought help from the village. When the villagers opened the grave, they found the body of the "deceased" sitting upright in the coffin. He was alive, but in under twenty-four hours, his hair had become grey and very long; his fingernails were curved like spoons. Poor fellow, the air had been knocked out of him and he had been buried alive. A family legend for sure!

The castle tower near Volkmarsen was the source of many scary stories. As children we loved the story about the vanquished enemies whose dead bodies were hung on hooks in the basement of the castle. Even in Clara's childhood she could see the congealed blood on the hooks!

---

[2] 1618–1648

Greetings from Volkmarsen.
Castle tower, lower right.

Clara sent me the following Hüneberg family anecdotes in a letter dated January 1976:

"...when I was small, visiting my grandmother Jenny Hüneberg in Volkmarsen, I got sick
and had to stay in bed. Grandmother sat by me and entertained me with stories (they were
called Dönikens). Among others of a fabulous ancestor of hers who lived to the age of 113
whom she remembered as a small child. She (Jenny Hüneberg) said he walked once a year
from Steinheim to Paderborn,[3] bought one pound of coffee, walked back, and the coffee
lasted all year.

I now think she must have referred—a bit vaguely—to her own great-grandfather
Herz-Marcus Katzenstein (1745–1854). He was not quite 109 when he died (and Jenny
neé Rosenthal in Geseke was almost ten years old) but his wife also lived to be 104 and
Grossmutter (grandmother) ... also mentioned that the Old Man in his later years did a
lot of chopping wood. Not that he needed to, but it supposedly kept him in good physical
condition."

---

[3] A distance of about 20 miles.

Clara's mother Emmy Hüneberg (1871–1927) came from Volkmarsen; her father Bernard Löwenstein (1867–1930) from Steinheim. I visited the area by myself in 1965. In 1994 Philipp, Aaron, and I visited there together. Both towns (some 60 kilometers apart) had a long history of including a few Jewish families.

In 1808, the Jews of Westphalia were among the first Jews in Germany to obtain Prussian citizenship. Think—this is only a little over two hundred years ago.[4] But Jews had lived in Westphalia for centuries. For hundreds of years intermarriage between Jewish families of Westphalia, "noble" or not, was almost a necessity. The families stayed close to home and didn't feel that anyone else was good enough for them. As mentioned, Clara's grandfather Hüneberg in Volkmarsen was a grain dealer; her grandfather Moses Löwenstein owned a large clothing store in Steinheim.

Emmy's education was typical for a bourgeois country woman of her time: she learned drawing, penmanship, literature, art, and European history. We do not know how Emmy met her first husband, Siegmund Zielinsky, who was evidently a rich confection manufacturer.[5] Around the turn of the century, Siegmund married Emmy and took her away from humdrum Volkmarsen to Germany's biggest city, Berlin. We do not know the exact year.

Their marriage was, alas, very short. The newlyweds took a honeymoon to Sicily. As they toured Mt. Etna on the small tourist train, Siegmund became quite ill and died quickly thereafter. It turns out that he had suffered a ruptured appendix.

His death must have been a huge shock for Emmy. She and Siegmund had settled in a lovely apartment building they owned in downtown Berlin. Siegmund was well to do, and their apartment was furnished with all the most expensive and fashionable items available. Her life was now uncertain.

Emmy felt she couldn't live alone as a widow in Berlin. She decided to return to her family home in Volkmarsen, to live in the little nest of a village that she had previ-

---

[4] Google books: Quellen Zu den Reformen in Den Rheinbunstaaten [Sources pertaining to the reforms in the Rhein states] by Klaus Rob...27 January 1808

[5] I found a tiny square scrap of business stationary in the family archive. On one side was a small colored pencil drawing showing a boat; on the other side of the paper, I can decipher "Zielinsky" and "Confection Export." Why did Clara save this? See Additional Materials at the end of this chapter.

ously so longed to leave. Her family lived in a large house on the town square. They were among the leading citizens of the village, a village old enough to have a handsome Gothic Catholic church that dates from the 13th century.

While Emmy was grieving and readjusting to village life in Volkmarsen, a Jewish country doctor, Bernard Löwenstein, from the nearby town of Steinheim, began to court her. The Löwenstein family had lived in the area for over two hundred years and were also members of the "Jewish nobility of Westphalia." Bernard Löwenstein was the son of shop owners. He obtained his medical degree after studies in Bonn, Göttingen, Freiburg, and Berlin. Among his teachers in Berlin were renowned pathologist Rudolf Virchow and bacteriologist Robert Koch.[6]

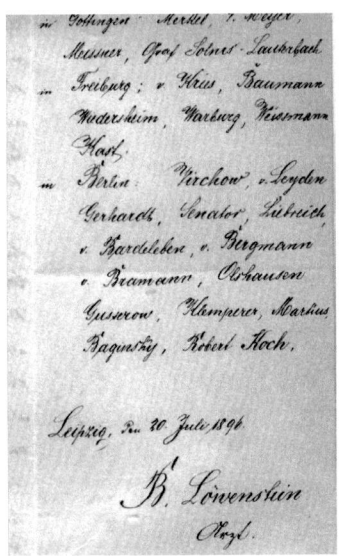

Page from medical article written by Bernard in 1896. Note the names of his Berlin professors: Virchow is the fifth name, Koch is the final name.

---

[6] Robert Koch (1843–1910) discovered the causes of anthrax and cholera, among other bacterial diseases. He is considered the father of bacteriology. Another committee member, Virchow, is considered the father of pathology.

After an intense courtship Bernard asked Emmy to marry him. She agreed with one condition: he should give up his country practice and move to Berlin. There she owned an apartment, part of her inheritance from her late husband Siegmund.[7] Emmy did not want to spend the rest of her life in Westphalia. Bernard agreed to her demands and gave up his thriving practice as a country doctor much loved by his many patients.

Emmy and Bernard, c. 1907.

They were married in Volkmarsen on April 18, 1906[8] and moved to Berlin the same year. They lived at Passauerstrasse 12. Clara often said that her father was the quintessential country doctor who never completely adjusted to life in the metropolis of Berlin.

---

[7] Evidently Emmy now owned the entire three-story apartment building. The rent from tenants was helpful later in the 1920s when the German economy collapsed.
[8] Emmy and Bernard's daughter Clara also married on April 18, but in 1935.

In October 1994 Philipp, Aaron and I visited Steinheim and Volkmarsen and their neglected Jewish cemeteries on our Bornstein/Löwenstein "roots" trip. In much of Europe and the United States, Christians and Jews had separate burial grounds (and still do today). There once was a large enough Jewish population to establish Jewish cemeteries in Steinheim[9] and in Volkmarsen.[10] We visited the Jewish cemetery in Steinheim first. It was still in relatively good condition, gravestones intact. The cemetery was surrounded by a fence with a locked gate, but a caretaker across from the cemetery had a key. He opened the gate so we could enter and walk around the Löwenstein headstones. The cemetery filled with trees and grass was a quiet, undisturbed and peaceful place.

The cemetery in Volkmarsen was another matter entirely. Almost all the headstones had been demolished to create a wall around the cemetery. Nothing green grew there. The only headstone remaining was that of Clara's grandmother, Jenny Hüneberg, with lettering in both German and Hebrew. We found a tiny piece of folded paper at the foot of her headstone. On the paper was a small, colored-pencil drawing depicting a swastika. What on Earth?

Jenny Hüneberg, Clara's grandmother (1844–1927).

---

[9] Steinheim population c. 2010 13,000.
[10] Volkmarsen population c. 2010 6,000.

When Clara was young, she and her brother spent a great part of their summers away from the stifling heat of Berlin, living with their grandmother in her Volkmarsen home. Clara said she was always happy in Volkmarsen, her mother's birthplace, and in Steinheim, her father's birthplace.

When I was a child, Clara would tell me stories about her grandmother Jenny Hüneberg. In photographs Jenny Hüneberg looks like a stern woman, but the tender letters and postcards she exchanged with her granddaughter give a very different impression. In them Jenny comes through as a warm, caring, and loving woman. Grandmother Hüneberg would often sit on her second-floor balcony, right on the town square in Volkmarsen. From there she could observe the townsfolk. If Clara walked across the square with a slouch, Jenny would shout from the balcony: "Clärchen, shoulders back. Straighten up." In those days good posture while sitting, standing, and walking was considered a sign of breeding and manners; slouching was a sign of physical and moral laxness.

Many relatives lived in or near Volkmarsen. Emmy had two sisters: Dina and Ida, and a brother Gustav. After 1933, as Hitler's anti-Semitic policies and laws penetrated even into the smallest villages, Clara's aunts and uncles and their children gradually left Germany. The Quakers found a safe haven in England for Aunt Dina Hüneberg Löwenstein, her daughter Hilda Hüneberg Sturmthal, and their families.[11] Ida Hüneberg Schuster ended up living in Los Angeles. I remember visiting Tante Ida in Los Angeles in the early 1950s. To me she seemed very tall, but then I was a short ten-year-old. Ida lived there with her daughter Anna and Anna's husband Feo[12] Dahlberg and their children Lotte and Traute.

During WWII Clara sent food packages from Chicago to her relatives in England. Her relatives were so happy when the packages arrived. In order to fill every tiny space in the package, Clara used marshmallows as packing material—the sugar in the marshmallows was the closest thing to candy that Clara could find. Unfortunately, her relatives had never seen this typically American confection. They threw away the white puffy fillers until Clara wrote them that marshmallows were spun sugar and quite edible!

---

[11] I visited in London with Hilda's granddaughter Gerda, a nurse, and husband Chico Clayton, a physician, in 1962 and again in 1994. They were absolutely warm and gracious hosts.

[12] Feo was probably a nickname for Teodor.

Jenny Hüneberg with her children and their spouses celebrate her 80th birthday, 1924.

—》《—

Clara had fond memories of her days spent in Westphalia and spoke of them often even as I sat next to her at her death bed in 1988. Sometimes Clara, her brother Hajo, and their parents spent a few weeks at the Baltic in the village Heringsdorf. We once had wonderful photos of Clara and her brother Hajo in crisp linen summer sailor outfits, but those photos disappeared after Clara passed away. As we will learn,[13] Clara grew up with her feet planted in two worlds: country Westphalia and cosmopolitan Berlin.

—》《—

In summer 1965 I visited Volkmarsen where a few of Clara's non-Jewish childhood friends still lived. I stayed with two Volkmarsen natives, Toni and her husband. Toni, daughter of the baker[14] had been Clara's playmate when the Löwensteins visited there in the summer. One afternoon during my visit Toni's husband took me on a walk around town and earnestly explained to me that it was the Communists, not the Fascists, who had caused the chaos of WWII and the expulsion of Jews from Germany. This was patently false, but what could I say to this well-meaning old man?

Steinheim and Volkmarsen were as lovely as I imagined when I was a child and listened to stories from Clara's endless repertoire. The villages seemed to retain the atmosphere from the time Clara left Germany in 1935—they were quiet, neat, and much off the

---

[13] Clara's childhood is dealt with in a later chapter of this family history.
[14] Clara would call her Des Bäckers Toni or Toni, daughter of the baker.

beaten tourist track. Volkmarsen was too small to have a hotel, so in 1994, Philipp, Aaron and I found lodgings in Steinheim, where the Löwensteins had lived. As Americans, my brothers and I were objects of interest there.

At breakfast, the waitress/barmaid could not restrain her curiosity. She came over to us, asking in halting English "Why are you visiting Steinheim?" She was amazed when I replied to her in perfect German (Philipp and Aaron spoke only rudimentary German with an American accent). I explained that I was related to the Löwenstein family who had lived in Steinheim for many years. The waitress became very excited because she knew exactly who the Löwensteins were. She suggested we arrange to meet the gentleman (whose name I've blocked) who now owned the old Löwenstein store. It had once belonged to Bernard's father, Moses Löwenstein, and later to Bernard's brothers. We contacted the store owner and made an appointment to meet the next day.

The next morning, we walked over to the store. The owner told us about the Löwenstein ancestors who were taken away by Hitler's soldiers. According to him, the Löwensteins asked the father of the current owner to take care of the store while they were "away." Of course, our ancestors never returned to Steinheim, and this helpful family has had the very successful store and mail-order business for two generations now.

As I roamed the store with Philipp and Aaron, the owner pointed out antique furniture from the Löwenstein days. He said the furniture added a bit of history to the aisles and shelves filled with new clothing. He asked me to pick out a piece of clothing from the store racks for myself. I demurred. My brothers didn't get why I was reluctant to accept his offer. The owner was so insistent that I finally gave in to shut him up. I grabbed into a clothing rack and pulled out a red sweater. I think the owner had absolutely no idea that I would consider any gift from him tainted by the death of my relatives. How could I say anything? I never wore the sweater though it was expensive and of excellent quality. When I came home to Austin, Texas, I wrapped up the unworn sweater and gave it directly to Goodwill.

After the store tour, we were invited to the owner's home on the floor above the store. We were served coffee from a beautiful silver urn; the cups and saucers were made of fine porcelain. Our hosts told us how glad they were that they hadn't missed our visit, since they were leaving the next day on a cruise around the world to celebrate their fiftieth wedding anniversary.

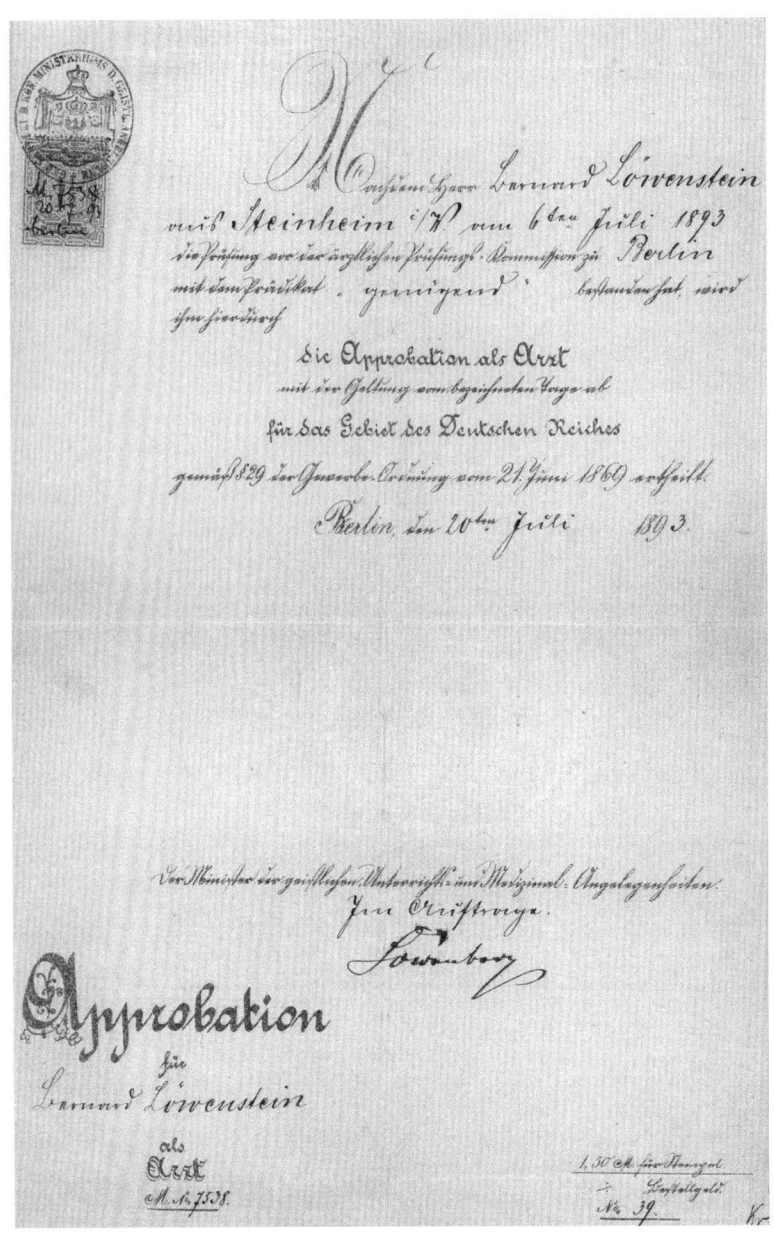

Bernard Löwenstein's license to practice medicine, 1893.

Heiratsurkunde.

Nr. — 8 —

Volkmarsen _____ am achtzehn _____ ten

April _____ tausend neunhundert undsechs _____

Vor dem unterzeichneten Standesbeamten erschienen heute zum Zwecke der Eheschließung:

1. der **praktische Arzt Dr. med. Bernard Löwenstein** _____

der Persönlichkeit nach durch den Kaufmann Gustav Hüneberg da hier der Persönlichkeit nach bekannt aner— fannt, mosaischer Religion, geboren am dreiundzwanzigs ten Maerz _____ des Jahres tausend acht hundert siebenundsechzig _____ zu Steinheim Kreis Höxter _____, wohnhaft in Steinheim _____

Sohn des Kaufmannes Moses Löwenstein und seiner in Steinheim verstorbenen Ehefrau Fanni geborene Löwenstein ersterer _____ wohnhaft in Steinheim ;

2. die **Witwe Emmi Zielinsky geborene Hüneberg, ohne besonderen Beruf**

der Persönlichkeit nach _____ be fannt, mosaischer Religion, geboren am neunundzwanzigs ten Dezember _____ des Jahres tausend acht hundert einundsiebenzig _____ zu Volkmarsen Kreis Wolfhagen _____, wohnhaft in Schöneberg Neue Bayreutherstrasse 2 _____

Tochter des in Volkmarsen verstorbenen Kaufmannes Salomon Hüneberg und seiner noch lebenden Ehefrau Fanni geborenen Rosenthal _____ wohnhaft in Volkmarsen _____

Form. Bb¹.

Marriage license for Bernard and Emmy. P. 1.

Als Zeugen waren zugezogen und erschienen:

3. der Kaufmann Gustav Hüneberg

der Persönlichkeit nach _____ bekannt,

____ 36 ____ Jahre alt, wohnhaft in ____ Volkmarsen, Pfortenstrasse No. 305
                                                                                            ;

4. der Rechtsanwalt Otto Löwenstein

der Persönlichkeit nach ____ durch den Kaufmann Gustav Hüneberg
                                         dahier _____ aner kannt,

____ 31 ____ Jahre alt, wohnhaft in ____ Cassel, Fulda-Brücke 8

Der Standesbeamte richtete an die Verlobten einzeln und nach einander die Frage:
    ob sie die Ehe mit einander eingehen wollen.
    Die Verlobten bejahten diese Frage und der Standesbeamte sprach hierauf aus:
    daß sie kraft des Bürgerlichen Gesetzbuchs nunmehr rechtmäßig verbundene Eheleute seien.

Vorgelesen, genehmigt und ____ unterschrieben
Bernard Löwenstein, Emmy Löwenstein geborene Hüneberg, Gustav Hüneberg, Otto Löwenstein

Der Standesbeamte.
H. v. Germeten

Daß vorstehender Auszug mit dem Heirats-Hauptregister des Standesamts zu ____ Volkmarsen
____ gleichlautend ist, wird hiermit bestätigt.
____ Volkmarsen ____ am ____ 28. März ____ 19 35.

(Siegel.)

Der Standesbeamte.
frenhövel.

Gebühren: _____
_____ der Rentr.

Marriage license for Bernard and Emmy. P. 2.

The Hüneberg and Löwenstein Families: From Westphalia to Berlin

Wedding Announcement/License, No. 8

This license is acceptable as proof of the marriage between Dr. Bernard Löwenstein, living in Stein-heim and Widow Emmi Zielinsky neé Hüneberg living in Schöneberg. Today both parties married in Volkmarsen on April 18, 1906.

These two people appeared at city hall to marry:

1. *Bernard Löwenstein, a practical physician attended by the merchant Gustav Hüneberg, of Jew-ish religion living in Steinheim, in the county of Höxter. Bernard is the son of Moses Löwenstein and his late wife, Fanni neé Löwenstein.*

2. *Emmi [sic] Zielinsky neé Hüneberg, widow, without profession, Jewish, born on December 29, 1871, in Volkmarsen in the county of Wolfhagen, currently living in Schöneberg, #2 New Bayreuth Street. Emmy is the daughter of the late Salomon Hüneberg and his living wife, Fanni [sic][15] neé Rosenthal living in Volkmarsen.*

These witnesses appeared before us:

3b. The merchant Gustav Hüneberg,[16] whom we know personally, 36 years of age, living in Volkmars-en at #305 Pfortenstrasse.

4b. The lawyer Otto Löwenstein,[17] whom we acknowledge is 31 years of age, living in Kassel at #8 Fulda-Brücke Street.

The city official determined that both parties wish to marry and that they are free of legal impediments. Document signatories include Bernard Löwenstein and Emmy Löwenstein neé Hüne-berg, Gustav Hüneberg, Otto Löwenstein.

The city official is H. v. Germenten. The marriage has been entered into the main register of the local officials, and is confirmed in Volkmarsen on 28 March, 1935.[18]

---

[15] Emmy's mother was named **Jenny** (not Fanni). A rare error in a German official document.
[16] Gustav Hüneberg was Emmy's brother.
[17] Bernard's younger brother.
[18] Clara obtained a typewritten copy of her parents' wedding license shortly before fleeing to the United States.

Berlin S.W., den

Beuth-Strasse 10.

Zielinsky

Name of
Clara's
mother's
first husband

– Confection.

Export.

Clue to name of Emmy
Löwenstein's first husband—
Zielinsky. Waste not want not.

On back of Zielinsky paper: Clara's drawing of boat with mooring.

CHAPTER 5

Jenny Barth Bornstein (1859–1951): Pioneering Female Physician

AFTER HER HUSBAND PHILIPP'S DEATH in 1891, Jenny was a thirty-two-year-old widow with three young children. Then Jenny's father, Israel, died in 1892. While Jenny had been taking care of Philipp in Dr. Fraenkel's sanitarium, she gradually became interested in studying medicine. Dr. Fraenkel, the husband of her sister Paula, encouraged Jenny to pursue her interest. Jenny's only education up to this point had been at a girl's high school which certified her as an elementary school teacher. Jenny apparently was able to attend university in Berlin to take required pre-medical classes. But she could not enter medical school in Germany—women at that time were barred from medical school admission. I have to assume that Jenny had the financial wherewithal to attend medical school in Switzerland. Inheritance? Assistance from relatives? I have no solid information, unfortunately.

In the second half of the 19th century the Swiss began developing new medical schools and they welcomed women from across Europe as students. Since many other countries besides Germany would not allow women to study medicine, the Swiss made a good business from educating foreigners. I have no idea what the cost of tuition was. In Germany, a university education was free, but that was not the case for foreign nationals in Switzerland.

During childhood Jenny's teachers called her Genie (German for genius, and a pun on her name Jenny). Her intelligence, combined with her persistence and determination, made her a good prospect for becoming a physician.

Imagine a widow with three children, perhaps a couple of servants, and endless amounts of baggage, traveling from Berlin to Zürich (in German speaking Switzerland). Can you imagine the determination and grit that pushed Jenny from being a kindergarten teacher to medical doctor? While she was studying medicine, her children were also advancing their education. I like to imagine the little Bornstein family: Jenny, her son Arthur, and daughters Therese (Röse), and Susanne all quietly studying at home together. Arthur was 17, Therese (Röse) was 15, and Susanne was 10. Arthur completed gymnasium in Zurich and was ready to begin his medical studies in Berlin. Röse and Susanne were still in school.

We can learn how rare it was for a woman to be awarded a medical diploma by studying Jenny's Diplom carefully. Where the printed boilerplate German diploma reads "his," an ink pen was used to strike out the masculine pronoun and to insert the feminine pronoun "she." That shows us how unusual Jenny's accomplishment was!

Jenny was awarded her medical degree in 1898. She was then 39 years old. After Jenny completed her medical studies in Zürich, she moved back to Berlin. Presumably her children, at least her two daughters, lived with her. We do not know her street address. Had the old family villa been sold at that point?

Jenny's Swiss medical license, 1898. The boiler-plate male pronoun "seinen" has been struck through and replaced with the feminine pronoun "ihren."

Sometime after Israel's and Philipp's deaths, the "Barth and Bornstein" business was renamed "Bornstein and Bütow." Wilhelm Bütow, like Philipp a son-in-law, married Jenny's sister Johanna (Hanne). According to my source Brigitte Wolman,[1] the business later went bankrupt. I have no further information.

Jenny undertook further medical preparation to obtain her German medical license. During this time, she worked at the Charité Hospital, founded in Berlin around 1710 as a charity hospital for the poor. In 1810 the hospital became associated with the University of Berlin, and still exists today with four large campuses.

When Jenny passed her medical boards in 1902, she worked in Berlin as an in-house physician for an insurance firm that provided health insurance for employees of department stores. She also had a private practice limited to obstetrics and gynecology until 1912, when the death of her daughter-in-law left her son Arthur a widower. Jenny's history continues in the chapter on her grandson, my father, Frederick Bornstein.

---

[1] A distant cousin in Israel who wrote me this information in 2005.

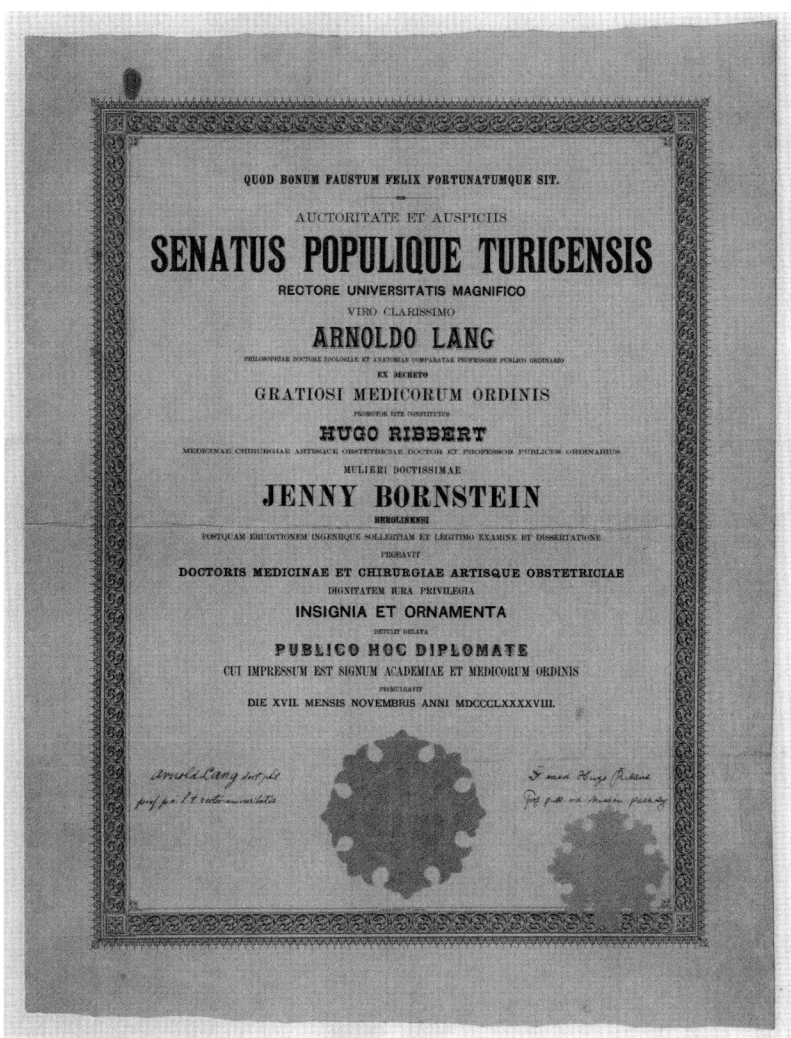

Jenny's Swiss medical diploma in Latin. 1898.

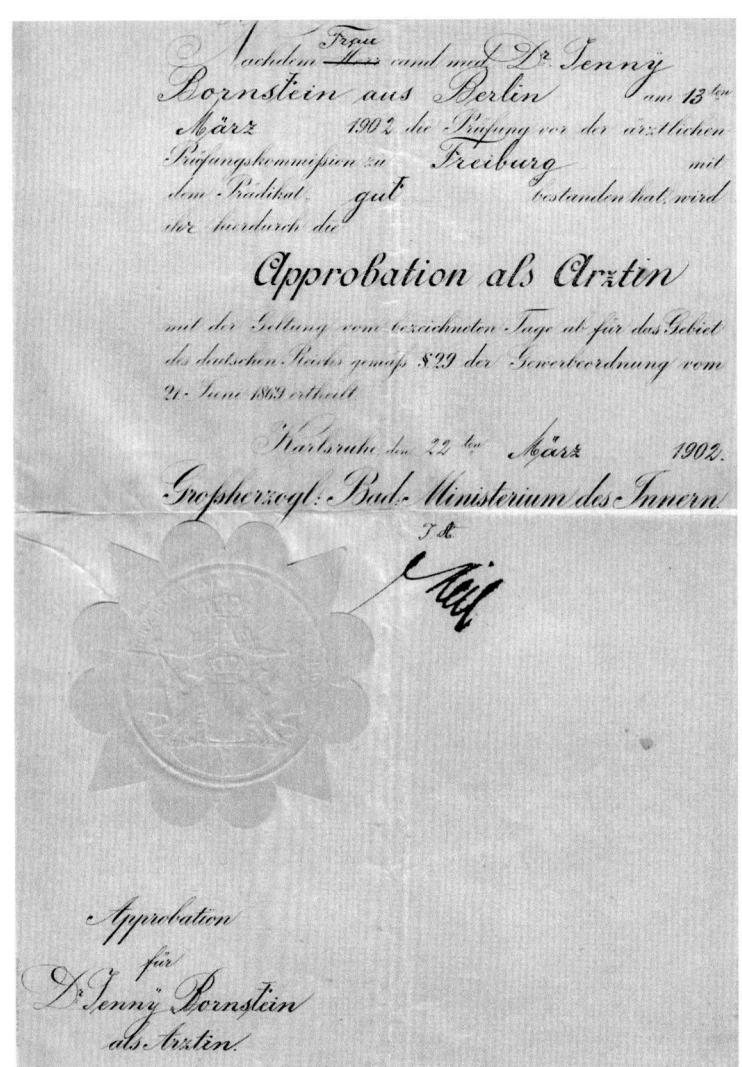

*German medical license
for Dr. Jenny Bornstein,
1902.*

Medical license for Dr. Jenny Bornstein, 1902:

*Dr. Jenny Bornstein, a resident of Berlin, took the medical boards on March 13, 1902, in Freiburg. She
was awarded the grade of gut (good) and thus is permitted to begin her medical practice in Germany
according to Article 29 promulgated on 21 June 1869.*

Karlsruhe, 22 March 1902.

The Department of Internal Affairs.

Seal. Next to the seal are the initials of the government official.

August 2, 1902

Mother and Son Are Physicians

Last night, a woman passed the medical licensing examination. She was tested by the Dean, Professor Englemann. The lady is a resident of Berlin, Dr. Jenny Bornstein. She was admitted to the examination by the Minister of Education. Several years ago, in Zurich she completed the M.D. degree and preliminary license. According to our sources, the "lady" received the grade of "good" on her exam. It is notable that her son has also achieved the M.D. title and can say with pride that his mother is a smart lady. His mother made a better score than all nine male candidates.

Mother and Son Are Physicians

Again last night a woman passed the medical licensing examination. The candidate is a resident of Berlin, Dr. Jenny Bornstein. She was admitted to the examination by the Education Minister after she attained her medical degree several years ago at the University of Zürich. Noteworthy is the fact that her son, Arthur Bornstein, also passed the exam last year. Yesterday he also became an M.D. and can say with conviction that his mother is one smart lady.

---

[2] Unfortunately, the original German articles are lost. Olga translated the newspaper articles in 1982.

CHAPTER 6

Arthur and Olga Adele Bornstein (both b. 1881): Husband and Wife, Physicians, Research Partners

Jenny's son Arthur is probably the most accomplished of the Bornstein/Löwenstein clan. He was born on April 14, 1881 as the eldest of Jenny and Philipp Bornstein's three children. He was named for Philipp's father, Aron Bornstein.[1] Arthur's younger sisters were Therese (Röse) Bornstein Brunstein (1883–?) and Susanne Bornstein (1888–195?). Susanne was employed by the *Berliner Polizeidient* (Berlin police department) as a social worker working with the underclass in Berlin and also Hamburg. In 1934 she moved to Cairo, Egypt where she was the nanny for the family of a British army officer. Suse followed the same family to Jerusalem, Palestine, when the officer was transferred there. Suse died in Jerusalem in 195?. Röse married Vladimir Brunstein, a brother of Olga Brunstein Bornstein. They emigrated to the Soviet Union and settled in St. Petersburg. Nothing was heard from them after 1937.

I have the short, handwritten autobiography Arthur wrote when he was a teenager. Arthur reports that Jenny supervised a small kindergarten in their home. He enjoyed taking things apart, shocking his mother one day as she entered the room where he was playing and found that he had completely dismantled an elegant clock.[2] He also writes that he'd go upstairs to his grandfather, Israel, to report his school grades. Since he had excellent grades, his grandfather would give him a gold coin! Arthur further writes in his teen-age memoir that their family was committed to helping others (*fromm*, moral or virtuous) but were not believers in God (*gläubig*). That point of view certainly rubbed off on his son Fritz.

Arthur and his mother must have had a close but complicated relationship as later events will demonstrate. Jenny loved all her three children, but I believe Arthur was her favorite. He was her first born child and only son, after all. Was Arthur influenced by his mother's ambition to excel?

After completing medical school, Arthur worked as a researcher with Nathan Zuntz,[3] a famous physiologist at the Royal Agricultural College in Poppendorf at the Baltic Sea. Zuntz is remembered today for his research on the effects of extremes in human

---

[1] Arthur was a substitute for Aron, a common practice. Parents wanted to avoid having names that sounded too 'Jewish'. For example, Moses might become Melvin; Solon might become Shelly; Baruch (Barack) might become Barry.

[2] An early sign of Arthur's deep curiosity.

[3] Nathan Zuntz (1847–1920). Interestingly, Zuntz was also Jewish. Was there a Jewish old boy network? I suspect so.

physiology and is considered a founder of aviation and sports medicine. Zuntz himself participated in experiments in high altitude physiology by rising 5000 meters in a hot air balloon! From him Arthur learned the value of strong, experimental methods and the need to be fearless in establishing limits by experimenting on himself. Both men continued the 19th-century tradition of heroic medical self-experimentation.

Arthur stands between Olga (in white hat) and his sister Susanne (in black hat) 1907.

Around 1905 Arthur went to Geneva, apparently as a visiting professor at the medical school there. At the same time Olga Brunstein from Odessa was close to finishing her medical studies in Geneva. Only upon careful reading of Jenny and Olga's Latin diplomas did I realize that Jenny studied in Zürich (German speaking Switzerland) whereas Olga studied in Geneva (French speaking Switzerland). It was in Geneva that my grandparents met and fell in love as Olga was finishing up her medical studies. I initially thought that Jenny had introduced Olga to Arthur. Not only was I wrong, but I hadn't noticed the difference in the year each finished her medical studies: Jenny in 1898, Olga in 1907.

We have little information about the Odessa Brunstein family.[4] Through close reading of documents was I able to sort out the following story: Olga Brunstein (1881–1912) was born to a well-to-do Jewish family in Odessa, Russia. I think her father Emanuel was a prosperous trader, perhaps in timber. There were perhaps thirteen children in the family, but we know nothing about them except for Olga's brother, Vladimir (Volodya), who married Arthur's sister Röse (Therese).[5] This was not an uncommon arrangement. The families were Jewish and probably had similar, bourgeois values. We know that when Olga finished her studies in Odessa she wanted to attend medical school close to home.

My grandmother, Olga Brunstein Bornstein. Undated photograph.

---

[4] The name Brunstein probably means well stone.
[5] We do not know when they met and married. Presumably around the time Arthur and Olga married. Vladimir and Röse had two children near in age to Fritz. The family moved to St. Petersburg Russia in the late 1920s. You will hear more about them in a later chapter.

Arthur and Olga Adele Bornstein (both b. 1881)

Unfortunately for Olga, Russian medical schools had a *numerus clausus* for the admission of Jews.[6] Thus, it was not unusual for Russian Jews to travel outside their country to study medicine. French was the language of the upper classes in Russia during pre-revolution times. Olga would have no problems with language when studying medicine at a French-speaking medical school in Switzerland.

We do not know how Olga and Arthur met. Perhaps Arthur was her instructor at the University of Geneva? From what I can gather from the few letters I have from Arthur to Olga in French and/or German, he encouraged her to finish up her dissertation so she could be awarded her medical degree. Olga knew some German but was not a fluent German speaker. She and Arthur corresponded mostly in French. Olga became fluent in German only while living in Germany after she and Arthur married.

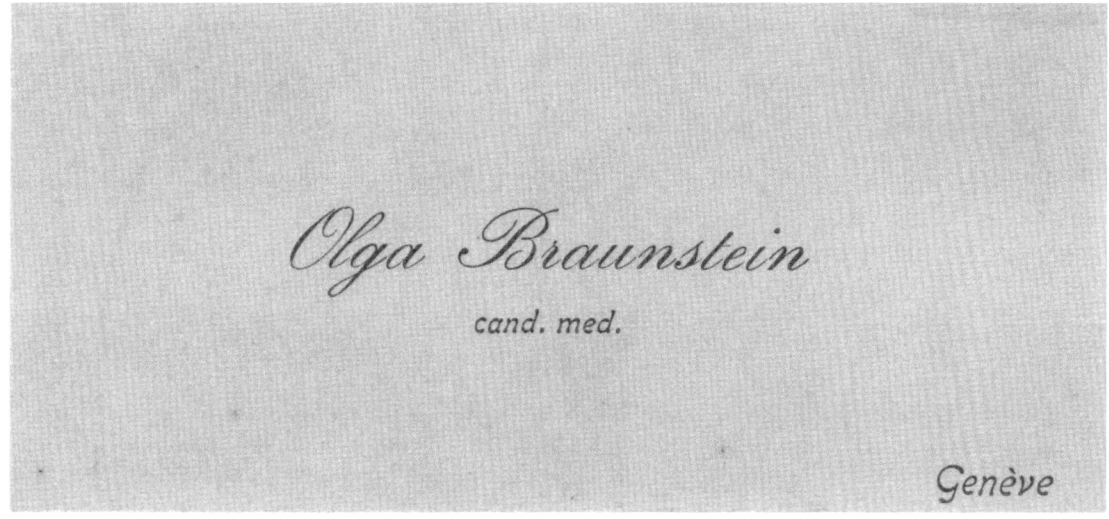

Olga's calling card before her marriage to Arthur.

---

[6] numerus clausus—Closed number, fixed maximum number in the admission of persons (or certain groups of persons) to specific professions institutions of higher learning, professional associations, positions of public office, etc.; frequently applied to Jews. The numerus clausus on the admission of Jews to institutions of higher learning was applied in the 19th century and into the 20th century especially in Eastern Europe.

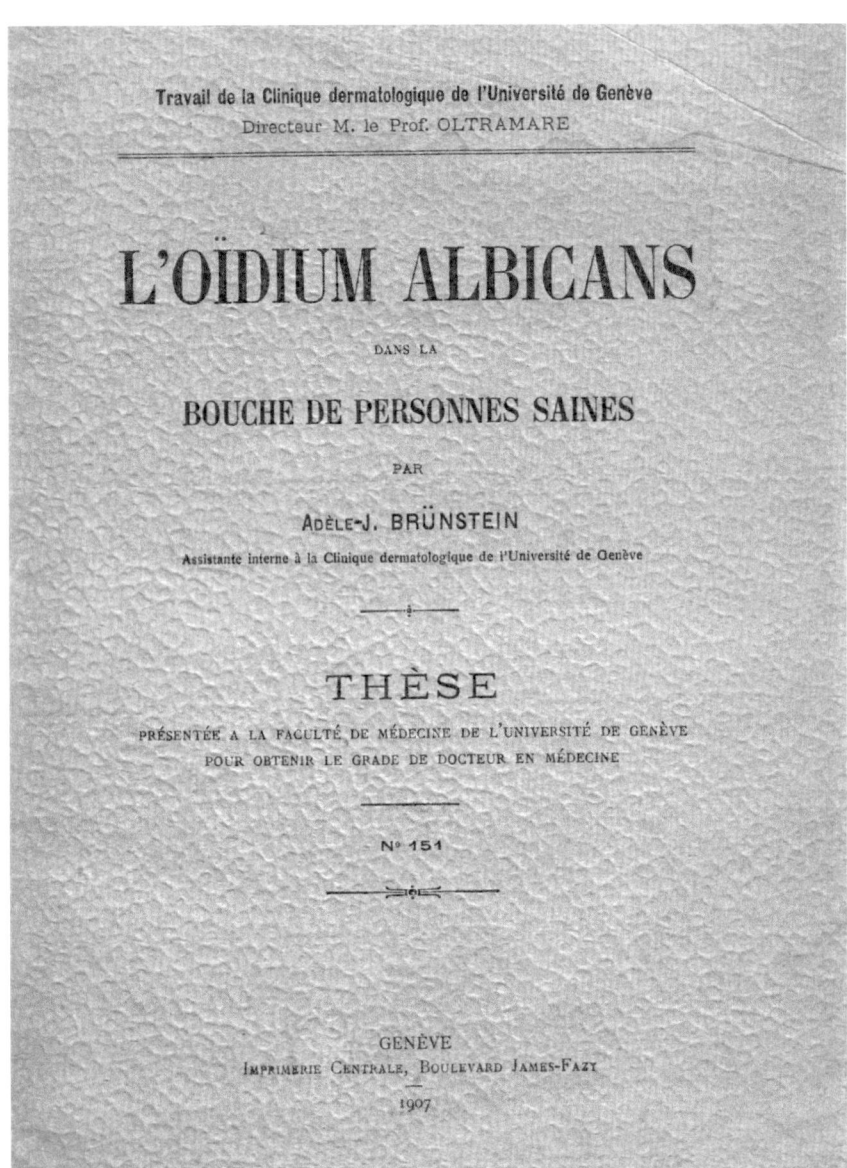

Travail de la Clinique dermatologique de l'Université de Genève

Directeur M. le Prof. OLTRAMARE

L'OÏDIUM ALBICANS

DANS LA

BOUCHE DE PERSONNES SAINES

PAR

Adèle-J. BRÜNSTEIN

Assistante interne à la Clinique dermatologique de l'Université de Genève

THÈSE

PRÉSENTÉE A LA FACULTÉ DE MÉDECINE DE L'UNIVERSITÉ DE GENÈVE
POUR OBTENIR LE GRADE DE DOCTEUR EN MÉDECINE

N° 151

GENÈVE
Imprimerie Centrale, Boulevard James-Fazy

1907

Olga's dissertation for her M.D.
"Thrush in the Mouth of Healthy People," 1907.

Olga's printed medical diploma, 1907. —»

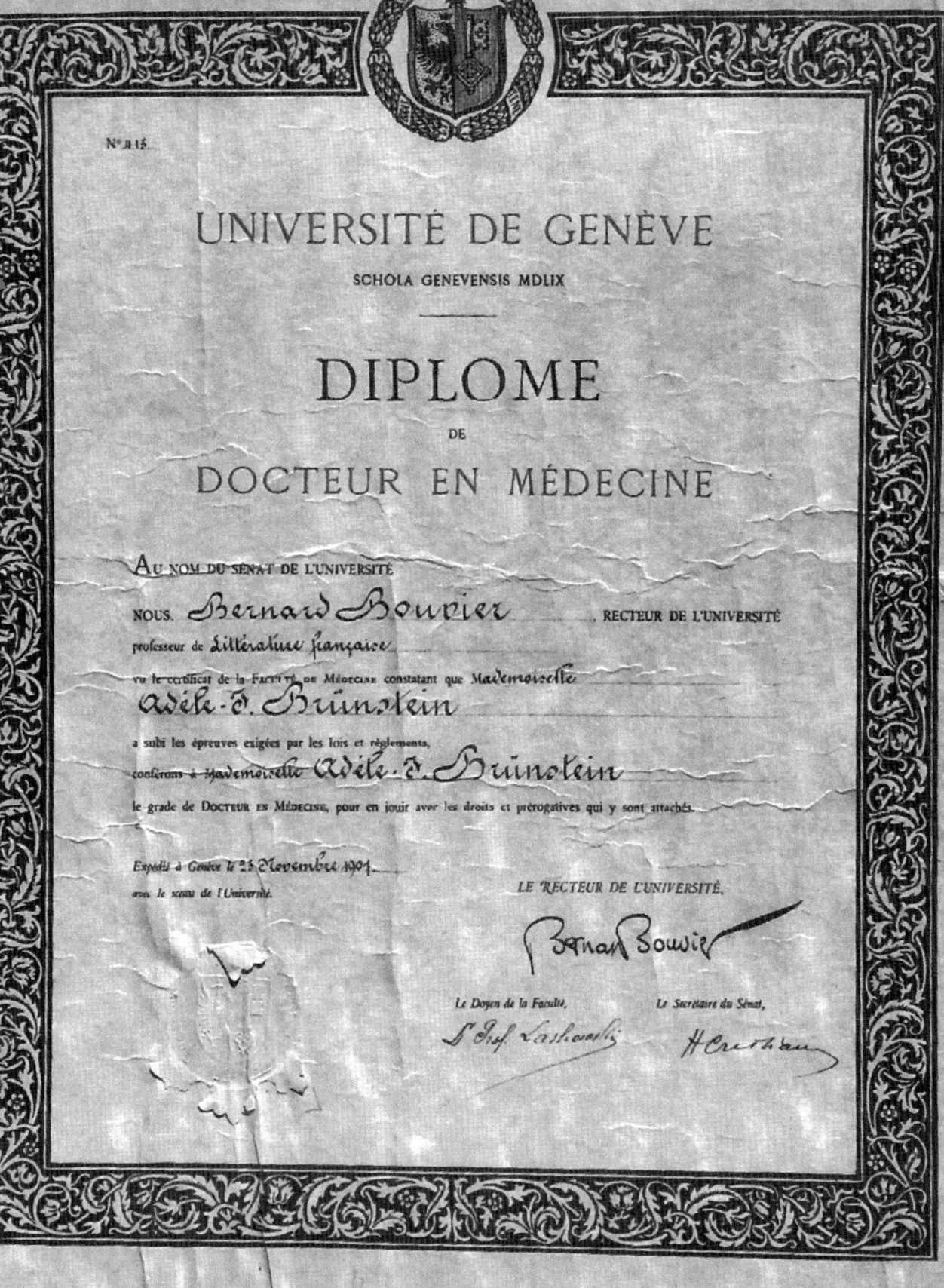

N° 315

UNIVERSITÉ DE GENÈVE

SCHOLA GENEVENSIS MDLIX

—

DIPLOME

DE

DOCTEUR EN MÉDECINE

AU NOM DU SÉNAT DE L'UNIVERSITÉ

NOUS *Bernard Bouvier*, RECTEUR DE L'UNIVERSITÉ

professeur de *Littérature française*

vu le certificat de la FACULTÉ DE MÉDECINE constatant que Mademoiselle

Adèle S. Brünstein

a subi les épreuves exigées par les lois et règlements,

conférons à Mademoiselle *Adèle S. Brünstein*

le grade de DOCTEUR EN MÉDECINE, pour en jouir avec les droits et prérogatives qui y sont attachés.

Expédié à Genève le 25 Novembre 1904.

avec le sceau de l'Université.

LE RECTEUR DE L'UNIVERSITÉ,

Bernard Bouvier

Le Doyen de la Faculté,

Prof. Laskowski

Le Secrétaire du Sénat,

H Crothan

UNIVERSITÉ   DE GENÈVE

FACULTÉ DE MÉDECINE

Genève, le 8 Janvier 1908.

Le Soussigné D^r en Médecine Professeur et Doyen à la Faculté de Médecine de l'Université de Genève, certifi par la presente que Madame Bornstein Adèle née Brunstein a fait toutes ses études régulières en Médecine dans notre Faculté et après avoir subi avec succès les examens de Doctorat et presenté une Thèse spéciale, elle a obtenu le Diplôme de Docteur en Médecine en 1907 Conformement à notre ancienne loi ce Diplôme confère à Mme Bornstein le droit d'exercer la Médecine dans la République et Canton de Genève.—

En foi de quoi je lui delivre sur sa demande le present certificat qui doit servir de qui de droit.—

Fait à Genève ce 8 Janvier 1908.

Dr Prof. Laskowski

UNIVERSITÉ DE GENÈVE
DOYEN A LA FACULTÉ
DE MÉDECINE

Handwritten certification. Olga Bornstein (neé Brunstein) can practice medicine in Switzerland, 1908.

Arthur moved to Göttingen where he had an appointment at the university as an entry-level professor. Arthur and Olga were married in 1907, almost certainly in Warsaw, then part of the Russian Empire. Their marriage certificate is in Russian. On August 9, 1907, the German Consul in Warsaw authenticated the certificate.

Arthur taught at Göttingen's medical school and embarked on what would be a fruitful career in research. The newlyweds lived together in Göttingen until Arthur was called to head a major project in Hamburg in January 1909.

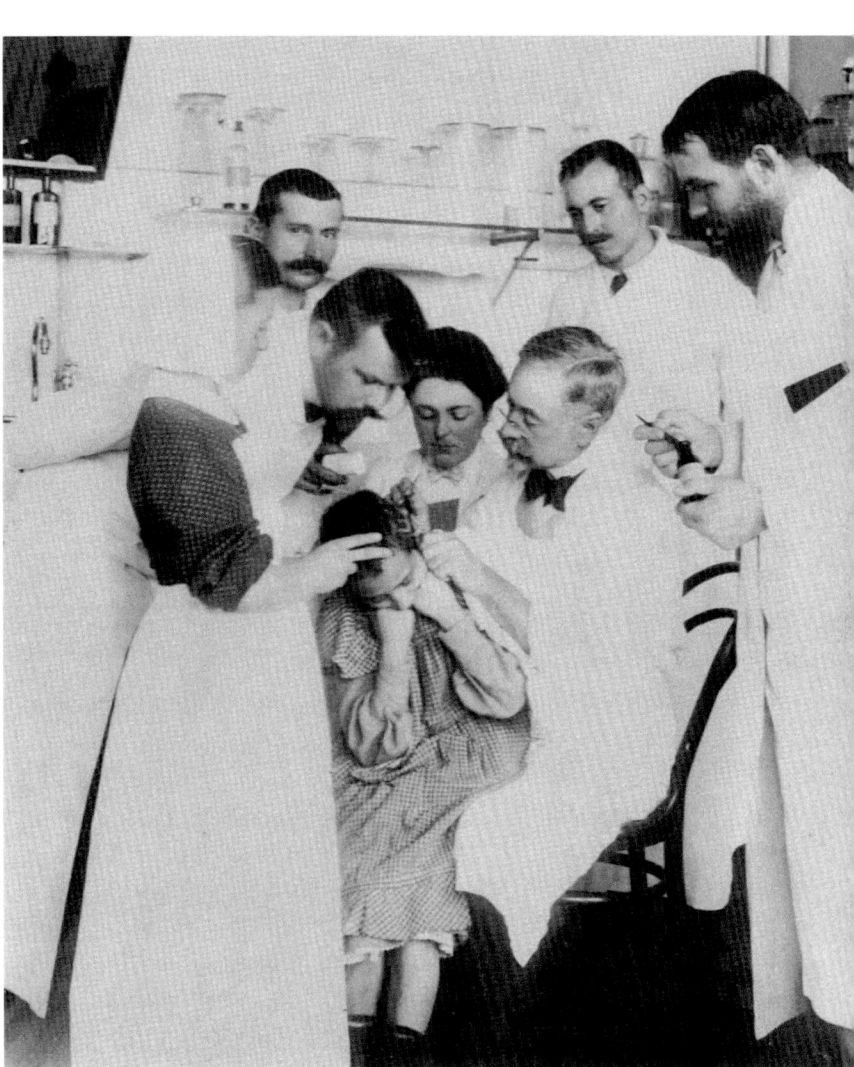

Olga, center, treating a patient. Note men surrounding her. c. 1909–1912. This photo was always in my room near my bed as I was growing up.

In 1907 the city of Hamburg broke ground on a tunnel under the Elbe River. Hamburg's huge shipyards lay on one side of the broad Elbe, but the workforce lived in St. Pauli on the other side of the river. Ferries inefficiently transported the workers to and from the shipyards. Planners had decided that a bridge over the Elbe would limit the size of the ships traveling up and down the river. A tunnel under the river for foot and vehicular traffic was an efficient and elegant solution and would allow more ship traffic to sail up the river from the North Sea. The tunnel project was a hugely expensive project and presented great technical difficulties.

After tunnel construction began, many laborers were incapacitated by "caisson disease" (the bends or diver's illness).[7] In the first year, three workers died from the bends as they worked in the depths under high atmospheric pressure. Hundreds were sickened. This brought the project to a complete halt.

Arthur's diving bathysphere with lab assistant and test animals. Note monkey.

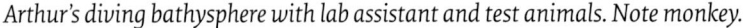

---

[7] The Bends is an illness that arises from the rapid release of nitrogen gas from the bloodstream and is caused by bubbles forming in the blood when a diver ascends to the surface too rapidly. It is also referred to as Caisson sickness, decompression sickness (DCS), and Divers' Disease. Divers must go through a decompression process after they come up from the depths.

Arthur and Olga Adele Bornstein (both b. 1881)

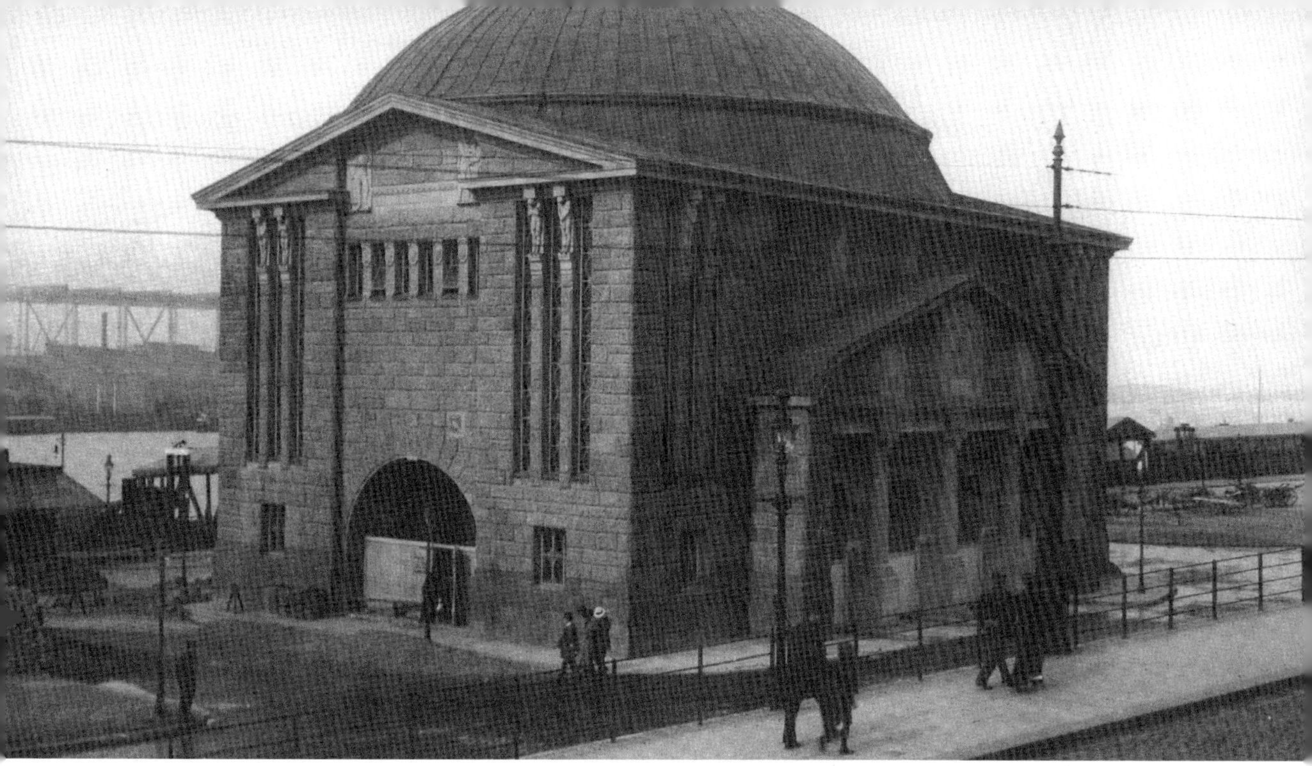

Exterior of Elbe Tunnel entry building and interior entrance to tunnel. Opened 1911.

Thus by the end of 1908, the city decided to hire a new project physician to ensure the safety of the workers. To lose even three workers was unacceptable. The city officials turned to Nathan Zuntz, Arthur's mentor in Berlin, to find a good candidate. Zuntz recommended his young protégé Arthur Bornstein, only 27 years old but already a specialist in physiology. Arthur was offered the position and accepted it. He and Olga took up residence in Hamburg.

Arthur and Olga were installed in a small house at the construction site on the far side of the Elbe. The couple conducted experiments to determine the physiological effects on the human body when it labored at high atmospheric pressure. Arthur made many investigational dives himself, increasing his knowledge about the cause of the bends and how to control the damage to humans when they were diving. Olga helped Arthur with the experiments, and they published scientific papers jointly.

Their work was very successful. No workers died while Arthur was the Elbe Tunnel doctor. The Elbe tunnel is still in working condition today. A favorite activity for the Hamburg locals (and visitors to the city) is to walk through the tunnel, which is closed to vehicular traffic on weekends. I made this walk alone in 1962, with my brothers Philipp and Aaron in 1994, and with my husband David in 2009. The green and black glazed tile work on the tunnel walls includes beautiful ceramic tiles that depict sea and river mammals and fish.

Sometime in 2008, on a whim, I typed Arthur Bornstein's name into a Google search box. Imagine my surprise when I found an entry for the *First International Arthur Bornstein Workshop on Medical Aspects of Deep Tunneling and Diving, 2001. K-P Faesecke, ed.* Goodness! What on earth was this? 70 years after his death, was Arthur still regarded as an authority on diving and high-pressure physiology? I immediately dusted off my librarian skills and found an e-mail address for a certain K-P Faesecke. Soon my long e-mail to him in German was on its way. In under 24 hours I received a reply from Karl Peter Faesecke, M.D., Ph.D., written in perfect English. It turned out that Faesecke had written his Ph.D. dissertation on Arthur Bornstein's work and had put together a symposium bearing his name.

I began a long correspondence with Faesecke that culminated in an invitation to David and me, all expenses paid, to the *Second International Arthur Bornstein Workshop on Compressed Air Work and Deep Diving in Tunnel Construction, 2nd International, Hamburg, Sept. 2009.* All I had to do was give a talk about my grandfather and his work. Luckily, I had already begun writing this family history and I could give a decent lecture in German. Even though I never knew my grandfather, I knew a great deal about him. And of course, I could refer to the large family archive which I had organized.

The highlight of the Hamburg conference was a tour to the newest underground tunnel being built in Hamburg for an extension of the subway system. We saw the huge tunnel boring machine as it cut through sand and rock. We met a special international group of tunnel doctors: all intensely interested in that specialized work whether across the Sea of Mamara (Istanbul), underground utilities (Hong Kong), on North Sea oil rigs, or gold mines in South Africa. We sat in the decompression trailer that workers use as they come up to the surface from the tunnel. Arthur's tables for safe diving and recovery are still in use today!

A German attendee asked me how I felt about being at the conference, knowing the sad years of German history during the Nazi period. I had to think a moment. Then I replied: "The entire Nazi period was dreadful for my family and many, many other Jewish families. But today we're in 2009. How can I let anger rule my life? None of the perpetrators of those great crimes against humanity are living today. I don't care to live with hate in my heart. I want to appreciate the recognition being given to Arthur Bornstein today."

Before learning about Dr. Faesecke's research I did not know how closely Arthur and Olga worked together on the tunnel project. It was Faesecke's idea to have the city of Hamburg give the name of *Bornsteinplatz* to the square on the south side of the river where they used to live to honor Arthur and Olga's work. How thankful we are to Dr. Faesecke for his efforts.

K.P. Faesecke on the Bornstein Platz on the south side of the Elbe Tunnel. Fritz was born near here.

Arthur and Olga's only child, my father, Frederick Philipp Emanuel Bornstein, was born on February 9, 1910. He was welcomed joyfully by his relatives in Germany and Russia. He would have a life journey that no fortune teller would have foreseen.

ADDITIONAL MATERIALS

Letter from Arthur to Olga before their marriage:

Berlin, June 29, 1907

My dear, dear Olushka:

I'm writing to urge you to come to Berlin as soon as possible...We are all very concerned about you. I'm going to try to find out today if we can be married at the border since you probably don't have time to do that. My mother agrees with that idea...we want you to come here from Odessa quickly. If you can, please answer the following questions:

1. *Can you tell me definitely when we will see each other?*
2. *Can you find out what the Russian legal requirements are for us to marry. What formal documents are required?*
3. *According to Russian law will you become a German citizen when we are married, or is there something else you must do to drop your Russian citizenship?*
4. *What kind of passport will you have after our marriage?*
5. *How will your Russian circumstances change, if our wedding takes place on the border? Will German functionaries accept our marriage?*
6. *What do we need to do to have our marriage recognized officially in Germany?*
7. *Can we get everything in order by August 8th?*

There's not much else to report from here. My opportunities here, as a Jew, are very unlikely. I've made visits to various professors. Prof. Laden told me that he's retiring but no successor has been named. We'll just have to see what happens. Many, many greetings, write soon, and remain my beloved.

Arthur

Marriage certificate for Olga and Arthur Bornstein, Warsaw 1907. Translation follows.

Olga and Arthur's marriage license translated from the Russian into German:

Translation from Russian of the notice #153, 1907.

Wedding license according to the civil registry.

We herewith certify that the physician, Arthur Bornstein, 26 years old, and the unmarried Adele Brunstein, 26 years old, were married on July 26 (August 8)[8] 1907 in Warsaw.

We certify that this marriage is legal. The marriage ceremony was conducted by Foszkowitz in the office of non-Christian marriages in the 8th district of Warsaw.

This certification is recognized by the German Consulate, declaring that the translation of the Russian marriage certification into German is correct and acceptable.

Warsaw, August 9, 1907

J. H. Defke

General Consul of the German Empire

---

[8] Depending on which calendar you are using. Check out the confusion on google.com

Program for the 4th International Arthur Bornstein Workshop

Arthur's granddaughter, Olga Bornstein Wise, presented at the workshop in 2012.

4ᵀᴴ INTERNATIONAL ARTHUR - BORNSTEIN - WORKSHOP
ON MEDICAL ASPECTS OF HYPERBARIC TUNNELING

"DIGGIN' EVER DEEPER - WORLDWIDE"

FOCUS ON CHINA: MEET THE EXPERTS
ON VERY DEEP HYPERBARIC TUNNELING

MARCH 10, 2012, 10 AM - 5 PM
AT THE HAMBURG MUSEUM OF WORK

IN CONNECTION WITH THE TUNNEL EXHIBITION
"100 YEARS OLD ELBE RIVER TUNNEL"

GERMAN SOCIETY OF DIVING AND HYPERBARIC MEDICINE

MUSEUM DER ARBEIT

SPEAKERS AND THEIR AFFILIATIONS

Dr. phil. Jürgen Bönig, Curator of the Hamburg Museum of Work

Olga Bornstein-Wise, Retired Lecturer, Austin, Texas, USA

Edwin Ching, Chief Resident Engineer – AECOM, Hong Kong

Dr. med. Karl P. Faesecke, Hyperbaric Medical Consultant, Member of the Board of „Gesellschaft für Tauch- und Überdruckmedizin"

Torsten Haux, President of Haux Life Support

Andreas Fischer, Germanischer Lloyd, Hamburg

Karsten Grimm, Dipl.-Ing., BilfingerBerger, Hamburg

Paddy Reijnders, IHC Hytech, Ramsdonkveer, NL

Claus Mayer, Managing Director of Nordseetaucher GmbH

Prof. Wouter Sterk, MD, PhD, Director Dadcodat, NL

T.P. van Rees Vellinga, MD, Dir. Medisch Centrum Hyperbare Zuurstoftherapie, Adm.de Ruyter Ziekenhuis, Goes, NL

Piers Verman, Project Manager - Lai Chi Kok Drainage Tunnel, Hong Kong, Leighton Contractors (Asia) Limited

LIST OF PRESENTATIONS

Karl P. Faesecke	*Opening Remarks*
Jürgen Bönig	*100 Years of Tunneling in Hamburg*
Olga Bornstein-Wise	*My Grandfather Arthur Bornstein*
Andreas Fischer	*Rules and Guidelines for Chamber Systems in Tunneling*
Karsten Grimm	*ESCSO Portland: C.A.W. in Greater Depths*
Claus Mayer	*Current Practice in Deep and Very Deep Hyperbaric Tunneling*

LUNCH BREAK

Piers Verman	*Hong Kong – Beyond the Regulations*
Torsten Haux	*Custom-made Hardware for Hyperbaric Tunnel Construction*
Paddy Reijnders	*Transfer Shuttles and Medical Chambers for Compressed Gas Workers*
Wouter Sterk	*The Use of Gas Mixtures during Deep Caisson and Tunnel Work*
T.P.van Rees Vellinga	*Practical Experience with Trimix-Saturation in Hyperbaric Tunneling*
Edwin Ching	*Closing Remarks*

ARTHUR BORNSTEIN AT THE TIME OF THE TUNNEL CONSTRUCTION

SOCIAL PROGRAM

Friday, March 9

ɔm	Guided bus tour through the port's largest container terminals; departure from hotel "Hafen Hamburg"
ɔm	Arrival at south entrance of tunnel, Walk through the Old Elbe Tunnel (450 m)
7 pm	à la carte dinner at hotel restaurant

Saturday, March 10

5 pm	Guided tour of tunnel exhibition at the Museum of Work
7 pm	Dinner at Museum restaurant "TRUDE"

Sunday, March 11

ad libitum, e.g. harbor cruise by boat (organized if demanded) or early-morning fish-market

---

FRONT PICTURE:

CUTTING WHEEL "**TRUDE**" OF 4TH TUBE ELBETUNNEL (1997 - 2000) ON PERMANENT VERTICAL DISPLAY AT THE HAMBURG MUSEUM OF WORK

CHAPTER 7

Fritz Bornstein (b. 1910)
Grows up in Hamburg

MY FATHER, FREDERICK PHILIPP EMANUEL (FRITZ) BORNSTEIN was born in Hamburg, Germany on February 9, 1910 to Olga Brunstein Bornstein and Arthur Bornstein. He was their only child. An earlier child of theirs had died at birth. Frederick is one of Germany's most historic given names. Between 1485 and 1918 nearly all of the Electors of Brandenburg and Kings of Prussia were named "Frederick," "Wilhelm," or some combination of the two names. Philipp was for Arthur's father, Emanuel for Olga's father. Obviously, patriotism took precedence over family ties. I will call my father Fritz, the German diminutive of Frederick.

Baby Fritz, 7 months old.

The new family was living together in the small cottage near the shipyard bank of the Elbe Tunnel in Steinwerder,[1] just across from the working men's district of Sankt Pauli. Once the massive construction project was completed in 1911, Arthur was no longer needed as the project physician. He took a position at St. Georg Hospital and continued his physiological research. His wife assisted him and co-published scientific papers with

---

[1] Very few people lived in Steinwerder. Even today, it remains mainly an industrial center and cruise ship terminal. Its famous shipyards no longer underpin the Hamburg economy.

him. Olga had additional training with Gerson Unna,[2] a pioneer in dermopathology and one of the founders of Beiersdorf and Nivea. During a brief stay in Hamburg in 1962 I met Dr. Marie Unna, his widow and also a dermatologist.[3] My husband David met her in 1971.

Marie Unna was the only person I ever met who talked to me about my grandmother Olga. Marie spoke a clear and elegant German. I remember her remarking, probably due to her trained eye as a dermatologist, that my skin was as beautiful as that of my grandmother, Olga. This obviously made a big impression on me, because I remember what she told me clearly after almost 60 years. In 1962 Marie Unna wrote my parents this short letter:

> *Bergedorf, Wentorferstr. 75. April 1962*
> *Dear Bornsteins:*
> *Your Olga was just here for a visit. We really enjoyed meeting this intelligent, interested, and resolute young woman. Fritz, her fresh spirit and enjoyment of life really reminded me of your dear mother. She also was so filled with the anticipation of all the wonders of life and completely open to all things beautiful and worth knowing. Your daughter has your nose, Fritz, and your grandmother Jenny's and Aunt Röse's bountiful hair. I cannot thank you enough for sending that sweet child to visit me.*
> *All best wishes,*
> *Maria Unna*

Many of the Bornsteins and Löwensteins born during the late nineteenth and early twentieth centuries bore first names that were familiar German or English names rather than classic Jewish names. Arthur was named for his grandfather Aron Bornstein, Frederick (Fritz) after the Prussian Kaiser Friedrich Wilhelm. Friedrich is a name that probably comes from old German: *Reich* (Rich) and *Friede* (peace), or rich in peace. How ironic that name proved to be in light of the tragic historical events to come.

---

[2] Dr. Paul Gerson Unna (1850–1929).

[3] "Marie Unna hereditary hypotrichosis" is named after her discovery of the condition. This is a disease characterized by sparse scalp hair at birth, with variable coarse, wiry hair regrowth in childhood, and potential loss again at puberty.

My two great grandmothers, Jenny Hüneberg and Jenny Barth Bornstein, had English first names, as did Clara's mother Emmy (Emily?). Clara and her brother Hans had prototypical German first names. Classic Jewish names such as Solomon, Moses, Sara, Israel appear only in the earliest branches of our family tree.

The first name you give your child is a very visible part of your relationship to the society you live in. Clara used to say you could tell if a Jew's first name had an underlying, classic Jewish name: Arthur for Aron, Bernard for Baruch, Melvin for Moses and so on. Olga Brunstein was called Adele on many documents to lessen the Slavic tone of her first name. I used to be confused because I thought Olga had a sister Adele. That was not the case at all! Here's a little coda to the naming of children: in Jewish tradition, you don't name children after relatives who are alive when your child is born. Clara and Fritz broke the tradition when they named their son Frederick (Fred) for his father, who was very much alive when little Fred was born.

Arthur, Olga and little Fritz may have traveled to Odessa to meet Olga's family, probably late 1910 or early 1911.[4] Odessa, founded in 1794, was a relatively new Russian city. In the mid-1700s, Catherine the Great[5] demanded that Jewish families move to the city to encourage trade throughout Imperial Russia, since Odessa has a fine port on the Black Sea.

We have several items at our home in Austin that probably came to the Bornsteins during that visit: first, a silver Russian tea glass holder and spoon called a *podstakannik*.[6] Engraved in Cyrillic letters on the outside of the cup is the word "Caucasus."[7] We also have a lovely cloisonné[8] demitasse coffee cup and saucer, and a little nesting Russian egg. Most nesting eggs, or *matroyshkas* depict women. The unique characteristic of this particular egg is that it depicts a man who becomes younger as the eggs become smaller. This doll must have had quite a bit of use before it arrived in the United States

---

[4] Actually, the Brunstein parents may have come to Hamburg. The trip to Odessa is supposition on my part.
[5] Empress of Russia 1729–1796.
[6] The podstakannik (Russian for "thing under the glass"), or tea glass holder, is a holder with a handle, most commonly made of metal that holds a drinking glass (stakan).
[7] For the Caucasus Mountains. The cup was also engraved with the initials EB for Olga's father Emanuel Brunstein.
[8] Decorative work in which enamel, glass, or gemstones are separated by strips of flattened wire placed edgeways on a metal backing.

Silver Russian teacup with glass.

Silver cloisonné demitasse cup.

Antique Russian nesting egg doll. The old man becomes younger as the eggs become smaller.

and became an antique. At least one of the nesting eggs is missing.[9] I remember being fascinated by the nesting egg when I played with it when I was a child.

From childhood on, I was intrigued by the idea of having a Russian grandmother. When the Bornstein family moved to West Texas in 1952, I was surprised to learn that there was also an Odessa in Texas.[10] When I was a teenager, I devoured Russian novels, imagining that I had a connection to Russian culture, especially as depicted in my grandmother's nineteenth century: *Anna Karenina, War and Peace, Oblomov, Fathers and Sons.* I was named, after all, for my Russian grandmother.

Postcard addressed to Olga in Odessa before her marriage, 1902.

In 2005, I took a Jewish heritage tour to Russia and the Ukraine. During that trip I visited Odessa. I had the Brunstein family's home address on a postcard dated 1902.[11] The street where the family had lived still bore the same name as in the early 1900s when Odessa was a lively seaport (and the home of periodic pogroms).[12] The home itself was now replaced by a nondescript modern store below a several-story apartment building, a block away from the main cathedral. When I asked to see information about the family in

---

[9] Perhaps Fritz brought these items with him to the U.S. Or was it more likely Jenny?

[10] Odessa, Ukraine and Odessa, Texas are in the Permian geologic time period. The name Permian comes from the Russian city of Perm, also with the same geological time period.

[11] Olga had an extensive postcard collection. The album resides in the large bookcase from Arthur in our living room.

[12] Many older Russian towns and streets were renamed after the Russian Revolution.

Fritz Bornstein (b. 1910) Grows up in Hamburg

the city archive, I was told that was not possible because the building was being remodeled. I didn't and still don't believe the excuse.

—»«—

Arthur, his mother Jenny, and even two-year-old Fritz were devastated by tragedy in 1912. Fritz's mother and Arthur's wife Olga died of cancer. Imagine, two doctors married for so few years, the husband unable to save his wife and the mother of their only son. What a sad time this was for the entire family.

Given the later Bornstein family history of cancer,[13] there has been much speculation on what type of cancer Olga had. Some family recollections say she had ovarian cancer, others stomach cancer. Upon her death, Olga was cremated. Jenny saved her ashes and those of Arthur[14] until around 1933, when Jenny realized she must arrange to leave Germany. She had a gravestone erected for both her son and his wife in Hamburg at the Ohlsdorf Jewish cemetery.

Olga and Arthur Bornstein gravestone.

---

[13] Fritz died of pancreatic cancer; his sons Philipp and Fred from colon cancer; his daughter Olga survived breast cancer; his son Aaron survived melanoma.

[14] Arthur died in January 1932.

Dr. Faesecke located Olga's and Arthur's grave and sent me a digital photo of it. Note that Arthur's name is chipped off the gravestone. Dr. Faesecke assumed that the erasure of Arthur's name was an anti-Jewish attack on both Arthur and his scientific work during the Nazi period. I was shocked by this violent and mean-spirited destruction and I am still stunned each time I look at the photo. Why bother to do this? But then how can we ever understand the depth of the Nazis' anti-Jewish hatred?

A short addendum about the gravestone: In Germany you generally only own a grave plot for 75 years. When the lease expires, the gravestone and plot are cleared to make room for the next occupant. In 2014 David and I tried in vain to find Arthur and Olga's grave as we trudged through the cemetery on a cold, rainy April morning. After much questioning in the cemetery's main office, we learned that Dr. Faesecke had taken the photo of the grave just before it was removed per the 75-year rule.[15]

Back to 1912. Who would take care of baby Fritz now? Arthur was very busy at his research institute, working harder than ever. By 1913 Jenny gave up her life in Berlin and moved to Hamburg to care for her son Arthur and grandson Fritz (sometimes called Fredi). Jenny's daughter Röse and her husband were perhaps in St. Petersburg. Susanne was working as a social worker for the Berlin police department. Jenny had no more maternal duties in Berlin. She gave up her work as a physician and closed up her household and medical practice. Later, Jenny's daughter Suse (Susanne) moved to Hamburg as well, working as a social worker with the Hamburg Police department.

From my perspective over a hundred years later, I find it almost impossible to understand how Jenny could give up her work as a physician. Think of the time, effort, and money she expended to attain her profession! How could such a unique accomplishment go to waste? One of the strongest Prussian beliefs was that a person must be dutiful.[16] Because of this belief, Jenny's automatic reflex was to help her son and grandson. For Jen-

---

[15] I assume the graves in Weissensee, a cemetery for Jews only, remained untouched either because there were too many to destroy or they were just neglected.
[16] Think of the British crown's motto: "Ich diene." I serve.

ny, family was more important than profession. Clara often said that she thought Jenny saved Arthur the trouble of remarrying. Why marry again when your mother is running the household?

When World War I broke out in August 1914, Arthur was called up as a medical officer in the German army. He served during the entire war on several fronts: Belgium and France and then later on the Eastern Front, in Romania.

Arthur Bornstein, WWI, on German army horse.

Arthur Bornstein, WWI, wearing Iron
Cross, First Class. About 35 years old.

Fritz Bornstein (b. 1910) Grows up in Hamburg

In a short biographical essay, Fritz wrote about his childhood:

> *I remember waking up in the morning in the big bedroom downstairs. On the night table stood a little photograph of my parents. Behind it, usually every morning, I found a piece of chocolate, where upon I had to say something like "I thank you mother dear, that you thought of me and that you brought me chocolate during the night." The attempt to implant in me a real memory of mother did not succeed.*

While Arthur was serving in the first World War (1914–1918), Jenny and Fritz moved to the "Giant Mountains" (*Riesengebirge*) out of harm's way. Here Fritz started kindergarten. Again, we learn more about how strong-willed Jenny was. She took some family business into her own hands, evidently without consulting her son. Jenny decided to have Fritz baptized as a Lutheran, in her opinion a practical decision having very little to do with belief but rather giving Fritz potentially more opportunities in an anti-Jewish culture. Baptism was commonly accepted as a way to fill out the blank in application forms requiring a statement of religious belief.

How can we understand German government officials who were interested only in seeing that a line, stating religion, on a bureaucratic form was filled in as Lutheran or Catholic?[17]

Fritz described the experience in a fragment he wrote on yellow typewritten paper when he was 68, shortly before his death.[18]

---

[17] Then again, for us in 2021, it is hard to believe that religion would need to be stated on a bureaucratic form whether it be a death certificate, marriage license, or job application. Today, race is still a confusing and problematic blank on forms. Interestingly, Jüdisch (Jewish) was not the word used to state religion. Rather the term of art was Mosäisch.

[18] I only learned about my father's baptism after his death as I was sorting through the family documents around 2006. I wish I could have talked with Fritz about his feelings regarding Jenny's insistence on baptism. Mother never told me about the baptism either. Did she ever know about it? We will never know. What we do know is that Fritz always had great doubts about the value of religion. For him reason and the scientific method did the best job of explaining the world.

September 22, 1977

From Fritz Bornstein (1910–1978) to his children (unsent letter)

Dear children:

Perhaps this day being Yom Kippur was the suitable occasion to interrupt my childhood rec-
ollections and talk about Jews since undoubtedly you are of Jewish descent from both sides.
I will not involve myself into long theoretical discussions of defining what was a Jew, but
limit myself to the purely practical consideration that both of your parents with over 99%
probability would have ended their life in one of the gas ovens before 1945.

As far as my own memories go back, one of the first ones was my baptism. I remember the
pastor very well. To me (at 4 years old) he was a tall man in a black robe with the same
folded Spanish neck collar which you have seen on your grandfather Arthur Bornstein's pho-
tograph as dean of the medical school in Hamburg. The preacher sprinkled me and spoke: "I
hereby baptize thee with the name Friedrich Philipp Emanuel Bornstein." I had no idea that
my father or grandmother (mother Olga already was dead more than two years) were not
baptized and the whole matter did not come up for several years.

The motivation—as explained to me by Grandmother Jenny many years later—was sim-
ply that in those innocent years baptism removed the Jewish stigma. The Kaiser had just
declared (August 1914) "I do not recognize any more parties, I only know Germans." And here
my father left this poor, motherless child behind, perhaps never to return from war (WWI)
so why not?

There was no real Jewish tradition (except for two women: Grandmother's stepmother
Therese Barth neé Meyer-Simon and my great-grandmother Sara Bornstein, neé-Philipps-
born).[19]

---

[19] The mother of Jenny's husband, Philipp Bornstein.

Fritz Bornstein (b. 1910) Grows up in Hamburg

I know so little about the maternal part of my family that I have to concentrate on the Born-stein and Barth parts. Both families came from that part of Poland which had a large Jewish population: namely the provinces of Posen and Upper Silesia. They probably had lived there for several generations. When Poland was divided up between Russia, Austria, and Prussia, they came under Prussian rule – which after the conditions under which Jews lived in the old Poland and Russia, must have been simply heaven. The Old Prussian law was certainly harsh, but the average (99.99%) Prussian official was incorruptible. There were, until 1812, definite limitations on what Jews could do, but they lived under a rule of law, and after 1812 a massive Jewish immigration took place. At the same time it was the time of religious loosening up—and "reform."[20]

My great-grandfather, Israel Barth, who was supposed to become a rabbi, ran away from home at age fourteen and ended up as a contractor and fabric store owner in Berlin. He had three daughters, none of which was baptized. The family still fasted on Yom Kippur, except for Israel Barth who was served a meal in his study.[21] Philipp Bornstein (married Israel's daughter Jenny) also ran away from home and worked in a shipyard in Stettin. Your grand-father Arthur Bornstein certainly was not baptized. So whatever religious tradition there was, was minimal – although as I discovered later, the fact of my baptism was not commu-nicated to grandmother's (Jenny) sisters in Berlin.

I knew I was Lutheran, but I never went to church. I was unaware that Christmas had anything to do with either God, whom I first met in 1915 (except for the strict order never to use his name) and Jesus Christ whom I first met in 1917. This automatically became involved with anti-Semitism.

I was sent to the Riesengebirge, now Poland, about 600-900 meters high, which, home of the then famous writer Gerhard Hauptmann[22] and was put into a boarding school. Most of the children were Jewish, but there were also a few Christians there. In those days reli-

---

[20] Government reform.
[21] Remember the story of Israel Barth and the pork roast?
[22] Hauptmann won the Nobel Prize for Literature in 1912.

gious instruction was part of the official curriculum, I received Christian (i.e., Lutheran) religious instruction, which tactful as I was at that time, induced me to make some snide remarks about those awful Jews who killed our Jesus Christ. This must have been reported to grandmother, who after all, lived in the village, and now had the disagreeable (I assume) job to inform me that I was the only "Christian" in a family otherwise exclusively composed of Jews. The incident was not further referred to, but to me it shows how deeply the roots of possible anti-Semitism can reach into the human mind, even if not specifically conditioned. The story of the "Passion of our Lord" was in itself enough to arouse righteous indignation, and even after 2000 years, to arouse anti-Semitic feelings.

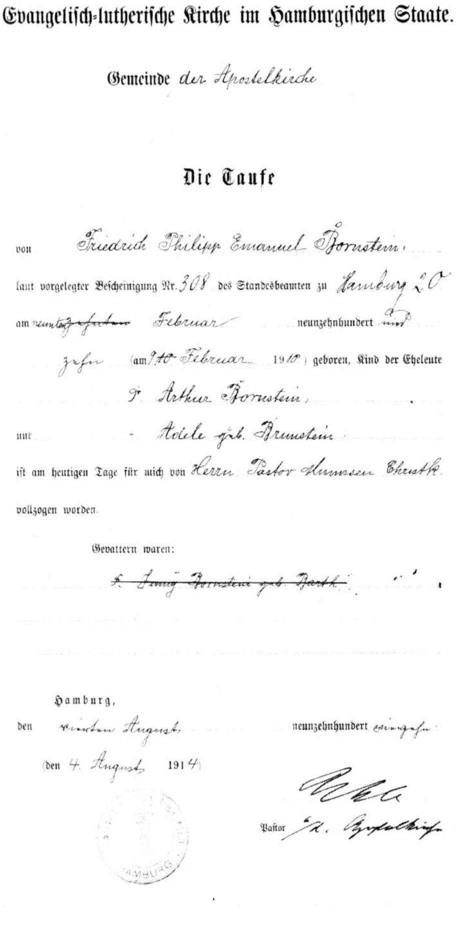

Evangelisch-lutherische Kirche im Hamburgischen Staate.

Gemeinde der Apostelkirche

Die Taufe

von *Friedrich Philipp Emanuel Bornstein,*

laut vorgelegter Bescheinigung Nr. *308* des Standesbeamten zu *Hamburg 20*

am *neunzehnten* Februar neunzehnhundert *zehn*

zehn (am *10* Februar 19*10*) geboren, Kind der Eheleute

Dr. Arthur Bornstein,

und *Adele geb. Brunstein*

ist am heutigen Tage für mich von Herrn *Pastor Asmussen Christb.*

vollzogen worden.

Gevattern waren:

x Familie Bornstein geb. Barth

Hamburg,

den *vierten August* neunzehnhundert *vierzehn*

(den 4. August 1914)

Pastor *J. R. ...*

Fritz Bornstein baptized August 4, 1914.

Fritz Bornstein's certificate of confirmation 29 March 1925.

→≫

I have no idea how Fritz's father Arthur reacted when he learned of Fritz's baptism when he returned home after WWI. I suspect he may have been displeased. According to a former student of his, Heinrich Necheles,[23] Arthur would fight duels with people who made anti-Semitic remarks. Arthur's laboratory at St. George Hospital in Hamburg was sometimes referred to as "*die heilige Jerusalem*" (holy Jerusalem) in reference to the many Jews who worked in Arthur's laboratory. The irony of all the conversion effort is that baptized Jews (*Taufjuden*) were always identified as such. So, the converts were still regarded as Jews. Consider how the issue of baptism must have created family discord.

---

[23] About whom we will learn more in a later chapter.

Jenny and sisters c. 1914. Jenny on the right. 4-year-old Fritz sits between Jenny and his father Arthur. I think that the gentleman with handlebar mustache on the left is Wilhelm Bütow married to Jenny's sister Johanna (Hanne).

As I think about our family's history, I am struck by how the reality of their Jewishness, the fact that outsiders regarded them as Jews, would never allow them to be seen as fully German. After all, Hitler's later policies made being Jewish impossible to disregard.

We know that Fritz grew up in a secular household where his family was identified by others as Jews even though they did not adhere to any Jewish religious practice. Fritz attended a famous Lutheran *gymnasium* (secondary school) still in existence today: the Johanneum, founded in 1529. The focus of the school today is still a curriculum based on the teaching of ancient Latin and Greek.

*Fritz on the first day of school, c. 1916.
Note classic sailor outfit.*

Fritz's grandmother Jenny ran the household; father Arthur was fully involved in his scientific work and was not very visible at home. Postcards and letters show that Arthur dearly loved his son. He never forgot his wife. A note in the family archive shows that Arthur wanted to establish a scholarship in his wife's honor. This note is dated almost twenty years after her death.

Arthur Bornstein became a prominent physiologist and pharmacologist, medical school professor, researcher, and dean of the medical school at the University of Hamburg. In 1925 the Nobel Prize committee asked him to suggest nominees for the Nobel Prize in medicine and physiology. Obviously, he should have suggested himself!

Arthur's research on the bends developed procedures, still used today, for preventing and treating the effects of the disease. Arthur also traveled to the United States in the mid-1920s. While preparing this history, I found a medal from 1925 given to Arthur at an international physiological conference at Clark University in Worcester, Massachusetts.

Arthur as dean of the medical school at the University of Hamburg, date unknown.

Arthur died unexpectedly in January 1932 of a severe heart attack. Throughout his life, Fritz was haunted by the possibility that he might die, as did his father, at age 50. Many thought that Arthur's own experiments on himself while diving may have weakened his heart.

His colleagues and his students, as well as Jenny and 21-year-old Fritz were devastated by Arthur's death. He had been working in Bad Oyenhausen, a well-known spa, several hours away from Hamburg. He'd established a Baneological Institute with other researchers there to study the medicinal properties of the spa's hot springs, a project that combined both his physiological and pharmacological interests. Many papers on the group's findings were published in annual reports.

I have always wondered how my father Fritz's life was affected by the death of his birth mother. His grandmother took excellent care of him and was probably at least as demanding as his mother might have been. But what of the loss of his father?

As an adult our father was quite bookish. I can visualize him as a lonely, only child reading volume after volume. As children we didn't need a home encyclopedia, we just would ask our father. He knew about history, science, astronomy, politics, literature, art, classical music and most anything else. Clara never forgot to remind us how smart her husband was! He was grounded in the basic knowledge required of a bourgeois gentleman of his era. Fritz could also be the absent-minded professor, completely unaware that his tie was crooked, that his pants and jacket did not match, or where he'd last put his glasses, wallet, and keys. If he found a conversation boring, he would float out of the room and would be found reading elsewhere. He had a keen enthusiasm for the things that interested him and an endless sense of curiosity about the newest ideas and facts.

He was really quite liberal in his political thinking and a supporter of the underserved (Blacks, Latinos). However, I was surprised to learn that he supported the Vietnam conflict. What? My father was pro-military? At that time I wasn't thinking of his service in WWII, the great patriotic war. I certainly was unaware of my German relatives' military service. Later Fritz made it clear that he wanted to disinherit me because of my involvement in the anti-war movement in the late 1960s.

Fritz was an excellent student at the gymnasium (except for handwriting). He loved mathematics and was tempted to study both philosophy and mathematics at the university. One of Fritz's university professors was the famous philosopher of science Ernst Cassirer.[24] Mother would tell me that it was hard for Fritz to grow up under the shadow of his well-known physician father much less that of his grandmother, one of the first female physicians in Germany, and of his physician mother.

The familial push to become a physician overwhelmed Fritz's desire to become a philosopher, and he began medical school in 1928. He was tired of being called "*der kleine Bornstein*" or the young Bornstein (in contrast to his father). Fritz sent this note on a postcard to his father Arthur from Marburg on April 26, 1928:

---

[24] Ernst Alfred Cassirer was a German philosopher best known for his work on the history and philosophy of science.

Dear Father:

I wanted to be accepted to the chemistry practicum but was not admitted because I had not been to any organic lectures. Besides I don't need to have to attend Strecker's lectures....for that reason, I think I will just skip chemistry and take anatomy. Otherwise, nothing was happening. Say hi to everyone from me.

Fritz

When Fritz transferred to the university in Berlin, he rented a room from Clara and her brother Hans Joachim Löwenstein. Fritz and Hans were Jewish fraternity brothers. The three college students lived together under the watchful eye of the elderly Löwenstein retainer, Auguste. It was a win-win situation: Fritz was a good friend who could pay badly needed rent.[25] Clara and Hans needed the money and enjoyed Fritz's company.

Hans Joachim (nicknamed Hajo) and Fritz's friendship grew after the death of Fritz's father in January 1932. Fritz was short, somewhat shy, and an only child. Hajo was gregarious, tall, and also a good medical student. After Arthur's death they went hiking together for a week on the north German heath. This short vacation cemented their life-long friendship.

Our story then took a new turn. Clara and Fritz fell in love. After fraternity fencing bouts, Clara cleaned, sewed, and bandaged dueling scars. Clara and Fritz traveled to the north of Germany and spent a holiday together on the Baltic Sea.[26] They probably became "promised" to each other or even engaged during this holiday.

At this point, there was no way to ignore the rise of Hitler and the Nazi party. Clara experienced the burning of the Reichstag in Berlin in February, 1933 shortly after Hitler took power. In May, 1933 one of Hitler's famous book burnings took place in Berlin on Bebelplatz, not far from Clara and Hajo's home on Passauerstrasse. It was clear now that Jews in Germany were endangered. Clara and Fritz needed to make plans to leave Germany.

---

[25] Remember these are the years of the lingering German economic depression.
[26] Perhaps 1932 or 1933.

ADDITIONAL MATERIALS

In Memory of Arthur Bornstein
by a member of the medical faculty at the University of Hamburg

Arthur Bornstein, Professor of Pharmacology died unexpectedly on January 25, 1932 in Bad Oeynhausen.

He was born in 1881 in Berlin, spent most of his youth in Zurich, where he also graduated from secondary school.[27] When he studied medicine in Berlin he worked closely with Zuntz[28] and Engelman. Zuntz was at that time the physiologist at the School for Veterinary Medicine; he was very influential in directing Bornstein's research, and always encouraged him in new directions. During his time with Zuntz, Bornstein worked intensively in the field of metabolism and other physiological questions, especially in the area of research in gas analysis.

In 1903 Bornstein passed the state's examination in Kiel; he also completed his Ph.D. on the topic of stomach aorta aneurysms.

After his "Approbation"[29] Bornstein was the assistant in the provincial mental hospital in Basel; later, assistant to the internist Bard in Geneva, and following that, he worked with Cramer,[30] a psychiatrist in Goettingen. When Bornstein worked in Internal Medicine and Neurology, he always kept close to the field of practical medicine, keeping interested in patho-physiological questions. His publications from this period demonstrate his interests: metabolism in patients with spastic paralysis; metabolism in dementia praecox; the lipid blood profile in persons with progressive paralysis; breathing in people with mental illness; and many other articles. Bornstein's method of comparing the heartbeat volumes, based on gas analytical determination of nitrogen intake, has become recognized as an elementary (essential) and error-free approach to the problem.

---

[27] Reifeprufung = Arbitur = graduation from a school that was essentially all of high school and what we would consider the first two years of university. When students began their university studies, they were already in professional school, for example medical or law school.

[28] Nathan Zuntz (1840–1920) http://www.luise-berlin.de/Gedenktafeln/cha/z/zuntz_nathan.htm
Zuntz was the founder of space medicine and a professor of animal physiology.

[29] Certification to practice medicine. Like passing the state medical board exams in the U.S.

[30] Johann Baptist August Cramer (1860–1912).

Since it became necessary to have medical supervision of the caisson workers during the construction of the Elbe (River Tunnel), Zuntz recommended that Bornstein move from Goettingen to Hamburg as medical supervisor of the tunnel project. In 1909[31] Bornstein went to work for the city's water works department. Bornstein was not only able to understand how to protect the workers and engineers from the bends, he was also able to gather a rich store of scientific data, which he presented in 1910 in Brussels at a conference on industrial medicine. Out of his work on the bends he was able to determine that a mittierende Decompression *(a gradual decompression) was a better approach.*

In recognition of his work in the service of the city of Hamburg, Bornstein was named the director of the chemical/physiological division of St. Georg hospital. In the beginning he had only cramped quarters and spotty equipment in the Simonds Institute. However, because of the support of Prof. Deneke he gradually was able to assemble a decent institute. Its accomplishments were soon known far and wide beyond Hamburg because of Bornstein's research ability and energetic work.

World War I interrupted his scientific research. Bornstein was the battalion doctor in Flanders. He was awarded the Iron Cross, First Class, after only one year in the army because of his fearless demeanor, his careful care of those wounded in battle, and his ability to work well with his fellow officers. Later Bornstein worked in the Carpathian Mountains, on the Isonzo-Front,[32] and the battles of resistance in the west.

At the end of the war Bornstein was named as pharmacology professor upon the establishment of the University of Hamburg. Some of the skilled pharmacologists may have been less than enthusiastic about the appearance of the demanding new professor, but their opinion changed quickly when they came in contact with Bornstein who was well-informed, smart, and clever—and also when they heard his presentations on his research at professional conferences.[33] Working closely with

---

[31] Arthur is only 27.

[32] Many bloody battles between the Austro-Hungarian and Italian armies in the Italian territory that is now in Slovenia.

[33] Among his students was Heinrich Necheles who did ground-breaking work in dialysis. He and his wife also helped Frederick (Fritz) Bornstein and his wife, Clara, in the United States. They gave a wedding reception in their home in Chicago when Fritz and Clara married in April 1935; cared for Clara and her children while Fritz was in the Pacific during WWII; and continued to be like family to all the Bornsteins and their children. See Heinrich Necheles entries in google.com.

his clinical colleagues Bornstein had an excellent instinct for the important contemporary issues in the field of medicine: his students and those of his colleagues worked in many different areas— diverse topics in pathology, metabolism, adrenalin, insulin, and other areas of internal secretion— researched to the finest detail. Some results of his work with animals, which related to human beings, Bornstein researched on his own body—undertakings which were often rather dangerous.

All of Bornstein's work demonstrated the basic characteristics of his character: complete dependability, thoroughness, and desire for the truth—which was not tampered with to look good— and often resulted in findings that were not desired—or that pointed out research failures.

Bornstein's last talk to a medical gathering was on the following topic: Morbidity in exophalmic goiter (Grave's disease) when taking sleeping pills (soporifics).

Prof. Hegler[34] gave an excellent eulogy at the hospital regarding Bornstein's relationship to the staff at St. Georg's Hospital. At the same occasion, Prof. Poll, Bornstein's successor as dean of the medical faculty, and Prof. Kestner gave an excellent overview of Bornstein's contributions to pharmacological and physiological research.

Bornstein had all the characteristics of an excellent manager: he was able to divide and distribute work equitably; his lectures were excellent; he was able to select excellent students to undertake research in the institute, inspire them, and have them work with him. A large number of well-known Hamburg physicians did excellent research in his laboratory; he followed their professional development with interest. They received an excellent medical and scientific education that assured that they would apply their knowledge to their patients. If you look at the festschrift that Bornstein's laboratory published on the occasion of the one hundredth anniversary of the founding of St. Georg Hospital (1923) you can only be amazed at the range and breadth of the work of Bornstein and his students. Bornstein was always supportive of his students, saw that they were able to develop professionally, and helped many of them a great deal. How the students feel about the death of their teacher was demonstrated in the memorial gathering at St. Georg, especially the well-phrased and beautiful comments of Mr. Griesbach.

---

[34] Karl Theodor Hegler 1878–1943. Listed as a doctor of internal medicine.

Bornstein was a simple and direct human being. His family life suffered greatly as he lost his wife over twenty years ago. His mother then took care of him and his young son. His mother was one of the first German female physicians, and practiced medicine again during World War I, when the supply of physicians was greatly diminished.[35]

When Bornstein finished work, he enjoyed reading the classics—since he was a passionate humanist. He always traveled with his Homer. When he went on vacation he liked to travel to the mountains, where he was a passionate mountain climber. Just a year ago he climbed the Morter-atsch glacier in the Engadin region, where he had to deal with a quite dangerous glacier crevasse.

Recently Bornstein complained now and then about heart pain, but his energy for work and his overwhelming sense of duty kept him from making a fuss.

In 1930 Bornstein's work responsibilities were expanded as he was named the head of the balneological institute in Bad Oeynhausen. Bornstein always had many interests and he always was curious about climate and bath research. He worked with Loewy in a Swiss research institute on the effect of high mountain climate and strong sun on human beings. In 1908 he worked with several co-workers on several detailed studies to see why the sea climate has such (salutatory) healthy properties—especially for those who have tuberculosis—only those physicians who have no clinical experience would keep their TB patients away from the seaside.

Thus, Bornstein was involved at the Balneological Institute to see how he could elucidate the salutatory effects of the baths more closely. He had developed the habit of traveling to Bad Oeynhausen on weekends. Just a few Sundays ago, after he took a long walk that morning in the heath with his son, he went on to Bad Oeynhausen. Here he set up his experiments for the following morning and went to sleep. He died there during the night. He most probably had an existing hardening of the arteries that suddenly caused a coronary.

If an individual is living with a painful life-ending disease, it is almost a miracle that they can live to the last moment of their life unaware of what lies before them...so that when death sneaks up unexpectedly on a person who is full of life and work, it is an enviable and fine fate. It is certainly

---

[35] Supposition on his part.

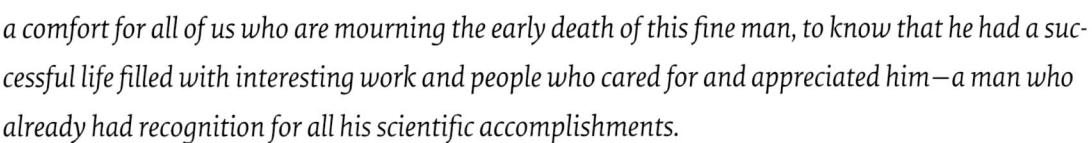

a comfort for all of us who are mourning the early death of this fine man, to know that he had a successful life filled with interesting work and people who cared for and appreciated him—a man who already had recognition for all his scientific accomplishments.

Oehlecker[36]

---

[36] Franz Oehlecker (1874–1957), pioneer in the development of blood transfusion for humans.

CHAPTER 8

Clara Löwenstein (b. 1909)
Grows up in Berlin

CLARA WAS BORN IN BERLIN on Sunday May 16, 1909; her brother Hans Joachim (nicknamed Hajo) on June 16, 1911. When Clara was born, Emmy and her husband Bernard Löwenstein were older parents: Emmy 37 and Bernard 40.

Emmy with Clara, a few months old.

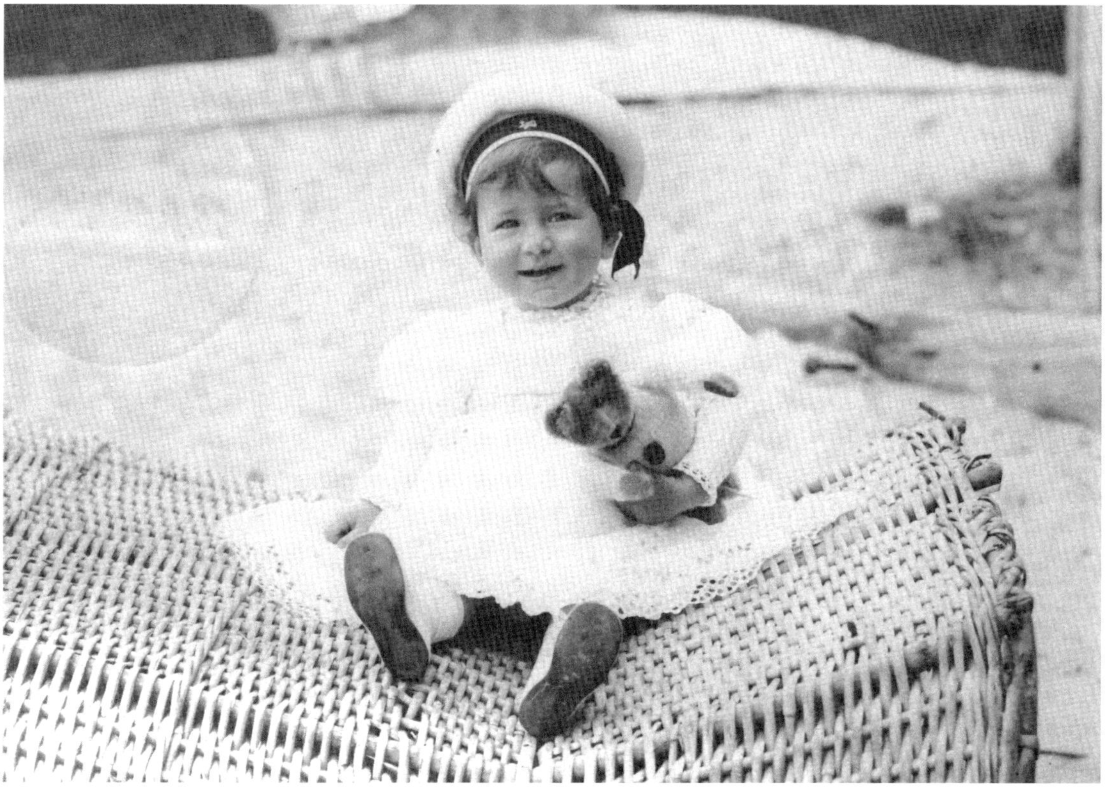

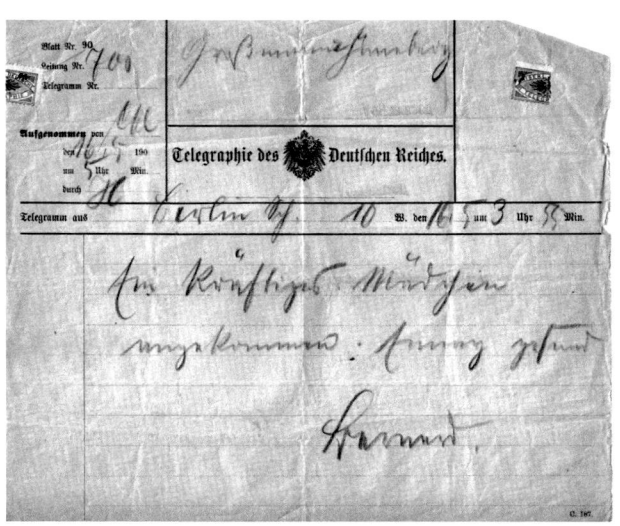

Clara, a year old, in Heringsdorf.

Blatt Nr. 90
Leitung Nr.
Telegramm Nr.
Aufgenommen von
den 190
um Uhr Min.
durch

Telegraphie des Deutschen Reiches.

Telegramm aus Berlin W. den um Uhr Min.

Telegram from Berlin to Volkmarsen announcing Clara's birth. "A strong girl was born today. Emmy is healthy. Bernard." Dated May 16, 1909, at 3:55 pm.

I think that these Löwenstein children were given typical German first names rather than traditional Jewish first names because of the distance their parents had from religious Judaism. The Old Testament names of Clara's grandfathers Moses Löwenstein and Salomon Hüneberg were not passed on to the new generation.

Emmy and Bernard lived in Berlin on the large second floor of a three-story apartment building. This multi-story apartment, in the heavy architectural style of the *Gründerjahre*,[1] was probably part of Emmy's inheritance from her wealthy first husband Sigmund Zielinsky. Built of light-colored stone and enhanced with other decorative elements, the apartment projects a bold image of bourgeois respectability and comfort.

Passauerstrasse 12, Berlin. Clara on balcony.

---

[1] Years of the rich industrial expansion in Germany in the late nineteenth century.

Clara Löwenstein (b. 1909) Grows up in Berlin

Emmy kept a detailed diary recording events in infant Clara's early life. The hand-written diary covers the first two years of Clara's life and gives us some insight into what was important to Emmy. Thanks to the efforts of our family friend, Alix Magnus, we have a transcription of Emmy's diary. In 1991, Alix lovingly prepared for me a 60-page, single-spaced typewritten transcription of Emmy's old *Fraktur*[2] handwriting from the years 1909–1913. Reading Fraktur is a skill that was lost before my generation.

Alix Magnus and her husband Werner were much like relatives to us. Alix's father was a pharmacist in Berlin who had studied with Arthur Bornstein in Hamburg. When Fritz came to Berlin around 1930, his father Arthur asked Dr. Magnus to look out for Fritz. Later Alix and Werner came to the United States and eventually settled in Ft. Worth, Texas. Clara and Fritz already lived in El Paso—so they were real Texas neighbors separated by only 600 miles! Alix became Clara's best friend. Between 1979 and 1984, when David, Jacob and I lived in Denton, Alix and Werner were the people with whom we celebrated birthdays, Thanksgiving meals, and family events including weddings and funerals. Ours was a strong and enduring friendship lasting until their death.

The opening lines of Emmy's handwritten diary tell us of Emmy's overwhelming joy upon the birth of her first child and daughter:

> *"Our sweet child was born on the Sunday afternoon of May 16, 1909, around 3:30 in the afternoon. It was a sunny May afternoon, the most painful and yet the most beautiful afternoon in my life. I scarcely have the words to describe my overwhelming happiness when I heard the first screams of my tiny, beloved daughter. In that very moment I knew that our deepest wishes had been realized with the birth of our beautiful daughter."*

Clara's birth took place at home with her physician father, Bernard, in attendance. By Tuesday, Emmy's mother, Jenny Hüneberg, arrived by train from Volkmarsen to greet her newest grandchild. What a heartfelt reunion that must have been: three female generations together in one room. Emmy was finally allowed out of bed after two weeks of recuperation. How things have changed! Today women are usually sent home from the hospital in under 24 hours after giving birth.

---

[2] *Fraktur* is an old form of German-language handwriting based on late medieval cursive writing.

Clara's first birthday in May 1910 was celebrated by a family visit to the grandparents in Volkmarsen. Clara grew quickly and by Christmas 1911, she was able to help decorate the Christmas tree, a common custom of assimilated German Jews of the period.

Emmy's sheer delight in Clara continued with the birth of her son Hans Joachim (Hajo), born two years after his sister. Emmy's diary of the first years of her children's life stops on June 30, 1913, at the end of their last summer stay in Heringsdorf. Emmy writes that she is about to start a second diary about her young children.

Heringsdorf today.

I can imagine that the second diary might have been more interesting since we would have known more about Clara's growing up. We could have read about her first words, her learning to read, and what her drawings were like. I'd love to know how my mother acted as a young child. I'm sure, like all children, she was energetic, smart, and delightful.

Emmy and the children spent most of the summer of 1912 at the shores of the Baltic Sea in Heringsdorf, north of Berlin. The cool sea breezes were so much more enjoyable than living through the stifling summer heat in their Berlin apartment. Bernard would visit on weekends from Berlin, only a three-hour train ride to Heringsdorf. In those days, the German nobility would also spend the summer there. Who knew whom you'd meet wandering the boardwalk? One day I hope to visit the village to enjoy the sparkling blue waters, the bright sunshine, and sample fresh herring!

Emmy and Bernard holding Hajo, Clara standing in front, c. 1913.

The Löwenstein household always had at least one maid and a nanny. Auguste (*Juste* in Berlin dialect) was Clara and Hajo's beloved nanny. She remained with Clara and Hajo until they fled Germany, maintaining the household after the death of Emmy (1927) and Bernard (1930).

As a child Clara traveled with Auguste to her family home in East Prussia. Clara told me stories about the wonderful food and freedom she had while visiting there. Auguste never married and devoted her entire life to the Löwenstein children—even when after the death of Emmy and Bernard, they were unable to pay her wages.

Clara sets the table at Passauerstrasse for her 16th birthday celebration.

In Clara's youth, the popular furniture style was that of heavy overstuffed chairs and couches fashionable before her birth. Later when Clara furnished her own home (no old furniture to inherit), she loved colorful, modern furniture in bright colors. A curved, plain chartreuse couch, for example, dominated our living room in Herrin, Illinois and El Paso, Texas.

The Löwenstein children had a bourgeois upbringing typical at that time: piano lessons, public school, visits with relatives in Westphalia, and summer vacations at the Baltic Sea. There is one detail from Clara's childhood that has always stayed with me: Clara and her brother ate their meals separately from their parents until about the age of 9 or 10. Their food was served in the nursery where the children ate with the nursemaid.

It was a proud moment when Clara and Hajo were deemed fit to eat at the same table as their parents.

By the early 1900s Germany had found its "place in the sun," as the Kaiser proclaimed. Germany towered over the rest of Europe as a leader in science, medicine, and the arts. In those days, it was a part of an advanced American education to study with the famous professors at German universities and learn the newest industrial and scientific techniques. Educated Europeans and Americans learned the German language, which in those years became the dominant international language of science, in particular.[3]

After WWI ended in 1918, Germany was a defeated nation, made even poorer by the financial demands of the victorious Allies. Everyday commodities were difficult to obtain. The country was overwhelmed by political unrest between the Communists, centrists, and the disappointed right wing. Riots in the streets were common. Inflation rose until the German Mark was issued in 1,000,000 Mark denominations.

Clara told me stories about daily life during those difficult times. For instance, her father would go out to buy some eggs for the family, paying for a dozen eggs with a literal cart filled with almost worthless money.

We do not know in detail how the Löwenstein family survived after the end of WWI. Bernard was presumably able to eke out a living as a physician, working out of his consulting rooms in the apartment on Passauerstrasse or visiting patients in their homes via streetcar. Of course, Emmy did not work. Perhaps Emmy had some money from her first marriage? Clara's reading record, saved in a small library pamphlet from the 1920s, shows that she was an avid reader of world literature. And of course, she saved money by using the library. The family had a life membership to the Berlin Zoological Garden, so they could enter as often as they liked, a special treat when the inflation of the 1920s wiped out the value of the German Mark.

---

[3] When I taught college German, I had the pleasure of teaching reading German to Ph.D. students, a remnant of the golden age of German science, technology, and the humanities.

Emmy Löwenstein's family entry card to the Berlin Zoo.

Clara was a clever penny-pincher her whole life long, always waiting for the next catastrophe or disaster to destroy her family's economy. Today I understand why: Clara experienced her first economic depression and its food shortages in Germany in the 1920s, then the Great Depression in the United States in the 1930s, not to speak of the privations of her early childhood during WWI.

As money became ever scarcer, Emmy took the children with her to Volkmarsen and Steinheim for the summer months. Bernard visited them now and then from Berlin. Clara always spoke with great fondness of her summers in the country with her relatives. I am sure that life in Volkmarsen was less formal and more relaxed than that in Berlin. Clara was surrounded by many loving relatives. She could play outside in the fresh air and, wonder of wonders, could swing from a tree in her grandmother's garden.

One Volkmarsen relative, Hilda, converted from Judaism to Catholicism when she married into a Catholic family. Clara was fascinated by the Catholic religious services she attended in the old Gothic church near the town square in Volkmarsen. She remembered especially envying the white dresses that girls wore for their first communion.

My mother had strong feelings, but only rarely shared her emotions. I think she combined Prussian stoicism with the common sense gained from her rural Westphalian family. She never spoke directly about her grief over the big losses she experienced: loss of parents and country. The stories she told us helped me understand why her childhood was so different from mine.

Clara and her brother Hajo attended *Gymnasium* in Berlin. *Gymnasium* was a German college preparatory high school. Upon passing the comprehensive final exam, *Abitur*,[4] they were ready to attend the university immediately. Studying for and passing the *Abitur* was a huge accomplishment. Clara spoke often about her anxiety before the *Abitur* exam and her relief when she learned that she had passed. When their university studies began, Clara enrolled in dental school and her brother, Hajo, enrolled in medical school.

Emmy's death on January 19, 1927 was a tragic loss for the seventeen-year-old Clara. I wrote about the cemetery book at the beginning of this family history. When I found that faded book on a hot July day in 1988, there was a yellowed page folded in the front of the book. It was a handwritten poem that Clara had penned at the gravesite, ten months after she lost her beloved mother:

Since mother's death the world is so lonely.
If only she could return and stroke my hair.
It is a long time since she died,
And I still do not comprehend
That only my memory of her remains along with
A little mound of dirt covered in ivy
Out there in Weissensee[5]
Reminding us that mother is gone forever.
What good does it do to cry?

---

[4] University entrance examination.
[5] The largest Jewish cemetery in Europe, located in the former eastern Berlin.

We must make the most of our life.

Others don't understand this.

But mother would understand, and she is no longer here.

I believe that I will never be completely happy again

I have prayed, but it doesn't help.

Our beloved God[6] took my mother away.

Why didn't he choose someone else?

Rather an old, sick, and unhappy human being

than my mother whom I loved endlessly.

I doubt that there is any justice.

There is beauty in the universe.

I will keep that thought in my heart.

My mother, as I do, loved beautiful things.

Now she is dead and will never see beauty again.

Ten months ago today we buried her.

She was the best we ever had.

From so many years ago, Clara's sad voice speaks to us, showing without shame how bereft and lonely she was. I think that there was a part of Clara that never overcame the deep sense of loss she felt when her mother died. Losing Emmy was the first of many losses she would experience in her long life. As writing this family history has taught me, much of life teaches us to live with losses, both great and small.

When Clara originally entered the university, she wanted to study medicine. Her father Bernard totally rejected that notion out of hand and told her that because she was good with her hands (she drew quite well), she must study dentistry instead. He also insisted that she take a gap year between gymnasium and university to study Latin with him. In Clara's opinion he required this of her because he missed Emmy and needed his daughter's company. Clara had never been close to her father, and I'm not sure that their joint study of Latin ever closed that gap.

When Philipp and I began high school in 1954, Clara and Fritz insisted we take

---

[6] An interesting line because Clara never spoke to me about a belief in God. Of course, then she was 17.

four years of Latin, so she evidently still felt her father's influence and that of Fritz's classical *Gymnasium*. In fact, all that Latin has helped me to learn other languages and figure out the origins and meaning of many English words.

Würzburg, 1929. From Clara's college photo album.

While her father was still alive, Clara studied in Würzburg and Freiburg.[7] At that time all the German universities offered similar curricula and were considered equally good. Part of the German student experience was changing universities every few semesters to experience new landscapes and cities. After her father's death in 1930, she returned to Berlin to live on Passauerstrasse and enrolled in the Kaiser Wilhelms University. By 1933 Clara had not yet finished her dental studies. The Nazis decreed then that Jews and non-Jews could not study in the same classroom or laboratory. Separate classrooms and labs were maintained for Jewish students. At this point Clara quit dental school, refusing to comply with these restrictions.

After their parents passed away, Clara and Hajo lived in the family apartment with Auguste, their family nanny. They were short of money and had extra bedrooms, so Fritz Bornstein eventually rented a room from them after he transferred his medical studies to Berlin. The lack of adult supervision gave these post-adolescents plenty of op-

---

[7] The same university where I studied during spring semester 1962. Freiburg is a lovely university town in the Black Forest.

portunity to become acquainted. Clara's brother Hajo had met Fritz Bornstein while they both were studying medicine at the Kaiser Wilhelms University in Berlin.

Fritz and Hajo were members of the same Jewish fraternity. Clara took part of the fraternity activities, including sewing up dueling scars. Until the end of his life, Fritz bore two dueling scars (*Schmisse*) on his cheekbones. These scars were a sign of the camaraderie of male German fraternity life. The students who dueled together were literally "blood brothers."

Clara and her friends went to the infamous Berlin night clubs like those depicted in the musical *Cabaret*[8] set during the early 1930s in Berlin. Telephones at each table allowed customers to phone someone at another table if they looked desirable and interesting. Clara and Hajo could also attend the Berlin opera free of change by working as stand-in members of the chorus. They would mumble "*rabarber, rabarber*," the German word for rhubarb, to fill in noise during crowd scenes. Clara experienced life during the famous "Berlin decadence." She was not easily shocked and had an earthy sense of humor. Those years prepared her well for her years as a mother of three earthy sons and one easily shocked daughter.

This is the time Clara and Fritz fell in love and became promised to each other on their trip to the Baltic. Clara's relatives in Westphalia were shocked when they learned she was going to marry Fritz. "*Aber er is nicht von hier!*" (But he's not from around here). Clara would tell me that her aunts and uncles were concerned about preserving their Westphalian Jewish heritage, and were not impressed by the fact that she was marrying a young soon-to-be physician from a prominent medical family. This at least is what she told me. Of course, that may have just shown her youthful perception of her country relatives.

More personal and political upheaval was to come. Clara and Hajo soon would be forced to leave Berlin and their relatives, abandon their studies and their chosen careers to flee from the Nazi government's increasingly violent anti-Jewish policies.

---

[8] Based on the novel *Goodbye to Berlin* by Christopher Isherwood.

ADDITIONAL MATERIALS

The contrast between the Barth and Bornstein gravestones and the Löwensteins gravestones is a perfect demonstration of how economic times in Germany changed between 1890 and 1930. The earlier tall gravestones are of marble and remain in mint condition. The Löwenstein parents have much smaller limestone gravestones that have deteriorated over the last hundred years.

Emmy and Bernard's small limestone graves, Weissensee Cemetery.

Letter to Clara at Passauerstr. 12, Berlin W. 50.

Fleeing Hitler: Clara and Fritz Come to the United States
1933–1935

IN 1933 LIFE BECOMES EVER MORE COMPLICATED. Clara is an orphan, no longer a dental student, living in Berlin. Fritz is in Hamburg, sorting out his education and future, knowing that he must develop a plan to leave Germany. Luckily, he has enough money to leave the country.

The Nuremberg Laws[1] are established in early 1933. The gist of the 1933 decrees is that no Jew can be in the employ of the German government. This law effectively cuts Fritz off from ever working in Germany.

Jews are no longer allowed to attend medical or dental school. Clara decides to go to Denmark to work on a farm where she can learn the skills to work on a kibbutz[2] in Palestine. Here her Westphalian roots come to the fore. She enjoys the hearty work on a beautiful farm on the Danish island of Bornholm. While cleaning out milk cans, Clara loses a ring Fritz gave her. Was this her engagement ring?

As Fritz considers his options, he realizes that his Lutheran baptism and confirmation make no difference to the Nazi government. He finds a rabbi who will "bring him back into the Jewish faith." Fritz knows quite well that his grandmother's decision to have him baptized as a Lutheran in 1914 won't make any difference to the Nazi authorities now.

The document stating Fritz's "reconversion" is included below. What I learned when I read this small piece of paper was a complete shock to me. At the time, I was still unaware of my father's earlier conversion. How could a piece of paper announcing Fritz's "readmission into the Jewish faith" simply convert him from one faith to another? Fritz was confirmed as a Lutheran in 1925 when he was 15 years old. Jewish? Lutheran? Fritz must have felt since he was regarded as a Jew, he might as well make it official.

---

[1] On April 3, 1933, Jewish doctors, lawyers, police, teachers and stores were boycotted. Only six days later, a law was passed, banning Jews from government jobs. These laws meant that Jews were now indirectly and directly dissuaded or banned from privileged and superior positions reserved for "Aryan Germans." From then on, Jews were forced to work at more menial positions, becoming second class citizens.
[2] Kibbutz—communal farm.

Rabbinat des Israelitischen Tempel-Verbandes.

Rabbiner Dr. Bruno Italiener
Brahmsallee 15
Fernsprecher: 55 89 22

Hamburg, den 24.April 1933

Bescheinigung

Herr Friedrich Philipp Emanuel B o r n s t e i n cand.med.,wohnhaft
in H a m b u r g,Papenhuderstr.45/47,der am 21.April 1933 seinen Aus-
tritt aus der evang.-lutherischen Kirche vollzogen hat,ist von dem
Unterzeichneten in das Judentum wieder aufgenommen worden.

Rabbiner Italiener

Frederick Bornstein readmitted into the Jewish faith, April 24, 1933.

Rabbi: Dr. Bruno Italiener[3]

24 April 1933

Brahmsallee 13

Certification

Mr. Friedrich Philipp Emanuel Bornstein, a medical student, living in Hamburg on Papenhudeerst. 45/47 completed his exit from the Evangelical-Lutheran church on the 21st of April 1933. I certify that he has been readmitted into the Jewish faith.

Signed, Rabbi Italiener

Fritz, unlike Clara, knew almost nothing about Judaism. In his later life, Fritz would have nothing to do with organized religion (a term he always used with disdain). He would not even enter the Strasbourg Cathedral when we were traveling together in summer 1962. All his secondary education was at a Lutheran *gymnasium* in Hamburg. He lived in the strange world of: "everyone knows I'm Jewish, but that religion does not mean much to me; however, I am concerned about the fate of the Jewish people."[4] Fritz, however, had received religious education and knew both the texts of the New and Old Testaments

---

[3] Rabbi Italiener (1881–1956) became a prominent Jewish rabbi and scholar in London after he left Hamburg in 1939.
[4] Fritz never visited Israel but was a strong supporter of the Jewish state. He adored his Israeli relatives the Wolmans and their children whom he saw when they visited the United States in the 1950s and later. At my first full-time job in 1965 I contributed to the United Way. Fritz said: Why didn't you contribute to the Israel Bond sales? Over the years Fritz became intensely pro-Israel.

well. Long before his death, he'd written out which Bible passages he wanted read at his funeral.

I do not know how Fritz obtained his visa to come to the United States in July 1934. He never spoke to us about it. We do know that his thesis advisor Friedrich Wohlwill was a Jewish neuropathologist at St. Georg Hospital in Hamburg. Wohlwill, a colleague of Fritz's father Arthur, somehow arranged for Fritz's graduation from medical school in July 1934 despite the fact that, by this time, Jews were no longer allowed to study or practice medicine or other professions. Documents concerning Fritz's work as a medical student state that he's interested in pathology, devoted to medicine, and has a scientific turn of mind. Interestingly, Fritz was awarded his medical degree with two stipulations: 1) he can never practice medicine in Germany, and 2) he must leave Germany immediately.

Fritz sailed to the United States on the Berengaria, a ship from the Cunard Line. Although Clara saved all the documentation regarding the ship on which she sailed: menus, passenger list, etc., I only determined the name of Fritz's ship from a newspaper article.

Fritz arrived in late July 1934 in New York City. He was interviewed by a reporter from the *Jewish Daily Bulletin* newspaper.[5]

Fritz sailed on the liner Berengaria for New York City.

---

[5] A newspaper for German Jewish speakers, published in New York City from 1924–1934. Now published in Zurich Switzerland.

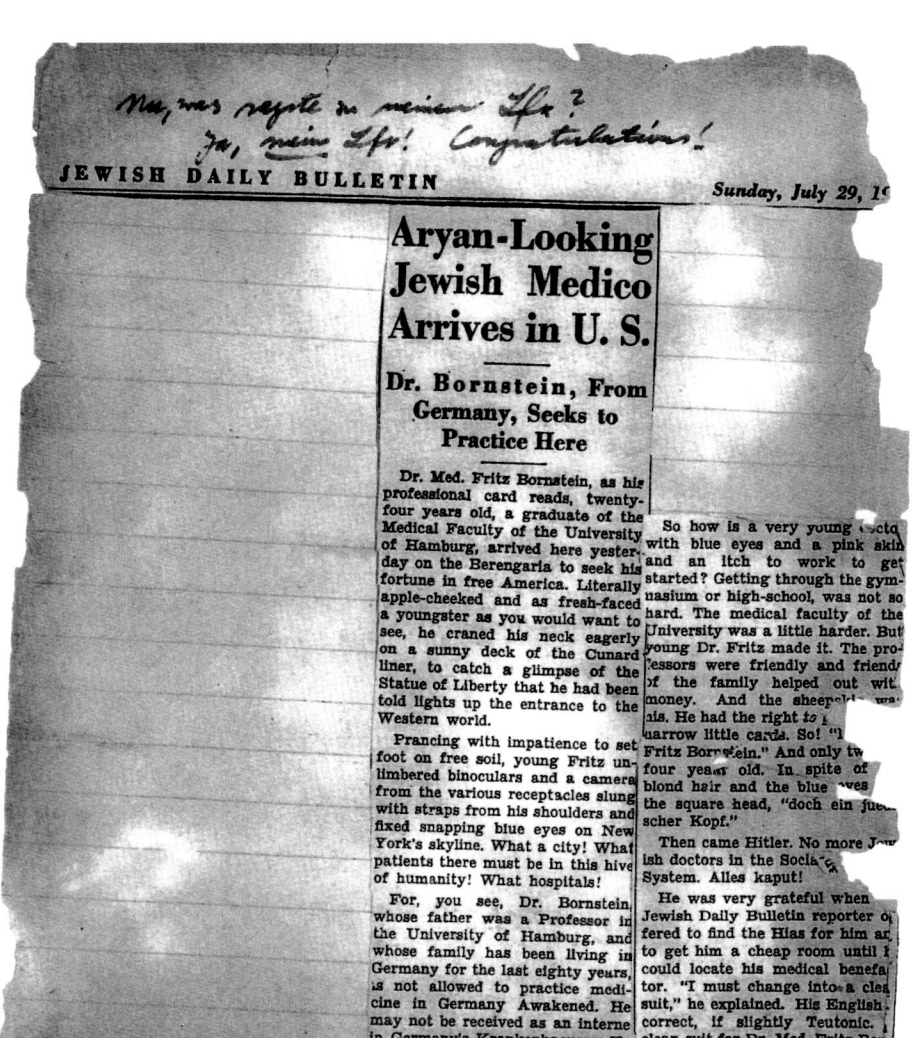

JEWISH DAILY BULLETIN   Sunday, July 29, 19

Aryan-Looking Jewish Medico Arrives in U. S.

Dr. Bornstein, From Germany, Seeks to Practice Here

Dr. Med. Fritz Bornstein, as his professional card reads, twenty-four years old, a graduate of the Medical Faculty of the University of Hamburg, arrived here yesterday on the Berengaria to seek his fortune in free America. Literally apple-cheeked and as fresh-faced a youngster as you would want to see, he craned his neck eagerly on a sunny deck of the Cunard liner, to catch a glimpse of the Statue of Liberty that he had been told lights up the entrance to the Western world.

Prancing with impatience to set foot on free soil, young Fritz unlimbered binoculars and a camera from the various receptacles slung with straps from his shoulders and fixed snapping blue eyes on New York's skyline. What a city! What patients there must be in this hive of humanity! What hospitals!

For, you see, Dr. Bornstein, whose father was a Professor in the University of Hamburg, and whose family has been living in Germany for the last eighty years, is not allowed to practice medicine in Germany Awakened. He may not be received as an interne in Germany's Krankenhaeuser. He may not attend patients of the state Social Insurance System.

So how is a very young docto with blue eyes and a pink skin and an itch to work to get started? Getting through the gymnasium or high-school, was not so hard. The medical faculty of the University was a little harder. But young Dr. Fritz made it. The professors were friendly and friendly of the family helped out with money. And the sheep-ski wa his. He had the right to narrow little cards. So! "I Fritz Bornstein." And only tw four years old. In spite of blond hair and the blue eyes the square head, "doch ein juescher Kopf."

Then came Hitler. No more Jewish doctors in the Social System. Alles kaput!

He was very grateful when Jewish Daily Bulletin reporter offered to find the Hias for him an to get him a cheap room until I could locate his medical benefactor. "I must change into a clean suit," he explained. His English correct, if slightly Teutonic. clean suit for Dr. Med. Fritz Bornstein, twenty-four—and then can tackle the new world.

Fritz interviewed by the Jewish Daily Bulletin.

As I reread the interview for the umpteenth time, I find the reporter's tone and perspective utterly astounding. "Snapping blue eyes!" (Do Jews have blue eyes?) Here we have a reporter's romantic vision of the energetic Jewish young man leaving an anti-Semitic Germany to find his future in America, where all are equal!

We do not know how Fritz somehow obtained a position at Montefiore Hospital in the Bronx. The hospital was founded by Moses Montefiore, a world-famous Jewish British philanthropist. Perhaps Hamburg medical friends made arrangements for Fritz to work there.

Fritz in white pants, wearing his movie usher uniform.

While Fritz worked at Montefiore, he also landed a part-time job as an usher at a movie theater on Times Square. His English improved daily. At least if someone became ill during the showing of the film, the young M.D. usher could help out!

Fritz left New York in late 1934 and traveled to Chicago. By the time Clara would arrive there in April 1935, Fritz was already working at a TB sanitarium in Naperville, Illinois, a Chicago suburb.[6]

Correspondence from 1934 and 1935 between Fritz and Clara, discussing their move to the United States, shows that Clara faced some difficult decisions.[7] She left Berlin[8] and spent some months in Denmark learning how to become a farmer. She considered a move to Palestine where she could work on a kibbutz. Though Clara was familiar with countryside living and farming from her summers in Steinheim and Volkmarsen, she was not completely convinced about going to Palestine.

At the same time, she wondered if she should make good on her promise to marry Fritz. It must have been hard for her to resolve the conflict. Clara never told me exactly why and how she decided she would join Fritz in America rather than emigrate to Palestine. Although quite secular, she grew up in a more Jewish milieu than Fritz. Still, it was

---

[6] I have no idea how he obtained the job.

[7] Clara saved the entire correspondence which I found bound with a tight string. It took me a while to undo the knots. Was I invading very private personal space? I looked at a few letters (Fritz's handwriting was absolutely impossible, Clara's somewhat better). I then tied up the packet again and put it away. I dare any interested party to take up the task of deciphering this 85-year-old correspondence.

[8] Exact date unknown.

hard to know how she might feel in Palestine. How long would it last until the charm of living and working in the desert to build a new country for the Jews wore off? To start a new life with Fritz in America had much more appeal—and was decidedly more practical. (A letter Clara's brother Hajo wrote to Fritz describes his life in Palestine and is included at the end of this chapter.)

Clara now faced several hurdles. Did she have the money for the ship fare? Could she obtain a visa to enter the United States? The United States requirements for entry were quite difficult. She had to demonstrate that she could support herself when in the U.S. by having work lined up or having someone who would support her. The U.S. officials were decidedly wary. These new immigrants could become a burden on the community. At this point Clara had not finished dental school and had no career. Her options for earning money were quite limited. But Fritz could support her.

Remember, these were the worst years of the Great Depression. Further, there was a U.S. government quota limiting how many German Jews could enter the country. In her quest to overcome the barriers presented by United States policies, Clara had help from one of Fritz's best childhood friends, Walter (Hörnchen) Hirsch, who had just completed law school in Hamburg. He guided Clara through the complex visa application process and arranged her interview with the American consul in Hamburg. Clara was terrified just thinking about the upcoming interview. Walter's advice to her: "Just imagine the consul naked in a bathtub, playing with this rubber duckie." Evidently the interview went well. Clara obtained the visa and wrote Fritz on February 26, 1935:

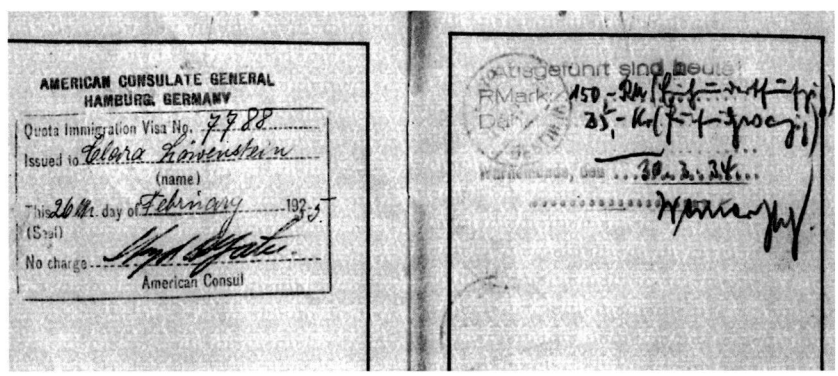

Clara's exit visa from the American Consulate General. Note Quota Immigration Visa No. 7788! Visas were quite limited.

Dear Fritz:

I've been in possession of my American visa for the last hour and a half!!! My reaction is one of complete disassociation.

My plan of attack is to stay for four or five days with Grandmother[9] to prepare for my trip. I'll take her to the ship in Trieste[10] after a short stay along the way in Geneva. We'll need to catch our breath. Then I'll come back [to Germany] and quickly visit Westphalia and Berlin (can't avoid this) so they can finish working on my teeth. I couldn't take care of my teeth earlier, since things had to heal. Then I'll get on the ship and come on over.

So, everything is ready for me to leave. Grandmother may get a ship ticket before March 15th. I hope I can come to you by the end of April. I wish Grandmother were gone already, so that I could leave without getting my teeth being fixed and going to Westphalia. Then I could be with you by the middle of March.[11]

I'm still in shock—I'm sure you can tell from my handwriting.

Yours, Clärchen[12]

Before Clara left Germany, she made a scale drawing of her apartment's layout and a detailed list of her household possessions. both of which are in our family archive. Most of the household possessions were later sold at auction to finance Clara's journey to the United States. An old boyfriend and schoolmate[13] of Clara's from dental school went to the auction and purchased a small beautiful wooden lacquered Russian box. When I met him in London in 1962, we visited together one afternoon in his living room. He gave me the Russian box telling me: "I always loved your mother." The box now sits on my knick-knack shelf in Austin in our dining room.

Clara packed up some precious family jewelry, linen tablecloths and sheets, and a special blanket given to her by Auguste to take with her on her journey. Jenny closed out

---

[9] Jenny in Hamburg.
[10] Jenny was traveling to Palestine to join her daughter Suse (Susanne).
[11] Clara actually left a month later than she had planned. There is so much detail to attend to when leaving your country for good.
[12] Clärchen is the diminutive of Clara.
[13] This boyfriend's mother was absolutely shocked when she came home one day and found Clara and her son frying a pork cutlet in the kitchen. Theirs was a practicing Jewish family. The relationship faded after then.

the Bornstein household in Hamburg since at this point her grandson had been in the United States for almost a year.[14]

Auguste stayed in the family apartment in Berlin after Clara left Germany. She was killed in a bombing strike late in WWII. One of the few times I can remember Clara crying was when she received a letter with the news of Auguste's death. My brother Aaron and his wife Jane have the indestructible wool blanket that Auguste gave Clara when she left for the United States in April 1935. It is as if Auguste were saying: "I am not with you, but I will keep you warm."

The apartment was destroyed in the bombing. On its site now stands a conventional modern apartment building housing a commercial enterprise on the first floor, as I saw on one of my many trips to Berlin.

Over the years I've told friends the story of our parents' exit from Germany for the United States. Often, they say: "Goodness, your parents were very foresighted to leave Germany when they did. They were so lucky to get out early." Fritz and Clara were definitely better informed than many Jews regarding how the emerging Nazi civil laws would affect them. They lived in big cities served by international newspapers. They could learn what the rest of the world was thinking about the persecution of Jews in Germany. They did not doubt that the situation would get worse for Jews. How correct they were!

There were other equally important elements in play. By 1933 neither Clara nor Fritz had parents who were alive.[15] Or as Clara would often say: "We were orphans." Fritz was an only child. Clara's brother Hajo had already fled Germany after his arrest by the Gestapo for anti-Nazi activities. He went to Latvia to learn a trade and then sailed to Palestine to find work on a kibbutz. Clara's many aunts and uncles would hopefully find their way out of Germany.[16] Still, both Fritz and Clara had relatives and friends who died during the Holocaust. Our parents never discussed those losses with us. I can't begin to know what a burden that must have been for them—to grieve and to talk only to each other or to friends who have had the same experience. We children were left out of our

---

[14] At the end of this chapter, you can see a listing of the Löwenstein household inventory.
[15] Arthur died in 1932; Emmy in 1927; Bernard in 1930.
[16] Some came to Los Angeles; others were rescued by the Quakers and settled in England.

parents' personal losses and grief. And perhaps silence helped close the door on the events that brought them to the United States.

Fritz and Clara decided that they didn't want to live in New York City with the other recently arrived, dispossessed German Jews. They were young, in their mid-twenties. They weren't keen on bemoaning their fate with fellow German-speaking refugees, many of them elderly. They were focused on becoming citizens in the United States. They wanted to jump into American culture with both feet and begin their new English-speaking life. How could they look back? A return to the country of their birth was now impossible if they wanted to stay alive.

Clara arrived in New York City in early April, sailing on the ocean liner S. S. Hamburg from Hamburg.

She traveled by bus from New York City to Chicago (cheaper than a ride on the Twentieth Century Limited, a famous train of the era).

Now began the times that Clara told us about throughout her life. Fritz never told us much about his childhood and growing-up years, or about his feelings regarding leaving Germany and starting a new life in the United States. Clara loved sharing stories about her life experiences, but her retellings were always quite matter of fact. Were these stories meant to teach her children how to live life? Be stoic and look ahead? To not let the difficulties of the past make it difficult to live in the present?

ADDITIONAL MATERIALS

1934 Inventory Household Passauerstrasse 12, Berlin

Clara counted on the income from this sale to travel to the U.S.

1. Dining room

buffet	lamp	bibles	tall lamp
coffee services	credenza	wall decorations	crystal glasses
round table	curtains	crystal plates	corner table
sofa	12 chairs	silver	luther chair
carpet	2 sets of decorative china dishes		

2. Living Room

sofa	lamp	bric a brac cabinet	curtains
bookcase	fire screen	writing desk and chair	four chairs
carpet	pictures		

3. Bedroom

two brass beds	two washbasins	curtains	dresser with mirror
two chairs	towels	wash table	lamp
other washing implements	brush and comb set	three night table lamps	sheets, pillowcases, and blankets

4. Sitting room

sofa	four chairs	bric a brac cabinet	curtains
carpet	four armchairs	crystal lamp	

5. Kitchen

kitchen buffet	table	ice box	2 chairs
coal box	warming shelf	writing table	wash table
wardrobe	sewing machine	grooming set	clothing wardrobes
three small tables	large table	gramophone	five chairs
clothes dryer stand	typewriter	sewing table	five bookcases
balcony furniture	piano	silk chairs	two floor lamps
telephone	heating pillows	electric iron	two cameras

Table silver[17]

18 spoons	18 teaspoons	18 large knives	18 large forks
18 small knives	18 small forks	12 fish knives	18 fish forks
12 fruit knives	12 fruit forks	18 dessert spoons	17 coffee spoons
1 large soup ladle	1 set salad servers		

From the physicians' examining room
(i.e., Clara's father Bernard's office)

desk	desk chair	instrument cabinet and instruments
bookcase with medical books	examination chair	instrument table

---

[17] This silver did come to America. Philipp inherited the silver initially and then gave it to Olga. At this point, the set is not 100% complete, but close to it. About half of the set is trimmed in gold.

Letters of Recommendation for Fritz

Letter 1:

Medical Faculty

Hamburg University

16 November 1933

Today, Mr. Fritz Bornstein, currently a medical intern, passed the oral examination on his disser-
tation. The granting of the license to practice medicine will take place after printed copies of the
dissertation become available. It is illegal [for him] to go by the title of doctor before then.

Signed Rothmiller,

Dean of the Medical School.

Letter 2:

Dr. Fr. Wohlwill, M.D.[18]

Hamburg 20

November 6, 1933

Alsterkrugchaussee 110

Certification

Until recently I was the head of the Pathology Institute of St. Georg General Hospital. Until my
departure Fritz Bornstein worked with me as an assistant and to complete his doctoral dissertation.
He is an energetic person, quite interested in scientific research, completely dependable and of course,
intelligent. While he was working on his dissertation, he was able to make excellent independent
judgments. I can recommend him without hesitation. I know that he will become an excellent
physician.

---

[18] Wohlwill was a colleague and friend of Fritz's father Arthur. He was Jewish, and as his letter hints, he was re-
lieved of his duties at St. Georg because of the Nurenburg Laws. Later he became a pathologist in Lisbon. http://
www.whonamedit.com/doctor.cfm/1011.html

Letter 3:

Office of the Medical Director

St. Georg General Hospital

Hamburg 5

17 April 1934

Certification

I hereby certify that Frederick Bornstein, born on February 9, 1910, has completed his assignment at St. Georg General Hospital. I certify [that this document] is valid for purposes of leaving the country.

The Medical Director

J. V. Ringel

Letter 4:

Office of the Medical Director

St. Georg General Hospital

15 June 1934

Certification.

Fritz Bornstein, born on February 9, 1910, worked as a medical intern under my direction in my department from 1 October 1933 until 3 March 1934.

I supervised him in his work in internal medicine. When I worked with him, I found him to excel in his devotion to his work, his general knowledge of medicine, and interest in all things scientific. In his last clinical semester, Bornstein was quite interested in experimental pathology and made great progress in his mastery of technical details.

Prof. D. Hegler

—»＂«—

Letter from Fritz to Clara as she leaves Germany

March 28, 1935 Naperville, Illinois
Edwards Sanitorium.[19]

My dear Clär,[20] beloved fiancée and soon to be wife,

Hopefully this will be the last letter in our memorable correspondence…I am writing you on this beautiful white stationary, the last of my stationary from Papenhuder Street.[21] Sometimes I just cannot believe how very far I am from there. I do hope that when you receive this letter it will be a welcome surprise. I can become philosophical about the fact that we've come this far. I've had time to think about things and realize that it was exactly a year ago that I asked you to marry me as we stood in front of the church in Wismar.[22]

In addition, when I think about that and other matters, I can hardly understand why you didn't say; "Why doesn't that guy just go away to the United States?" So please have patience with me—sometimes you will find me giving earnest lectures.

To more mundane matters: I hope that my fraternity brother Holstein will meet you at the dock (in New York) and take care of you. I'm full of worries about several things: Where the record player and the rest of the stuff will go, and whether I can get a permanent job here in Naperville. I don't have any firm answers yet.[23]

Yesterday after we had a temperature of 14 degrees Celsius,[24] it began to snow. We never know what kind of weather we will be having. Tomorrow I am going to Chicago to make preparations for the future.

---

[19] The sanatorium was founded in 1907 to care for TB patients. Naperville today is no longer a village but a large suburb west of Chicago.

[20] Term of endearment for Clara.

[21] Fritz's last residence before he left Hamburg. In a lovely locale near the Alster River.

[22] A city in northern Germany, on the Baltic Sea, known for its well-preserved medieval buildings. Wismar and nearby Stralsund are UNESCO World Heritage Sites. Both towns were members of the Hanseatic League (as was Hamburg).

[23] In addition to the record player, Fritz brought along the large bookshelf that is now in my living room, Oriental rugs, family silver, and many, many books.

[24] 57 degrees Fahrenheit.

Just now your sweet letter of March 16th arrived, and I realize what a dolt I am—the violets almost made me cry with homesickness. Just so you know—I put the lock of hair that you gave me in 1931 on the framed photograph I have of you. At the same time I also received a letter from grandmother[25] that contained letters from Hajo[26] and Suse.[27] Hajo has really become a stranger to me, since he writes so rarely. It is incredibly difficult for me to burn all my bridges behind me. But that is something we will have to get used to.

It is almost good that we will be so dependent on each other. I know what you mean to me, and I hope you know what I mean to you.

To more practical matters...I hope you received my check. If not I'll wire money to you in New York City. Every policeman will tell you that general delivery is at the downtown post office.

When you arrive in Chicago tell the taxi driver you want to go to Union Station. The taxi will cost about 30 cents. The train ticket to Naperville will cost 50 cents. You'll arrive in an hour and a half. I really do not approve of your having a one person cabin on the ship. As it is you won't know anyone on the ship. Besides you didn't sign your last letter "Your Beloved." What is all that about?

Regarding grandmother's most recent letter, she writes the following:

> *With everything you have before you, Clara will play an important role in your future. She is a lovely young lady.[28] I hope she will like the people she meets in her new country...I wonder how you two will get along—les estremes se touchant.[29] But no one but we will notice that. You are larvae who are about to come out of your shell. Here I'm surrounded by barbarians, and there are more every day.[30] There are signs of spring here despite the fact that it snowed yesterday...*

I am sorry that nothing came of the possibility of working in Rockford. To earn $125 per month would have been wonderful. On the other hand, if I get a position as a pathologist, it would pay only $50 per month. But I hope to have a better paying job a year from now. I'm making plans and can imagine us driving along beautiful Lake Michigan in the rickety Ford.

---

[25] Jenny Barth Bornstein.
[26] Clara's brother.
[27] Fritz's aunt; Jenny's daughter.
[28] Jenny is now 76 years old.
[29] Literally: the extremes touch each other; rather: you and Clara are as different as oil and water.
[30] Jenny is about to leave Germany for Palestine.

The typewriter ribbon fades out at this point, making the rest of the letter illegible. After the typing come all sorts of handwritten additions in Fritz's illegible handwriting. One closing phrase remains legible:

Your loving fiancé (Fritz)

–»«–

Hans Joachim Löwenstein writes from Palestine, November 17, 1934

Dear Ernst:

After I have become acclimated in a way to the new home, I find time to write to you and the other dear ones I left behind. Not that I feel like the "verstorbene Personlichkeit" (a dead personality) but we are going to be separated for at least two to three years, unless your practice permits you to visit me here in your own Mercedes-Benz in the meantime, which I wish from all my heart.

For the rest I can remark that such a visit would be worthwhile in every respect, at least as a permanent, highly interesting memory. I am convinced that the tourist in Palestine, despite the strong European percentage in the population, gives much the impression of being in the Orient—as if I were in Tehran or Cairo. As for the Europeans, they assimilate relatively quickly to the Orient; less in regard to culture than to certain ways of life which are customary here, like dress, mealtimes etc.

The skin color of the Europeans, especially the blond ones, changes only slowly as one protects oneself carefully from the rays of the sun. Nevertheless, even people who because of their fair skin never tanned in Germany and only turned red, well, they're tanning here. And the hair bleaches so that one hardly sees people of the medium blond type so common in Germany, but only very black-haired ones and platinum and light blondes. That all children are blondes here, as they say in Germany, that's not true. They become darker quickly.

To return to the beginning after this digression: the impression of being in the Orient is, as I said before, practically complete. Upon arrival in Jaffa one notices it at once. The dirty streets of this purely Arabic town, despite the strong tropical heat, are always somewhat humid.

One sees camel caravans heavily loaded in rows of 25 or 30, donkey drivers covered from head to foot with rags, stiff with dirt, mixing with noble Muslims wearing turbans or fez, in rich silken dress. There are a few German or English Europeans mostly administration officials in linen or khaki, with tropical helmets and the unavoidable little whip. Wherever you look: Orient. Palms, mosques, Arabic water vendors near the little cafe, seated in long rows or small circles on the ground, you see them silent in repose for hours. Only a few women can be seen. They're dressed entirely in black, deeply veiled. The veils on the face are doubled. If the women want to see something in the bazaar, they lift one veil above the eyes, never the second one. At the sight of male Arabs, they cover their mouth with yet another special veil. Otherwise the customary traditional mode of dress for Arab women is to wear many gold and silver coins on pendants or long chains. Sometimes you can see tattoos on the face. Men and women paint their faces a lot, especially the eyes are accented with blue. Their hands are reddened with henna.

The transition from Jaffa into the Jewish city of Tel-Aviv is quite strange. I can't imagine a stronger contrast. In Jaffa you see the narrow, nook-and-cranny Arab town with some half-ruined cave-like houses. In between, here and there, is the palace of a rich man. The palace has narrow windows, tightly encased in ironwork. In Tel-Aviv there are wide, bright streets, white houses with flat roofs, almost all recently constructed. The houses often have well-cared for gardens, in which palms and huge cacti grow with the wasteful splendor of the tropics. Here the Asiatic narrow-mindedness, despite long tradition; there development, a busy life which reminds one of American ways, and which is doubly remarkable because of the restfulness forced by the climate. Here the deeply veiled female Arabs, there the Jewish girls in shorts or fatigues, working construction. Here you'll find signs with Arabic inscriptions, there everything announces itself in Hebrew.

In contrast to the other Palestinian cities, the officials in Tel-Aviv are all Jewish: the bus drivers, the police, the magistrates, the postal employees—all of them Jewish.

I was only in Tel-Aviv for four days. Then I had enough of the noise and dust from the construction work. I took my luggage and got on one of those wonderful cross-country buses and rode for one and a half hours. First we were on well-kept asphalt highways. Later we drove through deep desert sand to Moshawal Herzliah, a village of 2500 people, where I now work and live.

The work is very strenuous. At present I am digging irrigation ditches and wells around the orange and grapefruit trees. I water the trees and keep them free of weeds. We all work an eight-hour day. Overtime is fully paid. The pay is not particularly good. It is sufficient for all necessities. With a modest budget one can even save a little. So I hope I will be able to visit you in two years with the money I have earned and saved. By then I hope to have my Palestinian citizenship.

I recently received the newsletter from the Brandenburgia[31] and read it with interest. Please don't forget, dear Ernst, to send more recent newsletters to me here.

I have a beautiful shower in the house where I live. One day after work, as I wanted to use it as usual, I found it unlocked but occupied by a young man getting dressed. When he saw me, he called out: "Just a minute dear fraternity brother." As it turned out, the friendly young man, named Goldschmidt, was a member of the Munich Thuringia, hailing from Stuttgart. He'd been in the fraternity for eight semesters and completed eight semesters of law school. Do you know him?

My current boss, attorney Dr. Bohm from Berlin is also a fraternity brother. We have lively discussions about the current "damned situation." Otherwise life here is going on in a rather pleasant fashion. Actually it is rather like my life in Germany.

After work I shave, bathe, dress decently, and go out to eat. Then I visit with friends, or am invited by families I know to have tea, play cards, or attend a musical soiree, or even walk along the seashore. Sometimes we get together for an evening, drinking the good Rischon-le-Zion wine.

Generally the Jews from Germany are strictly socially separated from the eastern Jews. Neither one of the groups can deny the distance between them due to differences in degree of education, civilization, culture, upbringing etc. Even in the next generation it won't be any different, for the children will be raised by their parents according to their values.

When you reply, dear, Ernst, please tell me also about yourselves, the fraternity brothers, the goings-on of the Brandenburgia, about our apartment, about my university affair,[32] in which I am still vitally interested.

...Pass on my letter to those fraternity brothers who might take an interest in it.

Most cordially and with many regards, your loyal friend, Hajo

---

[31] The name of the fraternity. Hajo and Fritz were members.
[32] Hajo's run in with the Gestapo, which forced him to leave Germany.

Haifa, 6th March 1938.

To whom it may concern !

      Mr. HANS JOACHIM LOWENSTEIN has worked from March 20th, 1936 until March 1st, 1938 as a head-waiter in this hotel. During all this time he has fulfilled his duties, both the plain every-day work and the arrangement of festivities at special occasions, to our utter satisfaction, by his outstanding efficiency as well as by his faultlessly honest conduct.

      He quits his job on his own request , because he intends to go to America . We take leave of him with great regret, for he has been one of the most *useful* members of the staff, and we wish him all his best for his further future.

Mathilde Teltsch

בית טלטש בע"מ הר הכרמל, חיפה

TELTSCH HOUSE LTD. Mt. CARMEL HAIFA

Mrs. Mathilde Teltsch

Manager of the Teltsch-house .

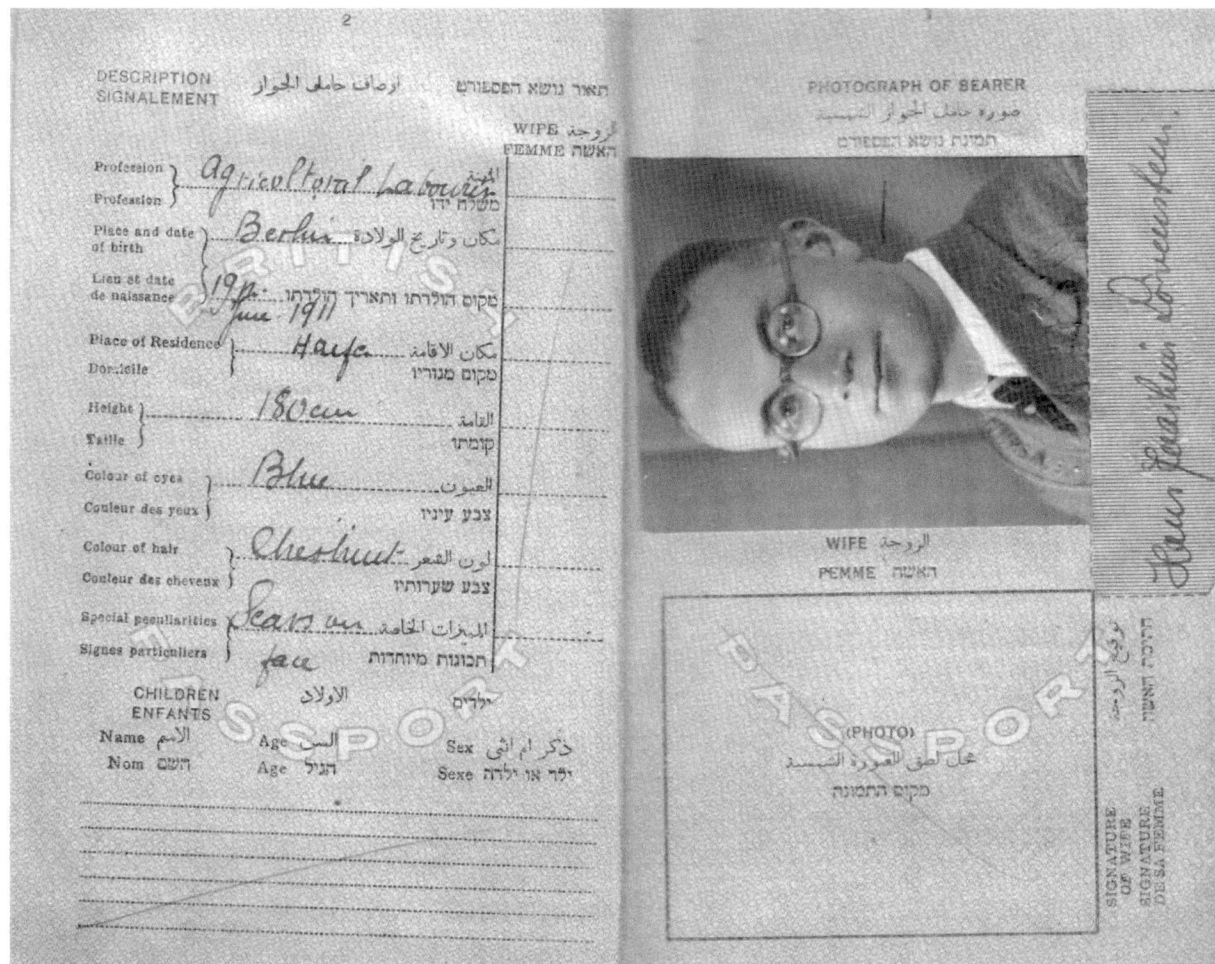

Hajo's Palestinian passport.

«— Letter of recommendation for Hajo
(Hans Löwenstein) 1938.

Bank of the Manhattan Company
40 WALL STREET
NEW YORK

CABLE ADDRESS
THEMANCO - NEW YORK

March 22, 1935.

Dr. Walter Hirsch,
Rothenbaumchaussee 12,
Hamburg, Germany.

Dear Doctor:

As requested by Dr. Friedrich Bornstein,
Naperville, Illinois, we enclose his check #10 dated
March 21, 1935, to the order of Miss Clara Lowenstein,
in the amount of $300.00, duly certified by us, which we
should appreciate your delivering to the payee.

Yours very truly,

Assistant Cashier.

JHS:MS
Encl.
c/c Dr. Friedrich Bornstein,
Naperville,
Illinois.

*Fritz sends Clara Money. She's ready to come to the U.S. and is
living with Jenny Bornstein in Hamburg.*

Clara's exit permit from the Hamburg police department, April 2, 1935.

NACH NEW YORK:

*Clara travels Tourist
class on the Hamburg.*

Frau Else Bender
Herr Karl Bergmann
Fräulein Anna Bischoff
Herr Albert Boettger
Herr Hermann Drach
Herr John Fenger
Frau Hanny Florin
Frau Ilse Florin
Herr Karl Fuchs
Herr Staatsanwalt
    Dr. Thilo Gante
Herr Baron
    Ulrich von Gienanth
Frau Lucy Gillette
    Georgie Gillette
Frau Sylvia Gordon
Herr Leopold Graubaum
Frau Leopold Graubaum
Frau Herta Groth
Frau Alice Gutmann
    Hans Gutmann
Fräulein Mathilde
    Hagenlocher
Herr Karl Heinen
Frau Karl Heinen

Herr Dr. Kurt A. Heinrich
Frau Kurt A. Heinrich
Herr Dr. Siegfried
    von Hinckeldey
Fräulein Margarethe Hinz
Frau Elisabeth Holle
Fräulein Mary Huettenbach
Frau Hildeburg
    Heubner-Junkermann
Fräulein Marion
    Ellen Junkermann
Fräulein Edith Kahn
Fräulein Anna Kaiser
Herr Herbert Knuppertz
Herr Fritz Kolesch
Fräulein Margaret Koopmann
Fräulein Else Kortebein
Herr Professor
    Dr. Alois Kraus
Frau Alois Kraus
Herr Adolf Levy
Fräulein Sophie Liebl
Fräulein Clara Löwenstein
Frau Else Lühdorf
Herr Frank Mahr

LIST OF TOURIST CLASS PASSENGERS

8

ON BOARD S.S. "HAMBURG"

Tuesday, April 9, 1935

Dinner

Fruit Cocktail

Cream of Tapioka
Consommé Vermicelli

Broiled Halibut, Paprika Butter

Larded Tenderloin of Beef, Mixed Vegetables
Duchesse Potatoes, Water Cress

Compote of Peaches

Pineapple Ice Cream, Wafers
Baked Bananas with Vanilla Sauce

Holland or Herb Cheese

Fruit

Coffee   Tea

*Dinner menu on the "Hamburg" from Hamburg
Germany to New York City April 1935.*

CHAPTER 10

Chicago and Downstate Illinois
1935–1941

A FORMER M.D. STUDENT OF ARTHUR BORNSTEIN'S, Heinrich Necheles,[1] whom we mentioned before, worked as a physician/researcher at Michael Reese hospital[2] in Chicago. After Clara and Fritz were married by a judge on April 18, 1935,[3] Hein and his wife Steffi held a small wedding reception at their home on South Kimbark, near the University of Chicago.

Now married and settled in Chicago, Clara wanted to resume her interrupted dental studies. She applied and was admitted to Northwestern University Dental School. But there was an insurmountable obstacle. When she asked the dean if she could work and attend dental school part-time, the Dean told her it was out of the question. The school would only accept full-time students.

Clara suggested to Fritz that they borrow tuition money for her to enroll. Her new husband said it was impossible. They were living in the middle of a huge economic depression[4] and they had no idea what their financial prospects were. As it was, they were barely living from paycheck to paycheck in a bleak, grim apartment. Secondly, debt was not a word in Fritz's vocabulary (and never was acceptable even later). In the late 1960s, I went with my father to a car dealership in El Paso. He wrote a check, paid for the car, and drove it home.

Clara and Fritz were often so short of funds that they walked to work past the famous Chicago Stockyards. The opening of Carl Sandberg's[5] famous "Chicago" poem (1914) makes it clear that Chicago was a rough-and-tumble industrial city:

---

[1] 1897–1979. His research was instrumental in the development of the artificial kidney.

[2] The hospital was founded in 1878 by a bequest from Michael Reese, a successful German Jewish immigrant. In its heyday, Michael Reese was one of the top research hospitals in the U.S. It closed in 2009.

[3] The same month and day as Clara's parents Emmy and Bernard were married in 1907.

[4] The Great Depression was the worst economic downturn in the history of the industrialized world, lasting from 1929 to 1939. By 1933, when the Great Depression reached its lowest point, some 15 million Americans were unemployed and nearly half the country's banks had failed.

[5] Carl August Sandburg (January 6, 1878–July 22, 1967) was a Swedish-American poet, biographer, journalist, and editor. He won three Pulitzer prizes: two for his poetry and one for his biography of Abraham Lincoln. During his lifetime, Sandburg was widely regarded as "a major figure in contemporary literature," especially for volumes of his collected verse.

Hog Butcher for the World,
Tool maker, Stacker of Wheat,
Player with Railroads and the Nation's
Freight Handler;
Stormy, husky, brawling,
City of the Big Shoulders:

The young couple was no longer in cultivated Berlin or Hamburg! The stench from the stockyards, more elegantly termed abattoir, was stomach wrenching. But the streetcar cost five cents per ride, so they could each save ten cents a day walking.

I am convinced that Clara would have been a marvelous professional and a much happier person if she could have completed her education to become a dentist. She was great with people, charming when she wished, down to earth, and snobbish only at home. But despite the examples of Fritz's grandmother Jenny and his mother Olga, women were not liberated in the 1930s, either in Germany or the United States.

As I became older, I was amazed when I learned how hard Clara and Fritz worked in the early years of their marriage. They were well educated and came from relatively comfortable upper-middle-class families, but were not too proud to accept menial jobs. Today it is almost impossible for us to grasp what life was like in those years of the Great Depression. How can we understand how grateful they were just to be alive, to be in grubby Chicago, where hard work for little money was standard.

What must it have been like to be considered *persona non grata* by the German government after both families had lived there for generations and contributed to the country? Then to become strangers in a strange land. Could you leave a comfortable life and live on the edge of poverty in an unfamiliar country and culture?

What kind of work did Clara find? She first worked at a cafeteria in the Chicago Loop, cleaning and chopping vegetables. At lunchtime, she could choose what she wanted for lunch, a considerable work perk during the height of the Depression. There was only one caveat: if she didn't finish the food she'd chosen, she'd have to pay for the leftovers.

Next, she was employed as a house maid by a well-to-do Chicago family on the elegant Near North Side of Chicago.[6] Clara had grown up in a bourgeois household that employed domestic help, so I am sure she knew what was expected of her as a house-maid. When we cleared out the El Paso house in 1988, I found a sheaf of instructions her mistress had prepared for Clara. The mistress did not leave things to chance.

I'm sure these notes were a source of information about the new culture in which Clara lived. Many of these household instructions became life-long habits for her.[7]

Clara did not know how to cook. That had always been Auguste's job in Berlin. Cooking was a skill she learned on the job in Chicago. As we grew up, we knew that Clara hated cooking. She would rather read a book or the latest issue of the *New Yorker* or *The Nation*.[8] She would say to us "I know that the one thing you won't miss when you leave home is my cooking." Well, she was wrong. She, in fact, became a decent cook.

Her children all had dishes they wanted her to prepare when we visited home. When I came home as an adult, she'd prepare a large platter piled high with her home-made meringues, served with stiff ice-cold, fresh whipped cream. She made the me-ringues by dropping spoonfuls of whipped egg whites and sugar onto a baking sheet covered with "parchment paper" made from old paper grocery bags. She didn't use fancy pastry pipes to form the meringues or expensive parchment paper. Delicious *baisers* (kisses): a huge spoonful of whipped cream between two meringues. We loved her choc-olate chip cookies, plum cake, cabbage rolls, red cabbage with apple, pickled tongue, and Berliner Pfannekuchen.[9] At Easter, she'd mail her grandchildren handmade sweet little fondant candies in white, pink and green: Easter bunnies with tiny chocolate eyes.

Later Clara landed a job cleaning rooms in the hotel where one of the Chicago baseball teams would stay when they were in town. I don't know if the team was the Cubs or the White Sox. The team owners were so impressed by Clara's energy and dili-gence that they made her an offer: "We'd like you to come to Florida with us for spring

---

[6] Clara probably obtained all her varied jobs from a Jewish Resettlement Service, set up to assist refugees find work.

[7] See additional materials for sample notes.

[8] *The Nation* is the oldest continuously published weekly magazine in the United States, covering liberal political and cultural news, opinion, and analysis. Began publishing in 1865.

[9] Not pancakes but jelly donuts. Clara would make batches when she'd accumulated enough grease to fry the dough in boiling grease. Who saves grease today?

training. Your husband can come along as a gardener or something." When Clara retold this story, she said that she and Fritz found the offer hysterically funny. Just imagine our intellectual, absent-minded father as a gardener! With good grace, Clara turned their offer down. Besides, the offer didn't meet their objective of setting Fritz up in medical practice.

Years later, when we lived in El Paso, Texas, Fritz and Clara were invited to the El Paso Country Club to have dinner with a nice Jewish couple transplanted from Chicago, Dr. Morton Leonard and his wife Judy. As the dinner conversation progressed, mother told the story of her work in the hotel and the offer from the baseball team.

What a surprise it was to find out that Judy's parents had been the owners of the hotel where Clara worked. They probably found Clara through a Jewish Aid Society. For Clara the story was proof that it was possible to get ahead in the United States. What would we say today?

Clara and Fritz led a simple life in their tiny apartment. She would stay home alone in the evenings while Fritz delivered babies on the South Side of Chicago or worked at Cook County Hospital, which served a large Black population.[10] She would play the old 78-rpm phonograph records Fritz brought from Germany. Beethoven string quartets were a favorite choice of music. And she would read the original German version of Thomas Mann's *Joseph and his Brothers*.[11]

Clara 1935. Posing as a Madonna. Fritz certainly adores Clara.

---

[10] Fritz and Clara had seen no Black people before they came to the United States. It is hard for us to comprehend that, living in the racially mixed world we live in today. Before WWII, Germany was nearly 100% white.

[11] A huge book, eventually four volumes published between 1933 and 1943. A deeply intellectual and complex work. I do not think the work has survived the test of time.

When I was a child, I imagined their Chicago apartment with bare walls, a basic bed with a metal frame, and a bare light bulb illuminating the room. It may not have been that grim, but it was still not fancy. Their Spartan existence did not diminish Fritz and Clara's need to nourish the mind. Even later, when they were much more financially comfortable, books, sprightly conversation, reading, art, and classical music made up the core of what was important to them. They were and remained genuine European bourgeois intellectuals.

Earlier, as Fritz and Clara prepared to leave Germany for the United States, Fritz told Clara, in no uncertain terms, that she could not bring many family possessions with her. They didn't know where they would live or how often they would move. So, Clara brought only a trunk with her that held, among other things, some china, the family silver, and many damask tablecloths. You can imagine her shock when she arrived in Chicago and saw that Fritz had set up their small household with his father Arthur's antique rolltop desk and also his large bookcase. (Not to mention a record player and many 78" phonograph recordings.) In 1935, it was filled with medical books and a complete German encyclopedia set. You can imagine the conversations that followed between the young married couple!

Today, the top shelf of the bookcase holds many of Arthur's antique books. The short books on that top shelf are the English Everyman Editions of Shakespeare's complete works. Arthur carried these books with him while he served in World War I. Arthur gave his mother Jenny the small, engraved tin picture sometime before he began medical school in Berlin. The drawer at the bottom of the bookcase contains Olga Brunstein Bornstein's extensive postcard collection from 1900–1905.

Fritz brought his family book-case to the U.S. with him in 1935.

Arthur's 3-volume Complete Works of Shakespeare next to the engraved tin of Chillon, where Rousseau once lived.

When Fritz passed the Illinois medical boards, it was time for them to establish a medical practice. First Fritz found work as a physician for a coal mining company in Kincaid, Illinois. Evidently foreign doctors (today called FMG, foreign medical graduates) often found such jobs. Ted Leon, of whom I will write later, told me that his father, a physician who was educated in Europe and lived in Palestine before coming to the U.S. in the 1920s, also worked first in a coal mining town in West Virginia before moving his family to St. Louis.

What I find striking about these early years in Illinois is that Clara and Fritz often spoke of them with great warmth. They didn't complain about being former metropolitans stuck in the provinces. They found the people interesting, and the reverse was also true. Most rural Illinoisians had never met people like them. Their accent was interesting and so were their stories about why they were in the United States. I think Fritz idealized the Illinois farmers and the other locals as "real people" and "noble tillers of the soil." Deep in his soul, Fritz was a true Romantic and quite sentimental.[12]

Around 1937 or 1938 Fritz and Clara moved to Rochester, Illinois, a hamlet of five hundred residents about ten miles outside Springfield, Illinois' state capitol. They purchased a house on Main Street which served as their home and office.[13] Clara handled appointments and general nursing duties.

The Great Depression was as bad as ever. Everyone was short of cash and patients gave items in barter for Fritz's services. The wonderful handmade cotton quilts we had as children date from those years. Clara's treadle sewing machine was payment for the delivery of a baby. This antique machine worked with foot power not electricity. Clara sewed countless curtains, tablecloths and dresses for herself and me on this machine.

Clara also decided to make use of her Danish Bornholm training to raise some goats and make goat cheese. Evidently the cheese was quite tasty. She once mailed a sample of her goat cheese to poet Carl Sandberg. He graciously wrote her a note, thanking her

---

[12] My husband David's upbringing conformed to Fritz's ideal of the Illinois farmer, a positive. Plus David was very smart. What more could he ask for?

[13] From my point of view in 2020, borrowing money for Clara's completion of dental school should have come before borrowing money to buy a home to start Fritz's medical practice. But hindsight doesn't change the reality of those times. A man's work came before that of a woman.

for the cheese, praising her cheese making abilities, and affirming their common love for feisty goats. Clara told me about the written exchange, but I haven't found it among the family papers.

Clara also mailed packages of homemade jams to the New York family whose affidavit had assured government authorities that Clara would be able to support herself in the U.S. I never learned the name of that family but presume that they were also Jews who were ready to support Jews who fled Fascism.

In Rochester Fritz tried his hand at winemaking, using locally grown grapes. He had studied chemistry and worked in laboratories. How hard could it be to make wine? The couple pressed the ripe grapes into juice, then carefully mixed the juice with the proper amounts of other ingredients. They put the blend into old bottles, corked them, lined them up in the kitchen and waited. One evening, a few weeks later, as they were falling asleep in their upstairs bedroom, they heard great popping sounds coming from below. They went down to the kitchen and turned on the light. What a sight greeted them! Purple liquid dripped down the ceiling and the walls—corks and fluid were strewn all over the kitchen.

Fritz with Bowser and his Ford sedan around 1937.

As a child, our son Jacob would describe his grandfather as a "humble country doctor," which in the 1930s he surely was. I don't know how Jacob came up with the phrase, but it fit perfectly. Fritz practiced medicine at a time when doctors made house calls. He had a Ford sedan to make his house calls and to care for patients. Fritz would tell us stories about his cases. I remember two in particular.

He was once called to deliver a baby in the Sangamon River bottoms, an area populated by the very poor and uneducated. When Fritz knocked on the door of the home to which he'd been called, he was greeted by a man holding a shotgun saying: "I ain't lettin' no strange man touch my wife." A few minutes later his wife delivered her new child into a chamber pot. You can imagine Fritz's shock. This was nothing he'd trained for in Hamburg or Chicago. In another case, he delivered a baby at home as the mother lay on the kitchen table. This family was just not going to the hospital where there were strangers.

Fritz had to do some research before he finally diagnosed a case of smallpox in the Sangamon River bottoms! He thought the disease had been eradicated all over the world. How wrong he was! Local doctors were impressed by his medical acumen.

Around 1937/38 Fritz's grandmother Jenny decided to leave Palestine. She had not been happy in Jerusalem living with her daughter Susanne. Suse, as she was known, had lost most of her own money when she fell in love with a confidence man in Egypt and even spent some time in debtors prison. Jenny did not adjust to the Middle Eastern climate and culture. Jenny left and Suse remained in Palestine.

When Jenny (aged 78) asked to come to Rochester, Fritz said to Clara: "No, Clara. You don't know her like I do." Clara replied: "It is our duty to take care of her. Her son Arthur is dead, her daughter Röse is in Leningrad with her children Ilse and Mila (Emanuel), and Susanne is a problem. If Jenny wants to live with us, we will take her in. After all, she gave up her medical career to help raise you."

Fritz had good reasons for his reservations. But these were times when old tensions had to be ignored. Jenny arrived in Rochester and promptly made it clear that she did not intend to live with them. She would rent a room in town and live on her own.[14] And so she did; she lived with a Mrs. Coe, down the street near the railroad tracks.

---

[14] I have no idea how Jenny financed her life. I have to assume she had money of her own.

Jenny was a known figure in town: walking down Main Street with her cane, her slight figure dressed in black. What a transition she made—from Jerusalem to the tiny town of Rochester! She seems to have made friends. I found a cache of greetings cards sent to her by her local acquaintances. We know that Jenny's English was good. Her main concerns during this time were her two daughters and their fate. A few very sad letters are included in the additional materials to this chapter.

What is the historical context for these letters between Röse and Jenny? There was severe censorship in Stalinist Russia, and discrimination against Jews had not stopped with the Russian Revolution. In 1917, Russia had one the largest Jewish populations in the world.[15] When Röse wrote to her mother, she was aware that the mail was censored, so she was very careful not to say anything negative about her life in Russia. There is little hard information in her letters, but she probably had a bleak and uncertain life. Her husband, Vladimir had died.[16] Her son, Mila, studying medicine, was ill. We do not know how she supported herself. These letters are the last news we have of her and the family. We can only think that she and her children were lost during the purges of the late 1930s or during the devastation of WWII.

Jenny was a woman born into comfort and affluence, who somehow gathered the energy to go against the grain of her times and become a physician. Yet every stage in her life was punctuated by tragedy: the disappearance of her birth mother, the loss of her beloved husband Philipp, the loss of Arthur's young wife Olga at age 31, the death of her son Arthur at age fifty, her forced emigration from Germany, the disappearance of her daughter Röse in Russia, and the inability of her daughter Suse to join her in the United States. I can only admire the strength and persistence of this diminutive lady who outlived all her children, adjusted to life in a new country, and lived to see her four great-grandchildren alive and well before she died at age 92. That is an accomplishment we should envy.

Clara's brother Hans Joachim also finally came to Illinois after several years in Palestine where he had worked as a farmer on a kibbutz and later as a waiter at a hotel in

---

[15] For more information take a look at the Wikipedia article: "History of the Jews in Russia."
[16] Vladimir (Volodya) was Olga Brunstein Bornstein's brother.

Haifa.[17] When he arrived in the U.S., he worked in Chicago as a laborer in a furniture factory. Most of his fellow workers were Black men. This was one of many new experiences for a former medical student! Hajo came down from Chicago to Rochester for a joyful reunion. The two siblings Clara and Hajo were together again, best friends Hajo and Fritz reunited after being apart for over four years!

Around this time, Clara and Fritz became friends with June and Wilson Park, who owned the local funeral home just across the street. June and Wilson were slightly younger than Fritz and Clara. The Bornstein and Park families would remain life-long friends. June would tell me how they loved to visit with our parents, drink martinis (her first), listen to music, and talk about politics and literature. In the late 1940s we would celebrate memorable Thanksgivings in Rochester with the extended Park family. We children would rid ourselves of excess energy by running around the huge casket display rooms after Thanksgiving dinner. Wilson's son Greg took over the business and still operates it. He arranged our brother Philipp's funeral there in August 2006. There we were again in the casket room!

In spring 1940 Clara and Fritz learned that Clara was pregnant at last! June Park told me about the day Fritz walked into the bookstore where she worked in Springfield to share the great news that they were expecting. They were so excited! They'd wanted children from the beginning of their marriage, but until now nothing happened. Fritz heard about a new pregnant mare serum that was being used to help women become pregnant. So Clara was given a shot—and boom—baby on the way. After having her first babies, twins, Clara never had any difficulty becoming pregnant again.

Both Fritz and Clara were naturalized as U.S. citizens in 1940. Their new nationality shielded them from deportation, but it also made Fritz eligible for the draft. The draft, abolished after WWI, was reinstated on September 16, 1940.

After a few years in Rochester, Clara and Fritz decide to move further downstate to Alton, Illinois where Fritz had found a job as a physician at the Illinois State Mental Hospital. He needed further training to qualify as a physician. Expectant parents Fritz and Clara also wanted to be nearer to the medical expertise in St. Louis.

---

[17] Translation of one of his letters from Palestine appears at the end of Chapter 9.

Olga in front of the administration building at Alton State Hospital, Alton, Illinois.

In late 1940 we find Clara and Fritz living on the grounds of the Alton State Hospital. Back then, State Hospital was the less threatening term for mental hospital or home for the insane. The couple had free housing and free household help from the hospital's patients. Fritz was hired to work there as a psychiatrist. He was always perceptive about people, but I suspect he worked more at Alton State Hospital as a general practitioner than a psychiatrist.

Clara loved to tell us the stories about the household help who were patients from the State Hospital. One lady wanted Clara to see her "trunks full of pancakes in her attic." Another called Clara excitedly as she was cleaning the bathtub: "Come here, look at the water circling down the drain." Clara must have enjoyed being free of the stress of helping to run Fritz's medical practice and watching over Jenny.

St. Louis was only twenty miles from Alton and now Clara and Fritz had access to classical music on the radio and in live performances.[18] They could visit the world class St. Louis Art Museum and the city's zoo. Here they also met Ted and Elizabeth Leon, a couple who became their life-long friends.

Elizabeth was an artist and also worked at the St. Louis Art Museum information desk. Later Elizabeth told me stories about noticing the intense couple who often visited the museum and would stop by the information desk with questions. Soon the two couples became fast friends. Ted Leon was finishing up his Ph.D. in German at Washington University. Ted and Fritz would play chess together and sometimes go fencing. After WWII broke out, Ted was one of the first members of the famous Office of Strategic Services (OSS).[19] When Ted retired, he was head of the translating department at the U.S. State Department.

On January 14, 1941, Olga Jean and Philipp Emanuel were born a month prematurely at Jewish Hospital in St. Louis. Olga was named for her paternal grandmother Olga Brunstein Bornstein. But why Jean? The new parents thought Jean sounded American. Philipp was named for his paternal great-grandfather Philipp and grandmother Olga's father Emanuel. Note the European spelling of Philipp's name, which would cause confusion throughout his life. "One L and two Ps. Not two Ls and two Ps."

Clara told us about Fritz driving her to Jewish Hospital in St. Louis from Alton. Mid-January ice covered the roads and snow was swirling fiercely as they drove over the old bridges above the Mississippi and Missouri Rivers. Philipp was born first in the delivery room. Then the obstetrician, a Dr. Drabkin, said: "Oh my God, there's another one in there!" So Olga was born seven minutes after Philipp. Clara stayed in the hospital for several weeks. The twins weighed only four pounds each at birth and remained in an incubator for a month. During their first year of life, their parents weighed them each day and kept track of their "intake and output" (very medical and thorough) in a special notebook now lost. The twins survived their first year in good health and thrived.

---

[18] Radio station KFUO was a classical music station sponsored by the Lutheran Missouri Synod Concordia Seminary in Clayton, Missouri, next to St. Louis. When David and I lived in Clayton in 1978, where we had an apartment across from Concordia Seminary, Jacob's babysitter was the wife of a seminary student.

[19] The intelligence service for the U.S. Armed Forces during WWII. Later the OSS became the Central Intelligence Agency (CIA).

Those of you who know Olga and Philipp would find it hard to imagine that these preemies were the shortest and thinnest members of their grade school class until eighth grade. Once the twins were born, Clara and Fritz realized that in the event they (Clara and Fritz) should die, they didn't have any relatives who could take care of their precious twins. They approached Ted and Elizabeth Leon and asked them if they would take on that responsibility. Elizabeth had been raised by her Austrian Catholic parents; Ted by his Jewish parents from Palestine. They were both educated and intellectual. Clara and Fritz thought that the Leons were the sort of couple who could take good care of Olga and Philipp should the need arise. The similarity in the Bornstein and Leon backgrounds would assure that the twins had a good upbringing. Ted and Elizabeth accepted the responsibility. Philipp and I always joked and called them our "godparents." The Leon home in Arlington, Virginia was always open to us, and later to Jacob and David. What wonderful friends they were.[20]

Short typewritten letter to Clara at 5540 Hyde Park Blvd. Broadview Hotel, Chicago, Illinois

Special delivery May 15, 1935 [on envelope] but letter is dated April 15 (three days before their wedding). However Fritz was absent-minded and an incredibly messy typist, so he could have meant May 15th, since the letter is signed "Your Husband." Evidently Clara couldn't live with Fritz at the Edward Sanitorium in Naperville.

I am enclosing a disappointing letter from grandmother that took nineteen days to get here.[21] I will be in Chicago filled with delight that I will see you again. There will be all kinds of business to take care of. My job is going great![22] I must get a letter to grandmother tomorrow morning. I have no idea why she hasn't received any of my letters. Those people have

---

[20] In 1978 Philipp and Ted took a trip to Central Asia together; Fritz died during that trip. How amazing that Ted was with Philipp. Later after Ted was gone, Philipp looked out for Elizabeth as she deteriorated. Luckily Philipp's experience as a geriatric psychiatrist helped him recommend to her neighbor and lawyer the type of home health care Elizabeth would need. Much later Elizabeth left Olga a significant bequest in her will.

[21] We do not have the letter, but we can assume that Jenny is disappointed with living in Palestine and the situation in which she found her daughter Susanne.

[22] *"Ist Knorke"*—Berlin dialect meaning great, wonderful, special, cool.

used up 1400 English pounds in six months. Wow! I'm delighted to hear the news about Hajo. Maybe we can still save him for humanity if the guy would only write. Does grandmother have 1000 Reichsmarks with her now? I just wish that everything weren't so damnably unclear. Frank[23] wrote a nice letter. So anyway, I'll see you tomorrow and send you my very best love. Your dear husband.

PS I'm awaiting your first letter tomorrow morning, so I'll know when and where to meet you.

–» «–

Housekeeping instructions to Clara when she was working as a housemaid on the near North Side of Chicago.

Please bake the apples in a bag. Use several teaspoons of sugar for each apple. Use the apple corer. Bake in moderate oven with a bit of sugar until done.

Wash the hairbrushes in the bathroom…Rinse twice in cold water.

My dear Mrs. Bornstein. Will you please do as much of the housecleaning as you can? Will you change the bedding, brushing the mattress? We use the whisk broom on the furniture. You'll find the pillows on the sofa are too dusty to clean in the room. They're hard to clean because they're made of feathers. We polish the furniture with the waxed paper which you'll find in the kitchen. Please follow instructions on the box. Mrs. K.[24]

---

[23] No idea who this is.
[24] Was Mrs. K named Kaplin, Kapirowitz, …

Jenny's daughter Röse with her children daughter Ilse and son Mila.

Röse writes to her mother Jenny in Rochester, Illinois

Leningrad, September [?] 1936

Dearest mother:

Just so that I don't lose my typing skills, I'm writing you today using a typewriter. If I get better at typing this summer, I think I will probably have to start figuring out how to earn some money. I received your last letter and was quite sad to learn that our dear cousin [illegible] passed away. Yes, people keep dying one by one. It all began with Arthur.[25] What is Luci doing? What do you hear from her? I'm glad to hear that Suse and Hilda are close to you.[26] I am glad to know that you are not alone. There is not too much new at our end. All three of us have a cold and are now only getting better. Mila[27] is in the middle of examinations and studies day and night. He gave a talk in Russian that was well received but he still has problems with Russian handwriting. However, even here he has made enormous strides. Ilse[28] is a bit better but she keeps getting fatter despite all my good efforts. She still has the same job and is comfortable with it. She has become more self-confident. She speaks a lot of Russian but makes many mistakes. The weather here is variable, sometimes cool and then

---

[25] Röse's brother; Jenny's son. He died in January 1932.
[26] Hilda Rosenberger was an old Bornstein family friend with whom David and I visited when we were in Jerusalem in 1990.
[27] Her son nicknamed Mila for Emmanuel. Mila is the son of Jenny Bornstein's daughter Röse and her husband Volodya (Vladimir). Vladimir is Olga Brunstein Bornstein's brother. Mila's mother is Fritz's aunt. Mila is Fritz's first cousin.
[28] Röse's daughter and Mila's sister.

warm. I still have not rented a dacha[29] because I am not sure when Ilse will be on vacation. Mila will have two months off but Ilse gets only two weeks. I have decided I will probably rent something nearby. That way Ilse could see us after work. I'm thinking of the house we rented two years ago when we arrived here, in case I cannot find something more fitting. My friends have also rented in that area although I would like to rent something a bit further out, since it is a bit cheaper there. I should go to the dacha but I have not. I cannot even work up the energy to go to the doctor. I really do not feel like your daughter anymore. I feel like someone took away my energy for life after Volodya died.[30] I have only the boundless desire to have you near me. But unfortunately that wish cannot be fulfilled. How is your health? How long will Suse[31] live with you? What are Hilda and Carl doing? Is Paula there?[32] Dearest mother, please stay well and write me soon. I want to know how Fritz and Clara are doing. I send you many deeply felt kisses.

PS. Your sweet post card just arrived. I was surprised to see how quickly airmail works. I do not think the money situation that you wrote about is as serious as you think. Please do not send me any money. I understand that you want to do something special for Ilse, so I'll find out if there are things you can send that are duty free. Dearest mother, the children send you their love. When a letter from you arrives, the children always fight to see who will get to read it first.

Handwritten addendum:

Dear Mother: This letter was lying around for a while, but not on purpose. I haven't been feeling well. Please remember that if I need any money, I will let you know.

I just learned that even old things have a very high duty on them, even things that are not gifts. Please mother, know that we love you very much.

---

[29] Dacha is the Russian word for a house in the country.
[30] Vladimir Brunstein, the brother of Olga Brunstein Bornstein, Arthur's wife.
[31] Reminder to the reader: Suse is Röse and Arthur's sister. Jenny is their mother.
[32] Paula is Jenny's half-sister. She settled in England.

Postcard from Röse to Jenny

Postcard from Yalta, Ukraine to her mother Jenny in Rochester, Illinois, 1936.

Röse's message to her mother on the back of the postcard from Yalta, 1936.

Translation of Röse's message:

Dearly beloved mother:

We're at the Crimea. We hope that being at the sanitarium will help Mila get better. It is really beautiful here. We hope you are healthy and doing well. Love from your daughter, Röse

Letter from Jenny's daughter Röse in Leningrad to her mother Jenny in Rochester Illinois, 1937.

Snomsk[33] 6 December, 1937

My dearest mother:

It seems to me that I haven't heard from you in a very long time and I find that quite unsettling. I've written to Leningrad asking that my letters are forwarded here but...thus far I've received nothing. I'm beside myself with worry. There's not much new to report from here. Barely a day goes by without rain. We're quite unable to take walks in the forest, thus very little exercise. That really puts a crimp in our activities. We just hope that Mila will get better soon.[34] He seems to become better because of the good food here. We're served fruit and fresh vegetables...[35] ...the children have a good appetite. We spend the entire day with friends and usually share lunch and dinner with them as well. If the weather gets better we might stay a little longer. Mila's temperature is still 37.2 (Celsius).[36] He's not happy at all about that. But he does look good. I just wish he were healthy again. Otherwise there is nothing to report. We eat, drink, and sleep. Those are our only activities. Mila plays chess all day long. Don't we have an easy life? Dearest mother, please let me know what is going on with you. How is your health? Does the climate agree with you? Is the summer beautiful where you live? When I walk on the beautiful forest paths here, I think always of you and how wonderful it would be if you could be here walking with me. How are Fritz and Clara doing with their new medical practice? We think of you and all those who are no longer with us. I haven't had time to visit Volodya's grave even once this summer. Mila's illness has taken over my life.

Kisses from Ilse and Mila.

---

[33] A later letter confirms that they are on Yalta at some sort of sanitarium. Yalta is at the tip of the Crimea on the Black Sea. The area is surrounded by a tall mountain range, but has a warm, humid subtropical climate.
[34] No information on what was wrong with him, but there is a good possibility that he had tuberculosis (TB).
[35] This detail is hard to believe. Probably included to please the censors.
[36] 99 Fahrenheit.

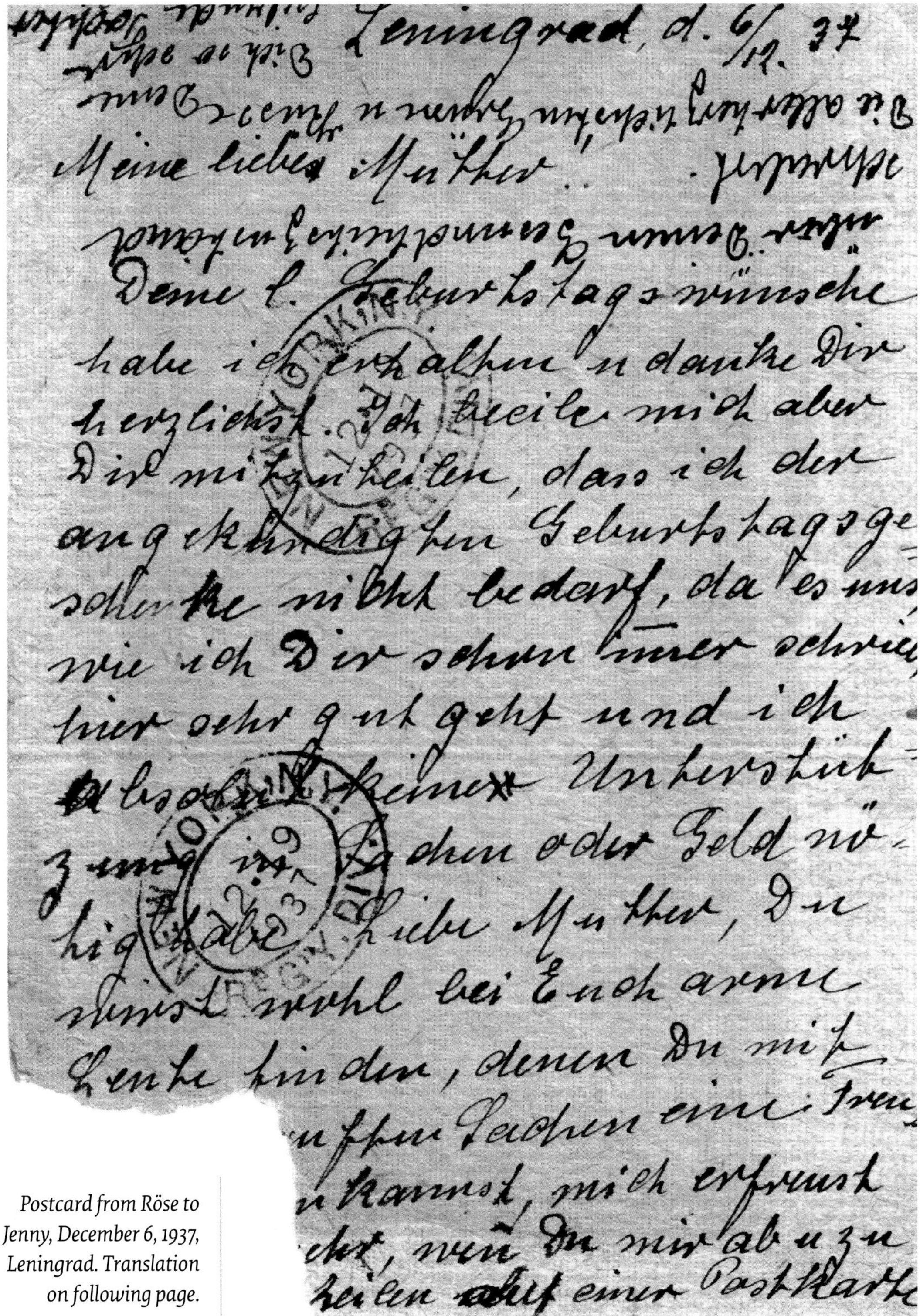

[Handwritten postcard, German]

Leningrad, d. 6/12. 37

Meine liebe Mutter!

Deine l. Geburtstagswünsche habe ich erhalten u danke Dir herzlichst. Ich beeile mich aber Dir mitzuteilen, dass ich der angekündigten Geburtstagsgeschenke nicht bedarf, da es uns, wie ich Dir schon immer schrieb, hier sehr gut geht und ich also keine Unterstüt-zung ... Sachen oder Geld nö... Liebe Mutter, Du meinst wohl bei Euch arme Leute finden, denen Du ... ... Sachen eine Freu... ... kannst, mich erfreust ..., wenn Du mir ab u zu ... auf einer Postkarte

Postcard from Röse to Jenny, December 6, 1937, Leningrad. Translation on following page.

Postcard from Röse to Jenny

December 6, 1937

Leningrad

My dear mother:

I received your sweet birthday wishes and thank you from the bottom of my heart. Am answering you right away to let you know that I do not need any birthday presents. I am doing well here and absolutely do not need any money.[37] Dearest mother, you probably have poor people where you live, to whom you could give money. If you only could send me a few lines on a postcard now and then so I have an idea of how you are doing. I send you my best love and kisses.

Your daughter who loves you very much,
Röse

PS. I would love it if you would send me a postcard now and then so I can learn how your health is holding up. I send you thousands of kisses. Your loving daughter, Röse.

1949 Application to the Jewish Congress by Jenny Bornstein

Jenny sent this application, handwritten in English, probably in 1949. Jenny never gave up trying to find her daughter and grandchildren.

I herewith apply to the committee of the Jewish Congress in Kawno (?) to undertake all steps to trace the whereabouts of my family members in the Soviet Union and in her occupied states in Europe. I understand that your humane and benefitted service may be rendered without charge but perhaps with post cash. My deepest gratitude and thanks for your helping hand.

Respectfully yours,
Mrs. Jenny Bornstein, 87 years old

---

[37] I find it very difficult to believe that Röse does not need any money.

Name: Therese Brunstein, familiar name Reese or Rose Brunstein. She had intended to live in 1938 in Odessa at her cousin. I hope the Russians overheard Reese in Neese or the writing has ....?

Date of birth: 1884 Dec. 09
Place of Birth: Berlin
Citizenship: Russia
Occupation before the war: housewife, typist
Date when last hear from her: in the year 1937–38

She has two children:

Emmanuel Brunstein a medical student in Leningrad, born Nov. 17, 1910 in Berlin. Russian citizen

Ilse Brunstein, born May 9, 1912 or 1913. Employed in Leningrad in a shoe factory. Mrs. Brunstein intended to live, after her son's M.D., in the Ukraine, maybe already in 1938–39.

From left to right: Mila, Röse, and friends, n.d.

Clara's goats

Geese flying south

The twins are born 1941

Old bridge over the Mississippi River

1935 Chicago

CHAPTER 11

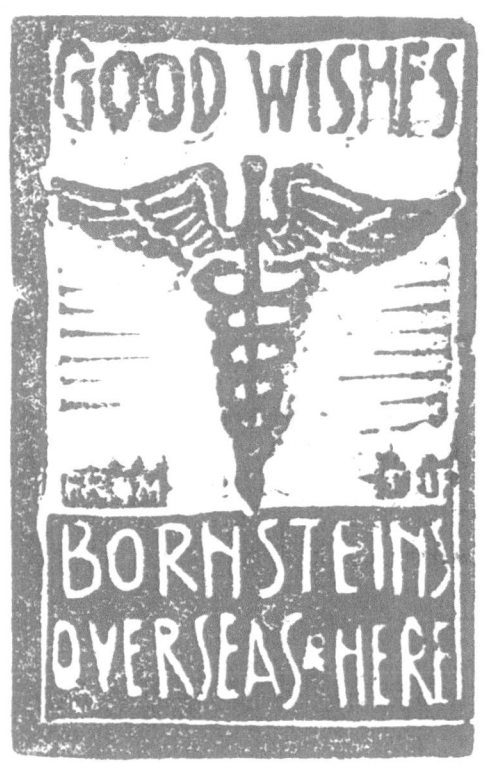

The War Years
1941–1946

Left to right: Fritz, Clara, Fred on Fritz's lap, Philipp standing next to Clara, and Olga seated, 1943. Olga has the ivory necklace Clara is wearing.

How did Clara and Fritz end up in Dallas, Texas of all places in late 1942? Perhaps this would not be the first choice as a place of residence for German-Jewish emigres. Why did they leave Illinois after almost ten years there? The reason: One of Fritz's best friends from secondary school and university, Walter Hirsch, left Hamburg in 1934 and landed in Dallas with his mother. Walter had studied law in Germany. Unfortunately, his German law degree was useless in the United States. Despite this, Walter found a good job with Sears and Roebuck in Dallas.[1]

Over the years Walter and, later, his wife Margot[2] were like aunt and uncle to us. We would spend holidays with them, meeting in Arkansas half-way between Illinois and Texas. Later when the Bornsteins became Texans, our visits took place in El Paso and Dallas. Walter and Margot were always lovely to us, perhaps because they never had children of their own. They treated us like their own relatives, attending our high school

---

[1] I have absolutely no idea how Walter ended up in Dallas. Help perhaps from a Jewish aid organization. In his 50s Walter went to law school at SMU part-time and earned his U.S. law degree. He lived in Dallas until he died at age 90+. I attended his jolly 90th birthday party.

[2] Margot's father Dr. Lippman was a well-known Hamburg radiologist and friend of Arthur Bornstein. He immigrated to Australia rather than the U.S.

graduations or putting us up overnight when we traveled through Dallas on our way east from El Paso. Walter's mother would send me packages containing little girl dresses from the sales rack at Neiman Marcus in Dallas. Her gifts were well-meant, but most of the dresses didn't work for me: I remember refusing to wear a chartreuse sun dress.

After the twins were born, Fritz decided to specialize in pathology. An internship in pathology was required before he could join the U.S. Army. Fritz's medical dissertation in Hamburg had been on a topic in pathology and was supervised by the famous pathologist Friederich Wohlwill. Wohlwill, also a Jew, fled Hamburg for Portugal and then the United States.

From 1942 to 1943 Fritz worked as a pathology intern at Methodist Hospital in Dallas. We were living in Oak Cliff in Dallas during the summer of 1943 when a great polio epidemic was in full swing. Fritz was determined to keep his children away from crowds to avoid the possibility of infection. It was difficult to stop the twins, now two and a half years old, from running around outside. Pregnant Clara hated the Texas heat. She was also heart broken when a small diamond timepiece from her mother Emmy was stolen from their apartment by a babysitter.

The twins were not old enough to understand why they were placed with neighbors while Clara gave birth in the hospital to her second son: Frederick Bernard born on July 14, 1943 and named for his father Fritz. His middle name came from Clara's father Bernard. Fritz or Clara were either unaware or indifferent to the Jewish tradition that a baby should not be named for a living person. Why? The concept was that you don't know how a living person will really turn out before she or he has died. So why give a child a name that may turn out to be tainted? While Clara was at the hospital giving birth to her second son Fred, the twins thought their mother had disappeared forever. When she returned home at last, they would not let her out of their sight. Olga would even cling to Clara's hand when Clara was sitting on the toilet.[3]

While the young Bornstein family resided in Dallas, Jenny was still living on her own in Rochester, Illinois. From there she sent Fritz and Clara a telegram in her idiosyncratic English: *"July 14, 1943: Dr. Frederick Bornstein Methodist Hospital Dallas. Wonderful Good Destinies Shall Protect Boys Lifeways. How feels Clara? Grandma."*

---

[3] One of Clara's favorite stories regarding fear of abandonment. It may tell as much about Clara as Olga.

The Bornstein family had now grown to five (one more child Aaron would arrive in 1946). While working at Methodist Hospital, Fritz found a new chess partner: Dr. Vincent Ravel from El Paso, Texas. In a decade, Dr. Ravel would be instrumental in convincing Fritz and his family to move to El Paso, Texas. In 1952 Fritz would set up the pathology department of a new hospital in El Paso: Providence Memorial.[4]

The Japanese attack on Pearl Harbor in December 1941 marked the outbreak of WWII.[5] Fritz and Clara had become naturalized citizens of the United States in 1940. It was a near certainty that Fritz would eventually be drafted. WWII became the great patriotic war, enthusiastically supported by all of America. The Nazis and the Japanese had to be defeated. Still this was an unbelievably difficult time. WWII impacted all aspects of daily life.

Clara and Fritz of course were familiar with crises and discomfort. They both had experienced the privations of WWI in Germany and of depressions in Germany and the United States. Our parents were ready to sacrifice to "make the world safe for democracy." But the prospect of a long family separation was not one they were looking forward to. At the same time, mother's only brother, Hans Joachim (Hajo) served as a medic in the U.S. Army in Europe. Another person to add to Clara's list of worries.

Clara's brother Hajo in U.S. Army uniform.

---

[4] Small world story: Vincent Ravel had a brother Irving who became a podiatrist in Austin, Texas. He founded the Karavel Shoe store, still operating today in my Austin neighborhood. I met Irving shortly after we moved here. He remembered Clara and Fritz well.

[5] The usual Sunday broadcast of the New York Philharmonic was interrupted by the announcement that Pearl Harbor had been bombed. Philipp and I were napping in our playpen. We were living in Alton.

After Fritz completed his internship, the family traveled from Dallas back to Rochester, Illinois for a short stay. They had to arrange for all their possessions to be placed in storage, to rent out their house and Fritz's former medical office on Main Street, and decide where Clara and the children would live while Fritz served in the U.S. Army. Fritz was commissioned as a Captain in the Army Medical Corps and sent first to training in Ft. Devens, Massachusetts. Clara, the kids, and great-grandmother remained in Rochester. Then Fritz was transferred to Fort Lewis, Washington where Clara and the kids would join him. Here Fritz had more training before being shipped to the Pacific Theater. Even though he was a captain, he received the basic training required of all soldiers. Had you known Fritz, you would find it hard to imagine him wriggling under barbed wire and firing a rifle. Fritz loved hiking in the outdoors and taking after dinner walks at home, but beyond that he was neither a regular exerciser nor a fitness buff.

One of my very first real memories was an incident from our family's short stay in Tacoma, Washington near Fort Lewis. Clara took me to the drugstore and she must have been carrying me in her arms. As she paid for her purchase, I leaned down and spied the Life Savers® on display next to the cash register. I grabbed a Life Savers roll, tore open the package and immediately began eating the candy. My mother was shocked and outraged, and later gave me a long speech about the evils of stealing. As a further indignity, she had to pay the clerk an extra five cents for my transgression. The incident left an impression on me. Later on when we lived in Herrin, Illinois, my brothers and I consistently filched change from her purse and from Fritz's suit jacket pockets. Mother again was shocked. To her dying day she kept her purse close to her, even putting it next to her bed at night so we couldn't get at it.

While Fritz served in the U.S. Army stationed thousands of miles away as a physician in the South Pacific, Clara would have complete responsibility for her three children in Chicago. How would she deal with this great responsibility alone?

Fritz was moved around in the South Pacific, to the islands of Saipan, Guam, and Iwo Jima. My best source of information are letters exchanged between him, Clara, and his grandmother Jenny. We also have a small stash of photographs and some photostats listing Fritz's laboratory inventory.[6]

I later learned that many German-speaking emigres serving in the U.S. Army were recruited for war service in Europe as interrogators, translators, general cultural resources, and even spies. Perhaps Fritz (or the army) thought that his medical talents were more important than his linguistic and cultural background?

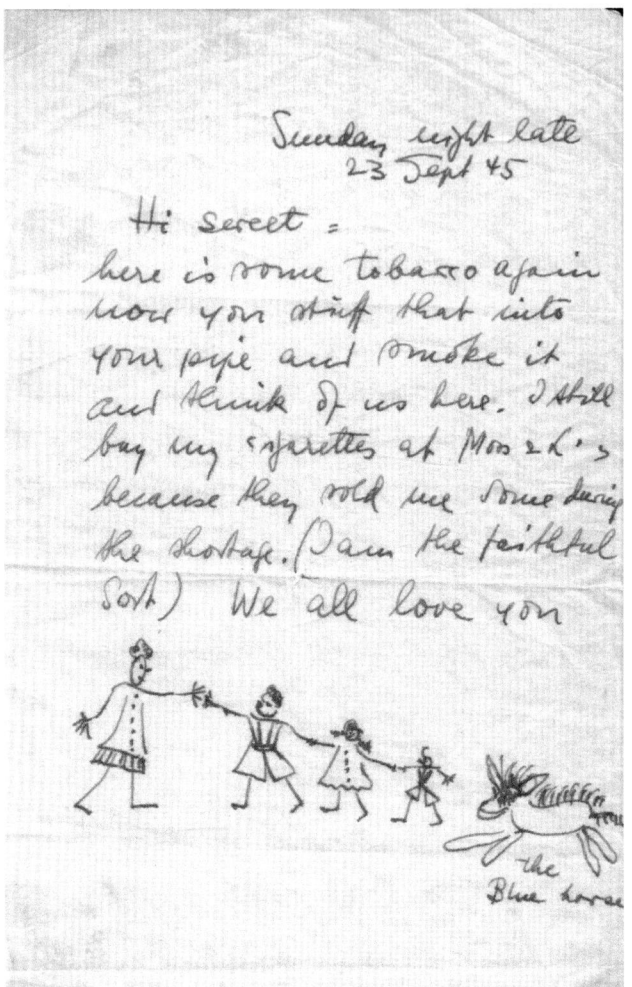

Clara writes to her husband, 1945[7]

---

[6] The Photostat machine, or Photostat, was an early projection photocopier created around 1910 by the Commercial Camera Company, later the Photostat Corporation.

[7] Franz Marc was a key figure in German Expressionism. Clara loved his paintings, especially Blaues Pferd (Blue Horse) 1911.

The War Years: 1941–1946

Franz Marc, Blaues Pferd (Blue Horse) 1911.

Letters from the Pacific theater to the home front were a special treat during the war. Even the smallest tidbit of information could connect the reader and the writer. Note the irony in this letter from Fritz to his brother-in-law Hajo:

10 December 1945. Somewhere in the Marianas.

My dear Hajo: Here we are safe and sound—no malaria after an elegant trip. Hospital in beautiful location. Life is pleasant; screened tents, electricity, B rations.[8] I bet you envy me and I can't blame you. The laboratory gets its roof today. So best regards, Fritz.

---

[8] B rations: a term used in the United States military for a meal provided to troops which was prepared using canned or preserved ingredients. 'B' ration meals could be prepared in field kitchens and served in the field or in garrisons without refrigeration or freezer facilities.

While Fritz was stationed far away from his wife and children, he mailed them original poems and his retellings of some Greek myths. These texts show Fritz's classical education and his continuing German obsession with the classical world. Clara certainly understood what he wrote. Do you think his children did?

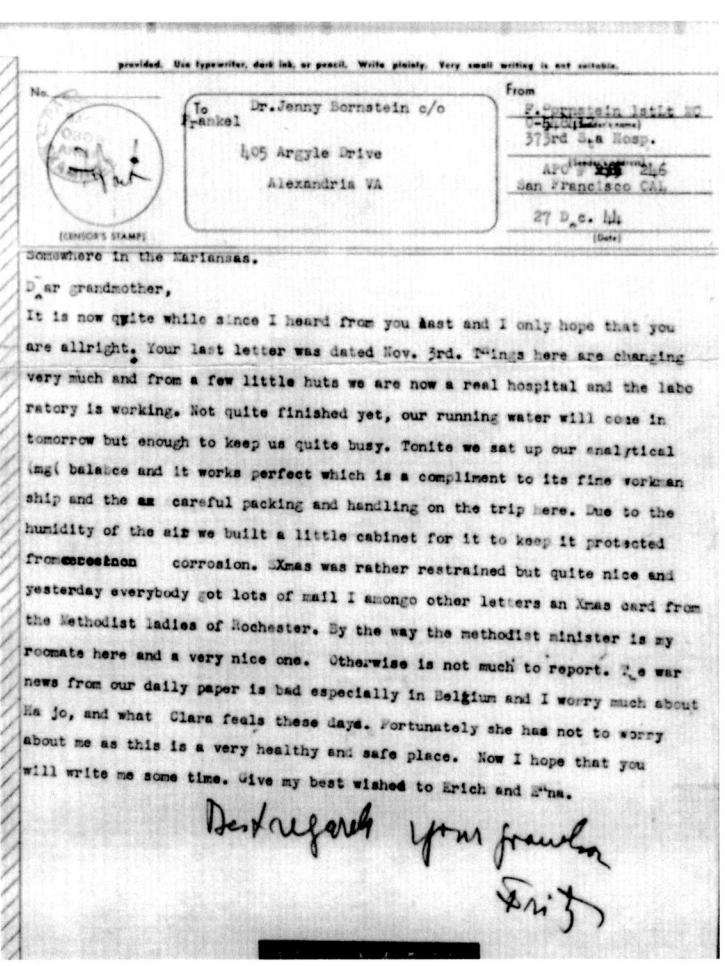

Fritz to Jenny, 1944.

The Bornsteins had been good Prussian soldiers for several generations. In Germany, Jenny's husband Philipp served in the 1860s and 1870s, Bernard Löwenstein in the 1900s, and Arthur in WWI on both the eastern and western fronts; now Fritz and Hajo served the U.S. in WWII. My three brothers would serve in the Armed Forces during the Vietnam conflict. Philipp served as the stockade psychiatrist at Fort Hood, Texas. Fred was a combat officer in the Signal Corps in Vietnam, and Aaron served in the Navy in Vietnam in various assignments including teaching English to Vietnamese officers.

In the late 1960s I was a "peacenik" working with my then boyfriend, David Wise, in the anti-war movement helping young men become draft resisters or conscientious objectors and avoid the draft. When my father learned about my activities, he threatened to disown me. He felt I should support the war in Vietnam because all his sons, my brothers, were serving in the armed forces. He thought I was disloyal but quickly forgave me.

Fritz rarely spoke about his war experiences but I do remember a few details. Soldiers stationed in the middle of nowhere drank if they could, and as much as they could. The officers drank in a bar reserved for them. Fritz often said it was a medical mystery why after the war some soldiers became lifelong alcoholics, and others came home and rarely touched alcohol again.

For a while during his time in the South Pacific, Fritz was billeted with a roommate who was a Methodist minister. I can imagine their conversations: Fritz the convinced atheist arguing intelligently with a believing minister about faith, God, and the future of mankind. Fritz knew the Bible quite well, knowledge gained from his years at his Lutheran grade school and high school. As a university student he loved studying philosophy.

Fritz Army pathologist, c.1944.

Fritz's field hospital in the South Pacific. Note Quonset hut architecture.

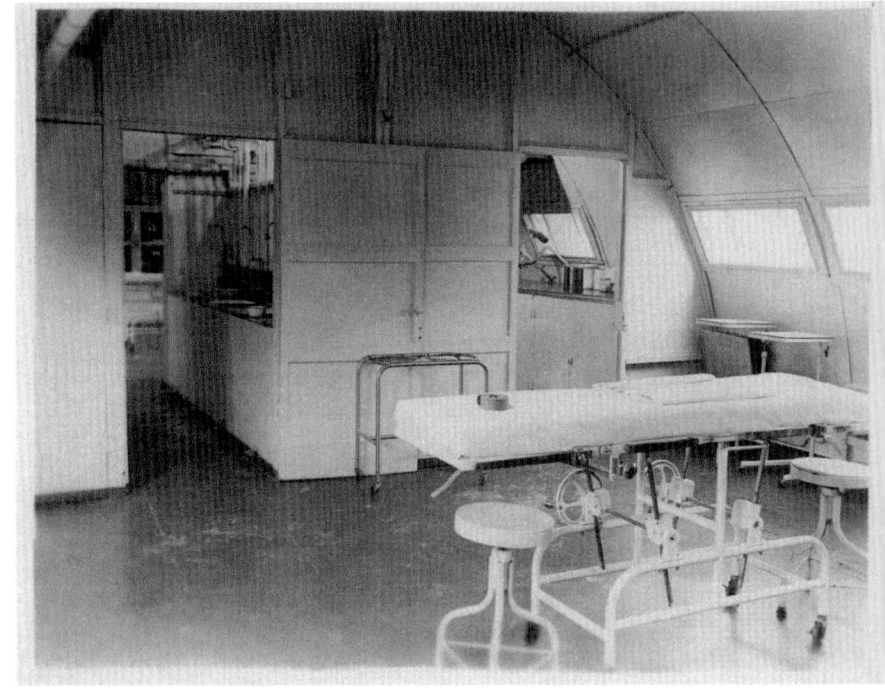

Around 1944 I can begin to draw on my own memories, rather than on the stories Clara told me again and again when I was a child.

After Fritz shipped out to the South Pacific (to places kept secret at the time by Army censorship), Clara and her three kids packed into a very small sleeping compartment on a passenger train headed east from Tacoma to Chicago. Clara brought along food for the trip; her tight budget did not permit expensive dining car meals. Two food items we ate on this trip entered into family lore: large rounds of Swedish hardtack (*knakebrød*, a bit like Rye Crisp) and carrots. And more carrots. Long, orange, and unpeeled. Was Clara concerned we might go blind? Or were carrots just cheap and easy to transport? There must have been a lot of crunching going on in that tight little train compartment.

I remember just one variation in our eating routine during the entire trip. Clara and her three children enter the elegant dining car. Mother has fresh coffee, and we all eat buttered toast. Perhaps we get a glass of orange juice too? Watch out scurvy! I was only three and a half, so this meal made a deep impression on me. Even today I can see the little metal toast holder on our table and the elegant Black waiter who served us while we stared out the window as the train raced toward Chicago.

Now it is 1945. Clara's challenges become extreme. How will she find an apartment for herself and her three young children, plus great-grandmother Jenny, 85-years old, soon to join them from Alexandria, VA. Clara was plunged into a rigorous crash course in single motherhood. She hoped Fritz would return safely and soon.

Heinrich and Steffi Necheles lived in a large house on the South Side of Chicago near the University of Chicago. They offered to take on the responsibility to be substitute parents to give us support while Fritz served overseas. Hein, as we called him, had been a doctoral student under Arthur Bornstein in Hamburg—one of Arthur's few Jewish graduate students.[9] As you will remember, Clara and Fritz married in Chicago. Hein and Steffi hosted their wedding reception in their home on April 18, 1935.

---

[9] He wrote his dissertation under Arthur on cockroach physiology. Hein collected the cockroaches for later dissection at the Hamburg Zoo.

Now there were no blood relations to depend on for support and help. Clara's brother Hajo was in the army in Europe; great-grandmother Jenny still lived in Arlington, Virginia with her nephew and his wife.[10] Even though Jenny was a spry 85-year-old, she was not up to caring for three energetic children under four years old.

Housing was hard to find during WWII. No new housing was being built and no landlord wanted to rent to a mother with three young children. Clara found an apartment, with cockroaches and filthy walls, on Chicago's south side at 4533 Lake Park, Chicago 15.[11] Later she moved us to an apartment on the second floor of a small yellow house at 5555 South Ellis Avenue. We had a front yard since the house was set back from the street. We could play outside, a special treat. This is the first home address I memorized and still remember today. The Necheles family lived close by on Kimbark Avenue. The downstairs tenant was Mrs. Klutz, unforgettable and not just for her name. Periodically she would pound on her ceiling with a broom. That's how she told us we were making too much noise. Otherwise, she was friendly to us. One day she brought us a freshly baked pumpkin pie, a new food for us all, including our mother. There had certainly been no pumpkin pie in Berlin. Clara took a bite and that was the last time she ever ate pumpkin pie. It wasn't like *Kuchen* at all.[12]

From our upstairs windows we could see across the street to a large brick building. I saw thin, elderly figures wandering about inside wearing what seemed like long white gowns. They seemed like ghosts to me. We never saw anyone going in or out of the building. The building was a sanitarium with the dreadful name "Home for the Incurables."

We always crowded into the tiny kitchen to watch Clara as she did the laundry. She had a wringer washer with a "mangle" to squeeze the wash water out of the clothes. I was terrified that my mother might put her arm through the mangle and crush it. This machine was one of the few conveniences Clara had as she tried to lighten her housework.

Our next-door neighbors were the Tanaka family, who had come from Japan.[13]

---

[10] Erich and Erna Fraenkel. Erich was the son of Jenny's sister Paula, now in England.
[11] Zip codes consisted of two numbers at the time. They grew to five numbers in the early 1960s.
[12] Kuchen is the German word for cake - generally a somewhat dry buttery cake. Not sweet at all.
[13] Mr. Tanaka was also our landlord as I learned from a rent check made out to him.

Their children were around our age. So there we were, two families with parents who were naturalized American citizens from the countries with which the United States was at war. The Bornstein and Tanaka families were loyal United States citizens. Still, neither family dared to speak German or Japanese outside their home.

While our father Fritz was in the U.S. Army in the South Pacific, Clara worked valiantly to care for three young children: Olga and Philipp were four years old and Fred two years old. To this ménage would soon be added our elderly grandmother, Jenny Bornstein, who decided to move from Arlington, Virginia to Chicago to be with her great-grandchildren. Just as almost ten years earlier, how could Clara say no to Jenny?

Clara struggled to feed us on her tiny budget. An army officer didn't make that much. Probably something like $1200/year. Today when I tell younger friends that most foods were rationed during WWII, they are amazed. Food rationing in the United States? War rationing began in the spring of 1942 and one ration book was issued to each family member. Ration stamps were like currency and they had to be securely guarded. It was the homemaker's challenge to pool the family's ration stamps and plan meals with the limited quantities of food available. Sugar, butter, coffee, and meat were especially scarce and valued items.

Philipp's WWII ration book. 1943.

One day Clara was out running errands with her three young children. Somehow, she lost her ration stamps. I think I may even have seen them fall out of her purse. What did I know? Clara was overwhelmed by anger, tears, and helplessness. How would she feed her family now?

Later Clara went to the Ration Board, with her three young children trailing behind her. She reported that she had lost her ration books. "Lady, everyone comes here with the same story," said the man in charge. Clara would have to wait until she was due new ration books. What did we live on until then? Cottage cheese, cow brains, sweetbreads, and other unmentionables would sustain us. Mother was angry, as if the loss of those ration stamps was concrete evidence of all her losses—parents, country, culture—and now she didn't even have decent food to nourish her little family. Yes, those were the days of stormy weather.[14]

In 1945, Fritz's grandmother Jenny came to live with us. Poor Jenny, now 86, was still looking for somewhere to call home. When she left Germany in 1935, she had been living comfortably in Hamburg for almost 25 years before emigrating to Palestine. In 1937 Jenny left Palestine and came to Rochester to live with Fritz and Clara. In 1940 when Clara and Fritz left Rochester to live in Alton Illinois, Jenny went to live with her nephew Erich Fraenkel and wife Erna in Arlington Virginia.

Jenny had two problems: her daughter Susanne was still living in Jerusalem and her daughter Therese (Röse) and family in St. Petersburg, Russia had disappeared. Fritz was thousands of miles away in the South Pacific and could do little for her directly. Clara had her hands full with her fledgling family in Chicago and no one had any extra money to help out relatives elsewhere.

---

[14] See words to the popular song at the end of this chapter.

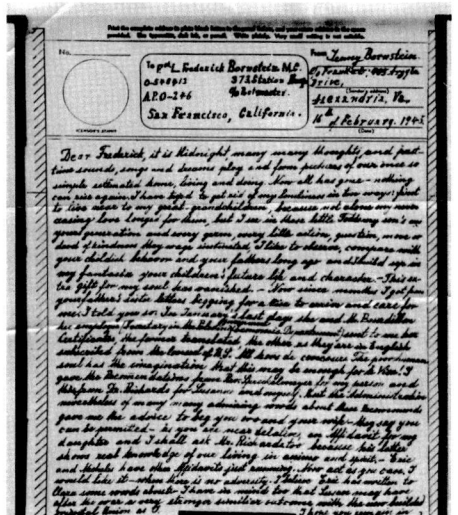

Jenny's letter to her grandson, Fritz.

Here are a few excerpts from Jenny's letter dated February 16, 1945, written on U.S. Army war letter stationary:

> *Dear Frederick, it is midnight, many thoughts and sounds, songs and dreams play and from pictures of our once simple estimate[15] home, living and doing. Now all has gone—nothing can rise again. I have tried to get rid of my loneliness in two ways: first to live near to my great-grandchildren...I like to share, compare with your childish behavior and your father's long ago.... This extra gift for me... has vanished...I would like to live where there is no adversity.*

She laments in frustration that she can't find anyone to vouch for Susanne's immigration to the United States. The Fraenkels are not close enough relatives to make a promise of financial support. Even Clara had been unable to bring her own aunts and cousins to the United States.[16]

---

[15] esteemed?

[16] Clara's aunt Ida is living in Los Angeles. Another aunt is in England, living outside London with her family.

Jenny wrote Fritz again on March 25, 1945 begging for help for Suse and hoping for a quick end to the war:

...I am troubled because I feel Clara does not understand that there would be never a menace to support me or my daughter. Your father, mother and my parents knew this very well. I still have enough for us both to spend our last days in an old-age home.[17] ... I only long for learning in many letters that you work with spirit and soul for our soldiers in good health and that your lovely children grow up in body and intellects (sic).

These letters must have been painful reading for Fritz. He knew that Clara understood the situation quite well. The U. S. Government made the immigration rules, and it did not want immigrants it would have to support.

Unfortunately her daughter Susanne never made it to the United States. She lived in Jerusalem while Palestine was under British administration, and after the founding of the state of Israel in 1948. Her last years were spent at the Montefiore Old Folks Home in Jerusalem. The last record we have of her is dated 1953. We assume she is buried in Jerusalem.[18]

Jenny pinned her hopes for the future on her young great-grandchildren. Jenny came to live with us in Chicago in 1945, and stayed until 1947 when the family moved downstate to Herrin, Illinois. She rented her own lodging there, not far from our house.

Here's a story told to me by my late Israeli relatives, Moshe and Brigitte (Bigi) Wolman: Suse lived with them as their babysitter,[19] and told them that one day a reparation from the German government would arrive in payment for her loss of her profession as a social worker.[20] They thought her hope for the money was just wishful thinking. Suse

---

[17] Jenny does not understand that there are all kinds of immigration rules that go beyond money.

[18] Unfortunately we do not know where.

[19] By then the Wolmans had three children. Dan and Naomi are close to me in age and we email often. I arranged for Dan, a famous movie director, to visit Austin and talk about his films. Naomi now lives in Culver City, California, and we have visited together both in Austin and California. Bigi Wolman's mother, Luci Koebbel, was related to the Bornsteins. Jenny was Luci's aunt. Jenny inspired Luci to become a physician. Later Luci married Max Koebbel, also a physician and not Jewish, a first for the family. Bigi met her husband Moshe at medical school in Italy. Bigi's parents lived in Berlin during the war, protected by loyal former patients. Max was the first German citizen to visit Israel after the end of WWII. He had a fantastic sense of humor: "I'll even get an adult circumcision if that's what's necessary to visit my daughter, her husband, and children." I spent a week with Max and Luci in Berlin in 1962. They were an absolutely warm, wonderful, and caring couple.

[20] She'd worked with prostitutes and ex-convicts at the Hamburg police department.

kept saying that when the money arrived, she was going to buy herself a ticket for a tour through the fjords of Norway. Surprise! The money arrived. Suse bought her ticket to Norway. But before she could embark on her trip, she needed a smallpox vaccination. And ironies of ironies, she had an adverse reaction to the vaccination! She died quite suddenly. Suse never fulfilled her dream of a trip to that green, moist, and peaceful country after over ten years in the chaos and parched heat of the Middle East.[21]

In Chicago, Clara and her children persevered. Clara was determined to stay strong for everyone. Now and then she took a day off for herself; a nice Black lady came to babysit us. Clara took the elevated train from the South Side of Chicago to the downtown Chicago Loop. While she was there, I'm sure she mostly "window shopped" as she called it, given how tight finances were. Perhaps she also visited the famous Chicago Art Institute.

I think Clara thought that an occasional babysitter was worth more than a new blouse or dress. Her German-speaking psychoanalyst, a certain Dr. Albrecht Meyer, was trained in the Freudian tradition. I am sure of this because of how she would frame stories and observations. I remember meeting Dr. Meyer once when I was 18 or 19 and I thought he was the ugliest person I had ever seen. I'm sure that he took Clara on as a pro bono patient. Clara never concealed her visits to Dr. Meyer from us though we could not have understood her need for those visits.

In the family papers I find occasional references to her visits with Dr. Meyer. I can imagine what their conversations covered: weighty topics such as loss of country, parents, raising children alone, worrying about Fritz and Hajo in the Army, so far away and in danger, and other dark feelings. Even as her life improved after the war ended, she was often depressed. By then depression was an integral part of her personality and not to be undone. I wondered later if one of the reasons our brother Philipp became a psychiatrist was because he had experienced the effects of Mother's ongoing depression as he grew up.

---

[21] I heard this story for the first time during our first visit to Israel in 1991. Moshe Wolman told David and me this story in great detail while he was driving us down the winding road from Jerusalem to their home in Tel Aviv in the dark.

Most of my memories from our years in Chicago are hazy. I remember playing with my rag dolls. My brothers and I dissected the only beautiful doll I had, scattering cotton all over our bedroom. Clara covered the windows in our bedroom with the old Bornstein oriental rugs so that we'd nap in the afternoon. The room became very dark. Clara always said our naps were more for her mental health than our need to rest. Fred, Philipp, and I slept in the same room. Where did great-grandmother and Clara sleep, I wondered.

One day I came into our kitchen where Clara was ironing. She was crying. I asked her why she was sad. The answer: She had just heard the news that our president, Franklin Delano Roosevelt (FDR) had died.[22] FDR had been her hero. He was the president when she came to the United States and his government provided safety from Fascism.[23] She knew that she and Fritz were among the lucky ones. And FDR's administration had made that happen.

The midway park at the University of Chicago was our playground. The park had steep embankments enclosing a broad rectangle of grass. At four or five years old, I found the embankments very steep, especially when I was doing somersaults. But when I revisited the Midway as an adult, my goodness, the embankments were not steep at all. I could get from the top to the bottom in a flash! How big they seemed to me as a child.

Philipp and I went to nursery school near our house. I think the school was in a church. We made new friends outside our cramped apartment. Later we attended kindergarten at Ray School in the heart of Hyde Park. The school still exists but in the 1960s the old school building was torn down.

Philipp and I walked to Ray School together alone without our mother. Our path took us by Stagg Field, the football stadium for the University of Chicago. Many years later we learned that the first nuclear reaction took place in an abandoned racquetball court

---

[22] He died on April 12, 1945.

[23] Michael Beschloss' book *The Conquerors* shows how Roosevelt privately refused desperate pleas to speak out directly against the Holocaust, to save Jewish refugees and to explore the possible bombing of Auschwitz to stop the killing. The book also shows FDR's fierce will to ensure that Germany would never threaten the world again. Near the end of World War II, he abruptly endorsed the secret plan of his friend, Treasury Secretary Henry Morgenthau, to reduce the Germans to a primitive existence — despite Churchill's fear that crushing postwar Germany would let the Soviets conquer the continent.

underneath Stagg Field on December 2, 1942. At the time, no one knew about this experiment or about the Manhattan project that produced the first atom bomb until years later.

What if one of the experiments had gone wrong and all of us had been blown up? Today such a dangerous experiment in the middle of a densely populated neighborhood would be impossible. The "War Effort" was all encompassing and secrecy was a big part of it.

I remember one event clearly: On the day that Philipp and I started off to our first day of kindergarten, Clara said to us: "If anyone calls you a kike,[24] punch them in the nose." Then she had to explain to us what the word meant. That was our early childhood introduction to prejudice. After we came home at the end of the school day, she asked us how the day went. We replied: "No one called us a kike."

Mother's admonition to us on our first day of school speaks volumes about her own harrowing experiences. She would tell us grim holocaust tales of human skins being made into lampshades and gold teeth being pried from the mouth of dead Jews in extermination camps. We understood very little at the time, but Clara knew the castle basement with its bloody hooks—her childhood horror—had become a modern reality.

Another memory from our first day of school: Philipp and I came home with our first-grade reader, *Fun With Dick and Jane*. We sat down and read through the entire book without any problem. Who knows how and when we learned to read?

Our pediatrician was another member of Chicago's Jewish émigré population: Dr. Helmut Seckel.[25] I do not know how my parents came to know him. Dr. Seckel had a copy of the famous Dürer etching of a hare on the wall in his waiting room. He was always very kind to us. When he gave us a shot,[26] mother would tell us: "You can't cry because your father is a doctor." We listened, and to this day we are stoic patients.

---

[24] A pejorative term for someone who is Jewish.

[25] Helmut Paul George Seckel, who came from a family of prominent academics was qualified in medicine at the University of Berlin. He specialized in pediatrics, but his career was interrupted by the Nazis. In 1936 he fled to the U.S. He was a professor of pediatrics at the University of Chicago Medical School.

[26] Imagine a physician giving a patient a shot! Today, a nurse administers injections.

Dürer's young hare, 1502.

Dr. Seckel took care of Philipp while he was hospitalized with a kidney infection. I remember standing outside below Philipp's hospital window waving to him because children were not allowed inside to visit patients. Philipp sometimes talked to me about his time in the hospital, where he had a "pet" rat that would visit him at night.

By the time Philipp and I started kindergarten, I think our father had returned from the South Pacific and was discharged from the Army around March 1946. He and an army buddy of his placed a bet to see who could father a new baby first. On November 14, 1946, our brother Aaron Claire was born at Michael Reese Hospital in Chicago. Fritz won his bet! Aaron was named for Arthur's grandfather, Aron Bornstein. "Claire" was a tip of the hat to Clara, and also the name of a famous WWII military figure.[27]

---

[27] Claire Lee Chenault (1893–1958), leader of the famous "Flying Tigers."

Fritz took us to our first real movie theater film: *Fantasia*.[28] Philipp and I loved it! Later we went to Orchestra Hall in downtown Chicago with our father to hear a performance of *Peter and the Wolf* with the Chicago Symphony Orchestra. It was overwhelming to be in such a big hall filled with marvelous music. Fritz started us on our lifelong passion of attending live classical music concerts.

Fritz had written to Clara from the Pacific theater that he wanted me to be wearing a blue velvet dress when he came home. Clara made me the dress. The fabric was beautiful and soft! Fritz was so pleased: Olga greeted him in her special dress topped with a lace collar, her curly blond hair fully unbraided flying in the wind, and her face covered in a big smile.

ADDITIONAL MATERIALS

Lyrics to the song "Stormy Weather," 1933
Written by Harold Arlen and Ted Koehler

Don't know why
There's no sun up in the sky
Stormy weather
Since my man and I ain't together
Keeps raining all of the time
Oh yeah
Life is bare
Gloom and misery everywhere
Stormy weather, stormy weather
And I just can't get my poor self together
Oh I'm weary all of the time

---

[28] Disney animators set pictures to Western classical music with Leopold Stokowski conducting the Philadelphia Orchestra. "The Sorcerer's Apprentice" features Mickey Mouse as an aspiring magician who oversteps his limits. "The Rite of Spring" tells the story of evolution, from single-celled animals to the death of the dinosaurs. "Dance of the Hours" is a comic ballet performed by ostriches, hippos, elephants, and alligators. "Night on Bald Mountain" and "Ave Maria" set the forces of darkness and light against each other as a devilish revel is interrupted by the coming of a new day.

The time, so weary all of the time

When he went away

The blues walked in and met me

Oh yeah if he stays away

Old rocking chair's gonna get me

All I do is pray

The Lord will let me

Walk in the sun once more

Oh I can't go on, can't go on, can't go on

Everything I have is gone

Stormy weather, stormy weather

Since my man and I, me and my daddy ain't together

Keeps raining all of the time

Oh, oh, keeps raining all of the time

Oh yeah, yeah, yeah raining all of the time

Stormy stormy

Stormy weather

Yeah.

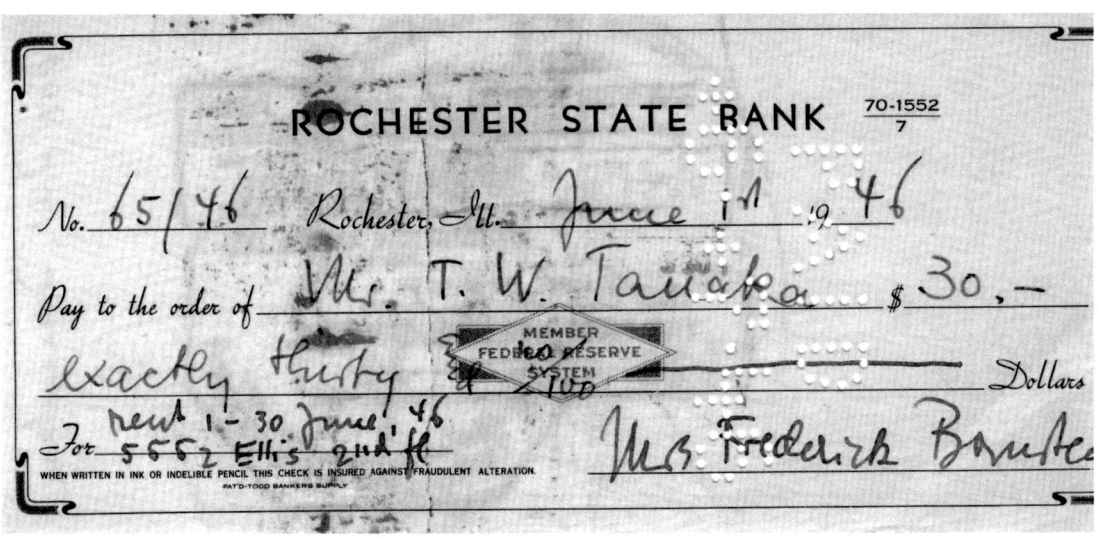

Rent check for our 2nd floor apartment at 5555 S. Ellis Ave. Mr. Tanaka was our next-door neighbor.

*Clara's brother Hajo poses on
Nazi war plane.*

A few days ago I had to go on a detail as interpreter which led
me to Wuerzburg, Schweinfurt, and Bamberg. It was very interesting but at the
same time made me a bit sad because Wuerzburg is completely destroyed,
I think beyond all repair. Only the Kaeppele Still stands. However I was glad
to see that the Germanen-Haus was all beat up. That will show the bastards
what it'll get them to smear shit on other people's door knob!

We stopped on our way in Randersacker and visited the famous
old Zehnthof in the vaults of which the still store the wine named after
the village. It was a most interestig visit, especially since we came away
with four bottles of Randersackerer Boxbeutel each. It is wonderful wine
even the damn Nazis could not change it.

*Excerpt from a letter from Hajo to Clara while
he's in the army, 1945*

Jerusalem, 25 October 1945—Letter by Employer Concerning Susanne Bornstein

The following letter was written by a senior British administrator in Palestine. Susanne Bornstein was Jenny Barth Bornstein's daughter, also the sister of Arthur Bornstein and Therese Bornstein Brunstein. Susanne was a trained social worker. She left Germany, lived briefly in Egypt, and settled in Jerusalem. She worked as a nanny for the family of the British administrator.

Dear Dr. Bornstein:

I'm writing you this letter to give you the most recent news about Susanne and hope that is okay with you that I've asked a friend of mine to translate my letter into German to be sure that I make myself perfectly clear. She just registered with the American consulate so that she can immigrate to America—and the consulate officer with whom I spoke, told me that it is very important that you send her another Affidavit before June. The reason for this is that the American immigration year coincides with the fiscal year, and the immigrant quotas are only good until the first of June. If Susanne were able to obtain permission before the first of June 1946 that would be to her advantage, since the quota for now has not been exhausted. The main requirement is that you obtain the Affidavits, so that they arrive here before the first of June 1946; otherwise, it will be very difficult for Susanne to obtain her immigration entry permit, since a lot of people are trying for the same thing in the coming year.

My wife and I are very concerned about this, since we are possibly leaving here in two or three months, and even though we are almost sure that we can find another position for Susanne, it will be difficult to find one that is as good as the one she has now. You must be aware of the fact that it won't be long before it will be almost impossible for her to find work. You must be aware of the fact that Palestine is a difficult country, and Susanne is way too independent to just take any job. She hasn't learned very much Hebrew, and for that reason it won't be easy for her to find a position when they learn that her current employment as a children's nanny is in an English household. Other work may be too difficult for her. We are both completely convinced that her only desire, which would also be the best solution for her, is to come to you in America.

Please don't worry—we'll take good care of her as long as we are here; and we will try our utmost to find her a new place of work; but please do your very best to obtain her affidavit as soon as possible, so that she can travel to you as soon as a boat is available. I am completely aware of the difficulties she has been having regarding the mortgage money, but I hope that she (in the meantime) has heard from D. Rosenberger, so that the Anglo-Palestine Bank can give her the money. Susanne has saved almost sixty pounds while working for us, but of course that won't be sufficient for the cost of her travel. She will try to earn some money to add to the amount she has saved, but if she could somehow obtain a little extra money beyond her savings, her travel would be assured. Please don't tell her that I've told you that Susanne needs money; she would be very angry if she were to find this out. We are fine and she is very happy living with us; and we're very sorry that we have to leave. But we must leave, and for that reason we are very concerned that she can fulfill her greatest wish—to come to you.

With best regards,
????

After the author of this letter and his family left Palestine, Susanne was out of work and lived with Brigitte and Moshe Wolman—watching out for their children (three at that time). Brigitte is the daughter of Jenny's niece Luci Koebbel, nee Bütow.

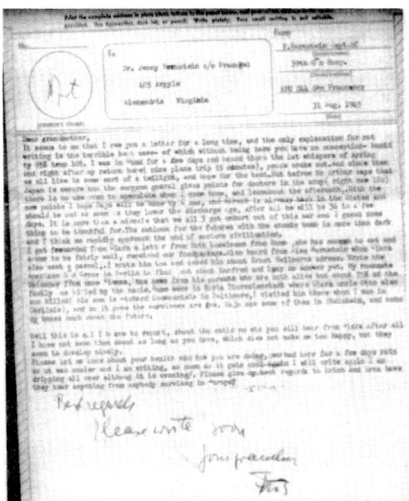

Fritz to Jenny, 1945.

Fred born 1943

Fritz in the U.S. Army

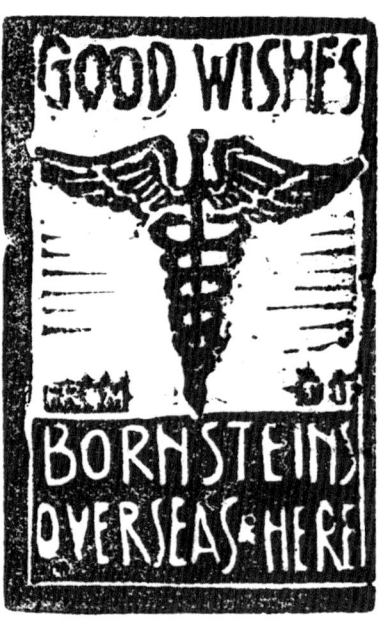

The War Years: 1941–1946

Aaron born 1946

CHAPTER 12

Herrin, Illinois
The House on 13th Street
1947–1952

WHEN FRITZ finished his training at Michael Reese Hospital in Chicago, it was time for the family to begin enjoying the rewards of a post-World War II life. Cars, appliances, housing, and many foods had been unavailable or in short supply during the war years. Now the merchandising floodgates were open again.

Soon we owned a car, a black Chevrolet. No cars of color were available then. Take a black car or nothing, okay? We moved to a small coal town in southern Illinois: Herrin, population 8,000. The town in Williamson County was notorious for the race riots and coal mine disturbances during the late 1910s through the late 1930s.[1]

Herrin is located in southernmost Illinois, known as Little Egypt, roughly between Cairo, Illinois and St. Louis, Missouri on the Mississippi River. The main enterprise in Herrin was a large Norge washing machine factory. The landscape is hilly, since the glaciers, which flattened the plains of northern and central Illinois, stopped a bit north of Herrin. Coal mines dotted the surrounding area.

We moved into a lovely 1910s prairie-style, four-bedroom brick house at 409 South 13th Street, in easy walking distance to our grade school: South Side School. The house had a dark basement where the glowing furnace worked to keep us warm during freezing midwestern winters. Clara took care of the furnace, removing the red-hot clinkers with a large shovel.[2] She tossed them into a bucket and carried them out to the far recesses of our back yard. The basement certainly wasn't Fritz's domain. Men go to work; women work at home.

Each winter, a truck load of coal was delivered down our coal chute, attached to the basement. Of course the house had no air conditioning to keep us comfortable on hot, humid midwestern summer days and nights.

Our wood floors glowed because mother would wax and polish them on her hands and knees. She often hand-washed the white living room curtains since they became dark with coal dust from the furnace. A Black cleaning lady came weekly.[3] My

---

[1] *Bloody Williamson: A Chapter in American Lawlessness* by Paul M. Angle. Knopf, 1952. In my personal book collection. Fascinating read.

[2] Clinkers occur in small stoves used for heating a home and in giant commercial/industrial boilers. Clinkers, also known as slag, consist of the noncombustible elements and minerals found in coal that melt and fuse together as lumpy ashes from coal combustion. Boiler operators consider clinkers to be miserable stuff.

[3] Mother always had household help, no matter how strained our circumstances. A carryover from her own upbringing.

Olga, Fred, and Philipp. Above the banks of the Mississippi River near St. Louis, 1947.

parents insisted that she join us at the table for lunch, something she was not happy to do. Only much later did I learn that Herrin was a sundown town.[4] Blacks were discouraged from socializing with Whites.

The house had four bedrooms. The front bedroom was reserved for Fritz as his study. He could close the hall door to his study to reduce the din the children made. Fritz spent long evening hours reading in his "den." Is this reading habit a remnant from his lonely childhood as an only child? His den closed with a sliding pocket door. The children loved to pull the pocket door in and out. You know what mother said to us!

---

[4] Towns where Blacks were not permitted to stay overnight but had to return home by sundown. A sign at the city limits stated the law.

The rest of the bedrooms were along a long hallway. The second bedroom belonged to Clara and Fritz. At one point they had a local artist paint a large abstract geometric mural in mostly pastel colors on the wall behind their bed—most visitors didn't understand this kind of art at all. [5]

The next two bedrooms were for the children: Philipp and Fred shared a room; Olga and Aaron shared the bedroom at the end of the house. We slept on old metal army cots covered with thin mattresses. Our blankets were quilts that Fritz had received in payment for his visits when he made house calls in the 1930s. Patients who could not pay their doctor bills with cash during the depression in Rochester would often pay him in goods: fresh butter, strawberries, goats, the aforementioned quilts, and other home goods. Our rooms were not decorated, just simply furnished for sleeping and playing.

There was only one bathroom in the house, located at the end of the hall. We didn't have a shower. We would close the bathroom door and the door at the opposite end of the hall and play ball, race up and down in winter, and generally make a huge ruckus. We kids also ruined our door jambs cracking the hard English walnuts from the tree in our yard. This behavior just drove Clara crazy. She thought we were destructive beasts and couldn't understand how we could be so evil and misbehaved. We were not well-behaved little Prussian kids, kept in line by the ever-present nursemaid. In Berlin, discipline was not the mother's work. As a child my mother and her brother Hajo never ate at the dining table with their parents until they were nine or ten, old enough to have acceptable dining deportment.

The right side of the house contained a dinette, kitchen, dining room and living room with fireplace, which we never used.[6] We had a lovely front porch where we would visit on hot summer evenings, waiting for the thunderstorms to crash in on us. Near the kitchen was a small stoop and a door with a screen door on the outside. Clara must have gotten tired of shouting: "Stop slamming the screen door!"

---

[5] Ruth Frey, wife of Ed Frey, a Norge engineer/inventor, designed and painted the mural. I wish I had a picture of the mural. Later the Freys moved to Ohio where Ed founded a scientific equipment company. Fritz was asked to be an early investor in the business and years later was delighted when he found that his investment had expanded at least ten times his original contribution.

[6] I think the fireplace tools conveyed with the house. The tools later sat before the unused fireplace in our El Paso house.

I had a terrible temper until I was 16 or 17. Once when I was really mad at Clara, I ran through the kitchen door, stood on the stoop and yelled: "Mother, stop beating me." Well, then I really did get spanked. Clara was furious that I would call her a child beater. Clara and Fritz were completely against corporal punishment. They made frequent use of what today we call "time out."

The walls of the house were filled with reproductions of art by famous European artists: The Four Horsemen of the Apocalypse (Dürer), Sunflowers (Van Gogh), and El Greco's View of Toledo. I always found the El Greco rather gloomy and couldn't quite make sense of it as a child. When David and I visited Toledo, Spain in 1993, I vividly recalled the El Greco painting. Obviously, it made an impression on me. We were raised to appreciate the classics of European art, expanding our visual knowledge by frequent visits to the St. Louis Art Museum, only a 90-mile drive from Herrin.[7]

El Greco's View of Toledo, c. 1596–1600.

---

[7] In 1979 when our son Jacob was about two years old, we took him to the same museum. His comment about the Greek statues was priceless: "Look. Men and women. No head or hands or feet."

Vincent Van Gogh's Sunflowers, 1888.

OUR LIFE AT HOME

There was one other Jewish family in Herrin, the Zwicks. They owned a department store. Some Zwicks still live in Herrin today. Mrs. Zwick's mother, Mrs. Goldberg,
had passed away shortly before we moved to town and her house on 13th Street was on
the market. Clara and Fritz were eager to begin family life in a house after ten years of
life in uncomfortable, squalid apartments. They purchased the house along with various
furniture items that the Zwick family wanted to sell. The Goldberg's large dining room
table, eight chairs, and a lovely china hutch became part of the Bornstein household until
Clara's death in 1988.

I often imagine Mrs. Goldberg presiding over her extended family at that very table during Shabbat[8] meals on Friday evening, Passover seders, break-the-fast meals after Yom Kippur, and of course Thanksgiving dinners. For the Bornsteins this table came to have many very different uses. Poor Mrs. Goldberg—her table was never meant for the ways the Bornsteins used it.

Later as Fritz's income improved, money became more plentiful for purchases beyond the household basics. Clara and Fritz purchased a new large, curved, chartreuse couch and two matching bedroom dressers.[9] Clara was so ready to have a colorful, modern home. She was finished with the heavy, Victorian *Biedermeier*[10] interiors of her childhood in Berlin. Later, in El Paso, Clara had our living room walls painted a light grey so that the chartreuse couch and a black couch made the room glow. By then there was also original, modern art on the walls, something to shock the neighbors.

Now and then the secular Jewish Bornstein family ate Friday evening meals at Mrs. Goldberg's former table. To my knowledge, neither of my parents had much experience with the traditional candle lighting ritual that takes place at the Friday evening Jewish sabbath meal. Clara and Fritz developed their own Friday evening meal routine. The large table was covered elegantly with one of our grandmother Emmy Löwenstein's damask tablecloths. Emmy's silverware replaced our usual metal utensils.[11] Candles were lit although no Hebrew prayers were recited. Then Fritz read us a passage from the Old Testament, with which he was quite familiar from his Lutheran education. We children weren't sure why the Bible was important but loved the terrific stories.

After the bare religious necessities had been taken care of, we began excruciating instructions regarding the proper table manners: where to keep our hands, not to cut a potato with a knife, never cut asparagus period, only use a fish knife for eating fish and so on. Our damask napkin belonged on our lap. Our hands belonged on the table.[12] We

---

[8] Shabbat = Hebrew for sabbath. Jewish sabbath falls on Friday evening.

[9] These are now part of Aaron Claire's household.

[10] A furniture style popular in German speaking countries in the mid-to-late nineteenth century.

[11] I inherited the silver after mother's death. It turned out that the silver is not real silver but rather "German silver" an alloy of copper, zinc, and nickel. I think the pieces are silver plated, because they polish up quite nicely. When he was a child, I would pay Jacob a penny per utensil to polish them.

[12] Clara maintained the hand-on-the-table custom dated from medieval times, i.e. if your hands were visible on the table, that meant that you weren't hiding a knife in your lap, ready at any time to murder one of your dinner companions. True? We children liked the bloody possibilities.

signaled that we finished our meal by placing our fork and knife in parallel across the empty plate. Some of the instructions were for obscure, nineteenth-century German table manners which had pretty much died out by the late 1940s. Have you ever seen a fish knife? Nonetheless this training in proper table manners held us all in good stead as we later entered into a wider world outside home.

Our parents were also very strict about our being on time. If we were even five minutes late for dinner, there was hell to pay. Prussians were famous for their obsession with being on time. On the other hand, when we became teen-agers there was no problem with our staying out until two or three in the morning, as long as we said that was when we'd be home.[13]

We were never allowed to reject food.[14] We had to accept all food offered at a meal and clean our plates.[15] Never far from mother's thinking was her worry about potential food scarcity.[16] At one point during our years in Herrin, guests who had been invited to Thanksgiving dinner were unable to visit because of an unexpected snowstorm. So, we had been eating leftover turkey for several days straight. On the nth day of turkey for dinner, the kids rebelled. They said they wouldn't eat any more turkey. The parental response: Until we relented, we were offered a diet of bread, milk, oleo and a daily glass of orange juice (BMOJ), so we wouldn't get scurvy. The BMOJ diet remained a definite food possibility for many childhood years whenever we children complained about the food or cooking.[17]

Another part of the food bargain was that at the start of each school year, we could choose a certain food as our "exception." The chosen food could not be a daily food item,

---

[13] Especially toward the end of El Paso High School with drinking excursions to Juarez, Mexico where tequila was five cents a shot.

[14] Yes, talk of the starving Chinese was mentioned, but their emphasis was having children who were open to all foods and not limited to a small menu of very familiar items.

[15] Jacob taught me how to let go of that old rule: He barfed up the dinner he didn't want to eat on the dining room table!

[16] In her life at that time Clara had experienced food scarcity in Germany during WWI and the German economic recession of the 1920s, in the U.S. during the Great Depression of the 1930s, and finally the lack of food choices during WWII. No wonder she acted the way she did.

[17] Later in El Paso, Clara finally had enough of the kids clearing out the cookie jar on the sly. Fritz used the knowledge gleaned from reading many Horatio Hornblower tales of the British Navy. When the sailors had feasted on food they weren't allowed, the captain made them all chew rice and spit it out. Supposedly any food crumbs still remaining would come out with the rice.

but one that appeared infrequently at the dinner table. I remember that my choice was liver sausage. I still don't eat it today almost 75 years later.[18]

However we could choose whatever we wanted to eat for our birthday dinner. I remember asking for frog legs one year. I think they tasted like chicken. Another year I wanted a birthday cake with blue frosting.[19] I had the cake all to myself.

Mother never really enjoyed most of the time she spent in the kitchen cooking for her large brood. She would rather have been reading novels or drawing or writing one of her marvelous letters, I think. So her excuse for her cooking was: "When you leave home, you won't miss my cooking."

Of course she was wrong. We loved her plum cakes, chocolate chip cookies, elaborate birthday cakes with piped multilingual inscriptions, her Königsberger Klops,[20] and her Berliner Pfannekuchen.[21] These jelly donuts were a great way to use up all the grease that she saved from cooking other fried dishes. Fritz's favorite North German specialties included boiled spinach topped by a soft-boiled egg or lentils with stewed prunes.[22] Barf to that! What did we know then about the strength of a childhood attachment to the taste of a familiar dish?

I was almost the only girl in my class wearing home-sewn dresses. Clara was an excellent seamstress. Her great invention for my clothing was a dress that had a button-on front for a tie-back apron. The apron gave me the ability to wear the dress more than once. When the apron was dirty, I could detach it, and have—voila—a clean dress. I remember the first time I owned a store-bought dress. Clara told me I came home from school in tears, because—oh sadness—another girl in my class was wearing exactly the same dress!

Our parents had NO rules about what we could read. Our house was filled with books. Of course we poked into them. In addition, we walked several times a week from

---

[18] Clara always recommended a sandwich spread thick with liver sausage before we went drinking. That liver sausage will coat your stomach and the liquor won't penetrate as quickly as it would otherwise.

[19] Right after WWII white oleo margarine came in a plastic pouch with some yellow food coloring. The lady of the house would squeeze the pouch until the white margarine turned yellow. One day Clara thought: "Why not try blue food coloring instead?" None of us would touch it.

[20] A kind of meatball cooked in a white sauce with capers.

[21] These are not pancakes as we know them. They are mounds of jelly filled dough, fried in oil.

[22] Those lentils might get us into BMOJ country. (Bread, milk, oleo, and orange juice).

our house to the library, which was across the street from Herrin Hospital where our father worked. After Philipp and I had exhausted pretty much every book in the children's section,[23] we wanted to read books from the adult section.

We asked Clara to talk with the head librarian about our desire. Clara didn't mind if we checked out materials for older kids or adults. However, the librarian never let kids read adult books, period. I'm not sure how Clara explained the situation to the conservative librarian, but soon we were reading whatever we pleased. I remember Irving Stone novels, retelling the lives of great men: Fremont, Van Gogh, Jack London among many other of my reading choices. Don't forget that television had barely made an appearance then and we certainly did not own one.

Our parents were not prudish at all. With great relish, mother would retell a story about her twins. One day we were walking home from South Side School. We told our mother we've seen a new word written in chalk on a tree trunk. Clara asks us: "What is the word"? We answer "FUCK." We ask: "What does that word mean?" Clara's response: "Something grown men and women do who like each other very much. It is more than kissing." So according to her we began naming all the couples we know: "Do Mr. and Mrs. Curry next door do that?" "Oh yes they do," mother replied!

THE BORNSTEIN FAMILY CELEBRATES CHRISTMAS

The December Jewish holiday of Hanukkah had always been a minor Jewish holiday until Jews began living outside the ghettos, mixing with Christians, mostly Lutheran and Catholic. Hanukkah became the American Jewish antidote to Christmas. Jewish children now had a way to be gifted presents (for eight days instead of one)[24] like their Christian friends. In those days Kwanza was still completely unknown.

Our small, live German Christmas tree graced Mrs. Goldberg's dining table. The tree was not in the living room because Clara didn't want the neighbors to see that we,

---

[23] Hardy Boys, Nancy Drew, Bobbsey Twins, Anne of Green Gables, Little Lord Fauntleroy, My Secret Garden, children's biographies of famous people illustrated with silhouette drawings and so on.

[24] An oil lamp burned on the altar for eight days after the Macabees expelled the Syrians from Jerusalem in the second century BCE.

as a Jewish family, were not only celebrating Christmas but had a Christmas tree. I think mother never recovered from her treatment when the Nazis came to power. Because of her experience, she felt all of us were labeled by others primarily by the fact that we were Jews.

One year Mrs. Goldberg's table was graced by a long Lionel electric train on a track encircling the Christmas tree, which was decorated with burning real candles. Santa Claus, played by one of Fritz's lab assistants, appeared at the appointed time carrying a pillowcase filled with presents. However, he confused us by wearing Clara's fake fur coat and an operating room mask. As astounded as we were by his outfit, for us this was Santa and we were delighted.

Clara and Fritz celebrated this holiday with all the trimmings of a genuine German Christmas.[25] The German Jews embraced the German folk aspects and Christmas holiday pageantry with full enthusiasm: the children were locked in a bedroom until the parents had put out presents and lit the candles on the tree. What rituals—a Christmas tree with real candles, a gift exchange on Christmas Eve, the singing of German Christmas carols such as *Oh Tannenbaum*," and the offering of Christmas bowls filled with candy, gingerbread cookies, and a single orange. We knew nothing of Christmas stockings, turkey and pie, or Christmas morning festivities. Our presents were never wrapped until many years later when we each had our own pile of presents and would take turns opening our gifts one at a time. There was no helter-skelter dive into presents as I saw later when celebrating Christmas with my friends, after I was no longer living at home.

SCHOOL DAYS AT SOUTH SIDE SCHOOL

We began attending South Side School in September 1947. Philipp and I were in first grade; Fred and Aaron were still at home. We walked to school down 13th Street, past an historical marker stating that Lewis and Clark passed through Herrin on their way west. We felt the street was famous!

---

[25] Jenny Bornstein's memoir: *A Jewish Girlhood in Berlin: 1859–1879*, devotes part of a chapter to a complete description of the German Christmas rituals.

School itself was no problem for us. We could already read without any difficulty. Miss Rollo, our first-grade teacher, began the school year by checking the eyesight of all her students. I had my eyes checked by a Dr. Loewenherz in Centralia, one of the old German-Jewish medical gang. I was astigmatic and needed glasses. Back then kids made fun of classmates who wore glasses. You can imagine how happy that made me. On the other hand, wearing glasses hinted, for some reason, that I was smart. I accepted that!

Later, Philipp and I were the only children in our second-grade class who did not attend Sunday school. Our teacher, Miss Corcoran, kept a chart on the bulletin board at the front of the room for all the students to see. This chart tracked our daily tooth brushing and weekly Sunday school attendance. The Bornstein twins' non-Sunday school attendance was there for all to see.[26] Our teacher also had us say the Lord's Prayer each morning after we finished the Pledge of Allegiance (without "under God" which was added later in the 1950s). Thanks to my teacher, I did learn the Lord's Prayer which proved to be useful later on.

The big event of second grade was that the presidential candidate, Harry Truman, visited Herrin, Illinois. We went downtown to see him. Everyone thought that Thomas Dewey, a Republican, would beat Truman. Some newspapers even claimed Dewey victorious before all the votes were in, but Truman won by a narrow margin. I remember seeing the newspaper headlines in a shop window.

Third grade was fun! We had a lovely teacher, Miss Norman. She read aloud to us each day after lunch. Our favorite books were a series about *Bomba the Jungle Boy*.[27] Of course we had no idea that the book was racist. We just loved the adventure stories. Miss Norman taught us to memorize the multiplication tables. A bookshelf in the room supplied us with books we could read when we were finished with our classwork. There was one book in particular that I loved about an early American Museum of Natural History

---

26 We really didn't know why Sunday school was important, only that the other kids went there. That added another layer to our feelings about being different from our classmates.

27 A common theme of the Bomba books is that Bomba, because he is white, has a soul that is awake, while his friends, the dark-skinned natives, have souls that are sleeping. Richard A. Lupoff, in his book *Master of Adventure*, a study of the works of Tarzan creator Edgar Rice Burroughs, describes the Bomba tales as more blatantly racist than the often-criticized Tarzan books.

expedition to Siberia, where the explorers are said to have celebrated their discovery of a frozen mammoth or mastodon by eating a meal of grilled mastodon steaks.

Fourth grade presented new challenges. We worked our way through a newspaper for kids called the *Weekly Reader*.[28] Philipp and I were always the first students to answer all the questions on the last page about current events discussed in the issue. Today I'm a confirmed daily print newspaper reader.[29] Perhaps that teaching idea did bear fruit.

Miss Kathryn Rollo, Olga's first grade teacher, signed this reading certificate in perfect Palmer Method handwriting. Back of reading certificate: Miss Rollo listed titles of books Olga had read as of May 1948. The future bookworm had found her calling.

---

[28] The *Weekly Reader* began publishing in the 1920s. The goal: to have elementary school students make newspaper reading a daily activity. They succeeded!

[29] Yes, I also scan the digital *New York Times* every day.

We had daily newspapers at home: the local newspaper, the *St. Louis Post Dispatch*, *Time Magazine* and *The Nation*,[30] which some people called a Communist publication during the fearmongering of the late 1940s. We lived in the height of the McCarthy era.

Clara and Fritz found McCarthy's accusations and widely publicized Congressional hearings completely terrifying. They saw how McCarthy was using the same tactics as the Nazi's false accusations that they had experienced before leaving Germany. I can't help but add that I think Donald Trump during his presidency was reading and acting from Joe McCarthy's playbook.[31]

In fourth grade I learned that parents and teachers were not always in agreement. There was an incident with our teacher, Miss Tschaikowsky. (She said *Tschaikowsky*; my parents said *Tschaikofski*.) At home we were told that our grandfather Arthur Bornstein fought in the spaghetti fields of Italy[32] during the spring pasta blossom season. Our grandfather told our father that nothing compared with the taste of fresh pasta, steamed directly after harvesting. At one point I told this story to my class. The teacher, dumbfounded, grabbed a volume of the World Book Encyclopedia from a nearby shelf and opened it to a photo of a bulky Italian matron, drying her freshly made, flour-based, spaghetti on a wooden drying rack.

I was perplexed and devastated by my teacher's act. My parents told me a lie! Today I love their story and lovely fancy flight of imagination! During our graduate school days, Philipp and I would hold forth about the advantages of hand-braided versus commercially braided asparagus.[33]

We had an old upright piano in our living room. When we were about seven years old, we began piano lessons from a teacher within walking distance of our house.[34] We grew up hearing old 78rpm recordings of Artur Schnabel[35] playing Beethoven piano

---

[30] *The Nation* is the oldest continuously published weekly magazine in the U.S. It had the reputation of being a liberal, even socialist publication.

[31] Roy Cohn, McCarthy's lawyer, was also Trump's lawyer until Cohn's death.

[32] In WWI, Grandfather fought on the Eastern and Western Fronts; we're not certain about Italy.

[33] Philipp later published a hilarious article in the *Journal of Irreproducible Results*, recounting the evolution of field-grown pasta.

[34] At the time piano playing was a skill for all well-bred children. Not today!

[35] Artur Schnabel (1882–1951) was an Austrian-American classical pianist, composer and pedagogue. Schnabel is known for his intellectual seriousness as a musician, avoiding pure technical bravura.

sonatas. The first time I sat at the piano and touched the keys, such disappointment! All I could play were very simple tunes. And even they were difficult!

We all loved going to piano lessons because our teacher displayed a big basket of comic books in her waiting area to keep us amused while we waited for our lesson to start. Our parents believed that silly comic books would taint our minds.[36] Piano lessons were our sole outlet for reading comics except for those in the Sunday edition of *St. Louis Post Dispatch* featuring "Prince Valiant" and the "Katzenjammer Kids."

 When we came home from school, we gathered around the radio in the living room and listened to the serialized adventure stories that were broadcast in the afternoon to amuse school children. We'd eat our peanut butter and jam sandwiches, listening with rapt attention to these tales of adventure and crime: *Dick Tracy, Sky King, The Lone Ranger, The Shadow.* I remember listening to shows on the car radio as we drove home from family trips to the drive-in theater: *Bob and Ray, The Jack Benny Show, Our Miss Brooks.* Fritz kept track of the soap operas when he went on long drives around Southern Illinois. I am always amazed that such an intellectual would enjoy these outlandish plots and circumstances. But, he also enjoyed reading Georgette Heyer's regency novels and the many novels in the Horatio Hornblower series.

Weekend entertainment often included attending live classical music concerts on the Southern Illinois University (SIU) campus in Carbondale, Illinois on Sunday afternoons. The adult audience members were amazed at our perfect concert behavior! Four children sitting quietly, book-ended by their parents. After the concert we would often eat at the only Chinese restaurant in the area. Fritz loved Chinese tea and often ordered jasmine tea.[37]

---

[36] Later television was treated the same way. Movies, however, were okay. What's the difference, I ask?
[37] Residents of Hamburg were great tea drinkers, probably due to the proximity of the city to England.

Our favorite painting by Siegfried Reinhardt, Screaming Eagles.

One day the family attended an art opening by a St. Louis artist at SIU. When the featured artist saw our baby brother Aaron, he came up to the family and said: "I must paint that child." My parents learned that the artist had an utterly German name, Siegfried Reinhardt.[38]

Siegfried and his wife Harriet quickly became close family friends. He drew portraits of all the Bornstein children in silverpoint as well as oil portraits of Clara and Frederick.

I clearly remember sitting for my portrait, not moving at all for long minutes. Siegfried drew me in his starving artist's apartment in St. Louis, near Washington University. He was very pleasant and talkative as he worked. A unique and thoroughly enjoy-

---

[38] Siegfried Reinhardt 1925–1984.

able experience. Later while I was enrolled at Washington University in St. Louis, I'd visit him and his wife.[39] We enjoyed late nights of long conversation together. Siegfried spoke a German filled with his parents' regional dialect. I'd never heard such spoken German, since Clara and Fritz always spoke a cultured, high German.[40]

The oil portraits of Fritz and Clara are now with my brother Aaron in Arizona. I assume the family of each Bornstein child owns their relevant silverpoint portrait. Siegfried became quite successful, painting murals for the Gateway Arch Museum and Lambert Field. Several St. Louis church windows are graced by his designs which I saw in 2012 on a tour during my fiftieth class reunion at Washington University. In an unexpected turn of fate in 1984, Philipp was at Siegfried's deathbed in St. Louis at Barnes Hospital. Philipp was head resident in psychiatry at Barnes at the time.

Clara Bornstein by Siegfried Reinhardt.

---

[39] By then they had a lovely art-filled home in the St. Louis suburb of Webster Groves.
[40] They spoke Hochdeutsch. Mother could do a Berlin dialect quite nicely; Fritz had the far north German accent at times, close to Plattdeutsch which veers into Dutch sounds. When I became a fluent German speaker, native German speakers would always label my German accent North German. I found that surprising, but who knows what echo I heard when I did speak.

BEING JEWISH IN SMALL TOWN ILLINOIS

Over the years, I have been asked, by Jews and non-Jews alike, if my brothers had a bar mitzvah. When I answer in the negative, they are usually shocked. Generally even the most assimilated, non-religious Jews will harken back to the tradition of having their son (and possibly daughter, a modern Reform Jewish change) enroll in studies at a Jewish Hebrew school so they can perform properly in the coming-of-age ceremony. This option was never observed by the Bornstein family. As previously mentioned, Fritz was ideologically opposed to any organized religion, to the point of often refusing to visit historical cathedrals while touring in Europe.[41] Further, Fritz spent most of his childhood and adolescence as a baptized Lutheran, attending a Lutheran high school. He certainly never had a bar mitzvah. Lastly, the closest Jewish congregation was 30 miles away in the coal-mining town of West Frankfort.

From an early age, our brother Fred was alert to American mainstream trends rather than our central European upbringing transplanted to the Midwest. Fred insisted on attending Sunday school since that was what his school friends did on Sundays.[42] Clara and Fritz respected Fred's demand and found a member of the previously mentioned Zwick family to drive Fred to West Frankfort with them each Sunday.

One spring, the congregation had a Purim festival.[43] The entire family attended since Fred had an important role in the Purim play.[44] I still remember the play, and a particular line in the play where Esther says: "Forgive me. I am a Jew. I know NOT what I do." I had had no Jewish education, so that is how I felt too. I felt kinship with Esther. How could I understand what was going on?

---

[41] In 1962 I was in Strasbourg France with Clara and Fritz. The main attraction is a beautiful Gothic cathedral. Fritz refused to enter.

[42] During the time that Fred was dying of cancer in the mid 1980s, he converted to Methodism. He is the only Bornstein family member buried in a military cemetery with a cross rather than a Jewish star on his headstone.

[43] A lesser Jewish festival held in spring (on the 14th or 15th day of Adar) to commemorate the defeat of Haman's plot to massacre the Jews as recorded in the book of Esther.

[44] Perhaps the Purim celebration was more the beginning of his acting career than his involvement in Judaism.

Clara was very conscious of the fact that we were a Jewish family. She kept us home from school on Yom Kippur[45] and Rosh Hashanah.[46] She felt that the neighbors would notice if we attended school during what Jews call the "high holidays." Realistically it is hard to believe that the neighbors would have noticed since most knew very little or nothing about the Jewish religion. I suspect Clara was responding to some habits ingrained during her youth in Berlin and to her self-consciousness about being Jewish.

Mother never spoke to us about her attending any Jewish religious services for these holidays during her childhood. However, her childhood public school curriculum included religious training. Most students in Berlin were Lutheran and received Lutheran religious education as part of the school curriculum. Jewish students attended Jewish religion classes and were even taught a bit of Hebrew. So much for the separation of church and state in Germany: importance was placed on a religious education.

We children didn't understand what these holidays were about since we had no Jewish religious training. We did stay home from school but that was pure agony. We weren't allowed to play outside. I like to think that having her children with her at home on those days made Clara feel better.

One spring my Brownie Scout troop asked Clara to make a presentation about Passover. She brought along some matzos[47] for the little girls to try after she told them the Biblical Passover story. They probably knew the story from their Sunday school, but the matzos? That was an exotic and different food for them to nibble on. Where did Clara obtain that box of matzos? Did she have to make a special driving trip to St. Louis?

I found her talk to the Brownies vaguely interesting but felt no special connection to the Passover story itself. To Clara the story must have had a very strong meaning: Jews driven out of their adopted homeland, suffering all kinds of privations and uncertainty along the way. She must have related completely to the main theme of the Old Testament's Exodus: calamity and survival.

---

[45] Yom Kippur—the Day of Atonement—is considered the most important holiday in the Jewish faith. According to tradition, it is on Yom Kippur that God decides each person's fate, so Jews are encouraged to make amends nd ask forgiveness for sins committed during the past year. The holiday is observed with a 24-hour fast and a special religious service.

[46] The literal meaning is "head [of] the year." Rosh is Hebrew for head. Hashana for year.

[47] Matzos are the unleavened bread the Jews ate when wandering in the desert. Actually matzos are thin crackers, about 8 by 8 inches.

What I knew about the meaning of being Jewish came mainly from the stories Clara told us: that the Nazis excluded her from the study of dentistry because she was Jewish. Then there is the story of how the residents of Steinheim, her father's place of origin, threw a dead pig into the local Jewish cemetery. I wonder if Philipp, Olga, Fred, and Aaron concluded that only bad things happened to Jews?

Much later in her life, when mother was widowed and living alone, she would fast on Yom Kippur—a very old Jewish religious practice. One year, as we talked over long distance, she told me that she had fasted on the day before Yom Kippur. Why? Because she had a dinner invitation on the day of Yom Kippur and did not want to miss a social gathering.

Upon reflection I now realize how difficult it must have been for Clara to explain to her children what she experienced in Germany before coming to the United States. She never wanted to return to visit Germany.[48] At the same time, she wanted to preserve both her Jewish and German cultural origins. That must have been a wrenching dichotomy for her. She clearly wanted her children to be aware that we were 100% Jewish via both parents. In her opinion, Jew-haters would always regard us as Jews. She didn't want us to have the same shocks she had in her late teens and early twenties when the Nazis began to take power in Germany. Still she understood that being German was something to which she also felt close. Though she was steeped in the German language, history, and culture, the Nazis had completely rejected her as a German since she was Jewish.

OLGA LEARNS ABOUT THE JEWISH RELIGION

In 1994, after our son Jacob graduated from high school, I visited my brother Aaron and his family in Show Low, Arizona. One afternoon on a flight with Aaron in his airplane, he and I had a very long conversation about our parents and why they insisted we call ourselves Jews.[49] I was of the opinion that during our childhood we lost out on

---

[48] In 1956 my parents returned to Germany for the first time since their departure in the 1930s. Fritz was all excited about seeing Hamburg again; he had to drag Clara along on the trip. She remained angry about the Nazis for her entire life. I do not know if they visited Berlin. Somehow I doubt it.

[49] In the late 1950s, students enrolling in classes at Texas Western College had to fill in their church preference. Philipp wrote "Gothic." I also remember filling out a small piece of paper saying I believed in God. Gracious, weren't those the days?

any positive aspects of being Jewish,[50] despite the fact that we never denied that we were Jewish.[51] We learned about Hitler and the holocaust, and almost nothing about Jewish religious belief and practice. Why is the Jewish religion different from Christianity? Aaron told me: "You aren't too old to learn about the Jewish religion now." He proposed an idea I'd never had: the possibility of learning about the Jewish religion as an adult. If I claimed my Jewish heritage, I might as well learn what that meant. In 1995 I joined our nearby local Reform Jewish Congregation. For about five years I maintained my formal membership in the congregation, the first family member to do so in many generations. During those years, I enrolled in an introductory class about Jewish history and religion,[52] took two years of basic prayerbook Hebrew on Sunday morning,[53] one semester of cantillation, as well as Saturday morning Old Testament Bible study.[54]

I attended Friday evening services regularly, mostly by myself. Sometimes my husband David joined me since he had taken the first two years of Hebrew with me, and picked up Hebrew better than I. After a while I had enough of it all. There was no way I could believe in God although I liked saying basic prayers in Hebrew.[55] The Friday evening service became comforting. I enjoyed sitting in a room full of Jews, living proof that not all Jews had perished in the holocaust. Still there was no way being attached to Jewish religious practice could become a regular part of my life.

---

[50] Except, of course, that Jews were smart. A curious self-prejudice.

[51] Of all the children, Philipp always regarded being Jewish as a religious practice only. Later when Case Western Reserve University was undertaking a study about Ashkenazi Jewish siblings and colon cancer, I enrolled myself, Philipp, and Aaron. Fred had already been dead for a couple of years. The research program director called me, confused: "Your twin brother Philipp says he is not Jewish. How can that be, aren't you twins?" So I had to explain that my twin brother had a very narrow take on what being Jewish was. Certainly Jewish genetics did not enter into the picture for him.

[52] Most participants were enrolled because they were considering conversion to Judaism. It had never occurred to me that someone would become a Jew by choice.

[53] At long last, Olga attends Sunday school!

[54] By then David and I had made our first visit to Israel, a strong motivating factor.

[55] David was insistent that I didn't just memorize the Hebrew but that I understand what the words meant. Otherwise he maintained Hebrew prayers would just be gobbledygook.

From left to right: Fritz, Clara, Aaron on her lap, Olga at her knee, Philipp standing, Fred, and Jenny. c. 1948.

JENNY BORNSTEIN IN HERRIN

Great-grandmother Jenny did not live with us on 13th Street. She insisted on living by herself nearby in a brick house where she rented a large semi-basement room. Since we were little children, we were hardly aware of the complex relationship that must have existed between Jenny, Clara, and Fritz. For us she was a tiny, little old lady in her eighties who wore false teeth, dressed mostly in black, and walked using a plain wooden cane. I was told that after the death of her husband Philipp in 1891, Jenny only wore black, but photos from the 1940s contradict that story.

Jenny always carried with her a small leather purse filled with coins. When she visited us, she would give each of her great-grandchildren a nickel for a frozen treat from the small mom and pop store down the street from our house. Such a treat that was! Candy and ice cream were quite rare for us. As Clara said: "Bornstein children don't ask for candy."[56] Clara and Fritz always believed that skinny children were healthy children. Fritz

---

[56] I imagine that Clara came up with this aphorism because she detested children who demand candy. But then there is the incident with the Life Savers in Tacoma: don't ask, just take.

would tell us about underweight babies born during WWII who grew up to be healthy adults and that Americans were fat.

We visited Jenny at her place and she at ours. We four children must have been a confirmation to her that life continued despite the disasters she experienced. She had lost so many beloved family members and friends.[57] Now she was far away from her original home, in her late eighties, an age when many people are living in their familiar home surroundings.

I always enjoyed visiting her in her large basement room. Her landlady's barking dog, a ferocious Spitz, would greet me. I was terrified of dogs all during my childhood.[58] Jenny had a subscription to *Reader's Digest*[59] and she would tell me the latest horror story she'd read there. One of them I remember quite clearly: an article stated that hot dogs were made from horse meat. Could that be why I've never liked hot dogs? I can't tell you whether Jenny and I spoke English or German. I do know I loved spending time with her. With her I almost felt like a special only child—Jenny's full concentration on me provided wonderful peace and quiet. I received her total attention.

My favorite memory of my great-grandmother is that of watching her braid her waist-length grey hair. There were still a few strands of her hair that remained blond, which just amazed me. She would braid her hair carefully from the top of her head down to the very tips of her long pigtail. Then she wound her braid at the nape of her neck and fastened it with long tortoise shell hair pins. She saved hair she had brushed out. She wound that bit of her hair around her index finger and then placed the little circle of hair in a small container. Nothing could be wasted. When she was a child did people save their hair for pillows? I would sit at Jenny's knee and listen to story after childhood story.[60] I always told her that if I were to have a girl one day, I would name her Jenny. Is Jacob close enough?

Jenny died in 1951 and was buried at the main cemetery in Herrin. I was supremely happy to find her father's and her husband's graves years later when I visited Weissensee Cemetery.

---

[57] As she mentions in her memoir, several died in concentration camps.
[58] I have no idea why, but even the sweet Cocker Spaniel of good friends terrified me.
[59] I liked all the jokes and the vocabulary quizzes.
[60] If you want to know these stories of Jenny's childhood in detail, my translation of her memoir, *A Jewish Girlhood in Berlin: 1859–1879*, is available on Amazon.

OUR FAMILY ADVENTURES OUTDOORS

Whenever possible weekends were devoted to family picnics and excursions outdoors: to either the many beautiful state parks or to nearby Crab Orchard Lake. I remember one freezing Christmas dinner outside around a picnic table at Giant City State Park. Our main dish was a canned chicken, heated in the can over a blazing campfire. Were there side dishes? Maybe a warmed up can of Boston baked beans or a can of salty green beans?

During these outings, our mother developed her love for fossils.[61] During hikes, she'd study the ground for ammonites while we clambered up the boulders and cliffs. She'd return to the car, happy to have her pockets bulging with large and small fossils embedded in rock.

During the five years we lived in Southern Illinois, Fritz always took off an entire month from work for his summer vacation, usually August. The European vacation habit of a month off in August dies hard. While he was away, my father hired a substitute pathologist to take charge of running the Herrin hospital laboratory and performing autopsies throughout southern Illinois.

We never camped but stayed in motels,[62] occasionally even one with a swimming pool. We ate yummy tidbits such as warm, canned corned beef packaged in Argentina, canned fruit salad, and breakfast cereal covered with warm evaporated milk, no sugar. Of course we had no cooler. Mother would make herself a warm cup of instant coffee from the motel bathroom sink's hot tap water.[63] The only restaurant meals I remember from any trip are the steak dinners we ate in Kansas City every year as our four-week trip came to an end. That was a total treat and great celebration!

---

[61] About 15 years later, Clara would become a part-time college student majoring in geology.
[62] In those days motels were called tourist courts.
[63] Once, an irate tourist court operator ran after mother yelling: "No cooking in my hotel." But then Clara was always ready to keep things simple and cheap.

When traveling in the hot and dry Four Corners country,[64] our drinking water came from a canvas water bag hanging on the car's hood ornament. Every now and then Fritz would line his children up and give us each a teaspoon of salt so we wouldn't become dehydrated traveling in the desert heat. He followed the salt ceremony by giving us each a small sip of water from the weird smelling canvas waterbag. Of course the car had no air conditioning. We'd have an occasional cold carbonated beverage as a treat, one bottle split by two kids. Our candy bar ritual was a bit more complex. One child would split the bar, the other child could choose their half of the bar. My father thought this system would make us split the bar more fairly. He gave us a great lesson in fairness and sharing.

The Delicate Arch, Arches National Park.
Photo courtesy of Wikicommons.

---

[64] The spot on the U.S. map where Arizona, New Mexico, Utah and Colorado meet.

Between 1947 and 1952 we covered an enormous swath of the western United States in our Studebaker:[65] Inscription Rock, the Grand Canyon (both north and south rims), Monument Valley, Arches National Monument,[66] Zion and Bryce Canyons, Yellowstone, the newish Big Bend National Park,[67] Capitol Reef, the California Redwoods, and San Francisco. I missed the hike to Delicate Arch. I was sulking in the car by myself, reading *Heidi*.[68] The list of parks went on and on. Even as adults, all of the Bornstein kids have loved to travel, especially in the West.

Studebaker Champion. Photo courtesy of Wikicommons.

---

[65] Clara loved the Studebaker designed by Raymond Loewy (1893–1986) a Franco-Jewish industrial designer. We had various models of the Studebaker. I remember the Champion and the Commander.

[66] Now Arches National Park.

[67] The park opened in 1944. We stayed there overnight around 1949. At the time, the park rented large army tents and cots to visitors. We were right at home!

[68] "Olga is reading *Heidi*." A favorite family refrain. Perhaps I was channeling great-aunt Susanne: take me to the green, cool Alps of Switzerland rather than condemning me to the heat and dry of the southwestern United States. The book was written by Swiss author Johanna Spyri and published in 1881.

We visited mother's cousin Fred Schuster in Holbrook Arizona, where he operated a large trading post. Fred had left Westphalia in the 1920s to seek his fortune in America. He lived as a bachelor in a tiny white house and drove a huge Cadillac almost as big as the house. Fred claimed to be friends with Barry Goldwater. He was always delighted to see the band of Bornsteins pull up. He would fix us a meal of eggs scrambled with real butter (a special treat).[69] I still have a silver bracelet that Fred gave me from the trading post. On one trip to Holbrook, Fred also gave my parents a large Navajo Indian blanket. The red, hand-woven, patterned wool blanket now resides with my brother Fred's family in Westlake Village, California. The family joke was that Fritz called Fred Schuster "my cousin" even though he rarely acknowledged mother's other relatives that way. The two Freds really liked each other. On our western trips, we would also visit Clara's aunt, uncle, and cousins who had resettled from Germany to Los Angeles. Their importance in our life was very vague to us—but they did feed us candy.

On one trip we were walking along the South Rim of the Grand Canyon. We noticed that our baby brother Aaron was veering very energetically toward the canyon's rim. What was going on with him? In those days, c. 1949, there were no fences or railings to protect tourists walking close to the edge. When we arrived back at the cabin, Clara discovered that Aaron had finished off her entire thermos of black coffee before we left on our walk. He was wired!

One day in the late 1940s, we had just crossed the San Juan River north of the Monument Valley. We stopped at the trading post in Mexican Hat (very close to the Four Corners). Fritz exited the car wearing his usual canvas shorts, leather sandals, and a rumpled nylon shirt.[70] When the manager saw the Studebaker with the four waifs in the back seat, he asked Fritz: "Are you a migrant worker?" We all thought the manager's comment was hysterically funny—a physician masquerading as a migrant worker?

The back seat of the Studebaker had side pockets for storage. We all wanted to sit near the side pockets, close to the window, so our parents devised a rotation plan to avoid lots of squabbling among the kids. When Aaron was still in diapers, Clara washed them at

---

[69] Clara was of the strong opinion that butter was a waste of money. Oleo was just fine. Is that why I love cooking with butter today?
[70] Used when traveling because when washed, those nylon shirts dried in almost an instant!

Clara and brood (Olga, Aaron, Philipp, Fred) at the edge of the South Rim of the Grand Canyon. There is no fence behind us, c. 1948.

Herrin, Illinois. The House on 13th Street: 1947–1952

the motel, and then dried them flapping in the wind, secured tightly in the car's side vent windows as we made our way down the road. Disposable diapers were invented in 1948, but why just use something once and throw it away? That was a key idea in Clara's world view. Today I think that her outlook provided good training for our adulthood. Be spare and use only what you really need.

When we were adults on our own, all of us enjoyed the outdoors and often returned to the many places we had visited as children. Our parents instilled in us the joy of being out in nature, away from the tensions of more urban daily life.

WE MOVE TO EL PASO, TEXAS

After Jenny's death in 1951, Clara and Fritz began to contemplate a move. They just loved the desert southwest. A friend from their year in Dallas was living in El Paso. Vincent Ravel asked Fritz if he'd be interested in becoming the pathologist for a new hospital opening up in El Paso. We had visited the Ravel family several times on our trips out west from Illinois. And Clara's brother Hajo also died in 1951, just as he was about to complete medical school in Buffalo, New York. Yes, it was time to start a new life in a new location. The Bornstein family was on the move again.

Fritz, back row, second from the right. Staff of Anna, Illinois State Hospital.

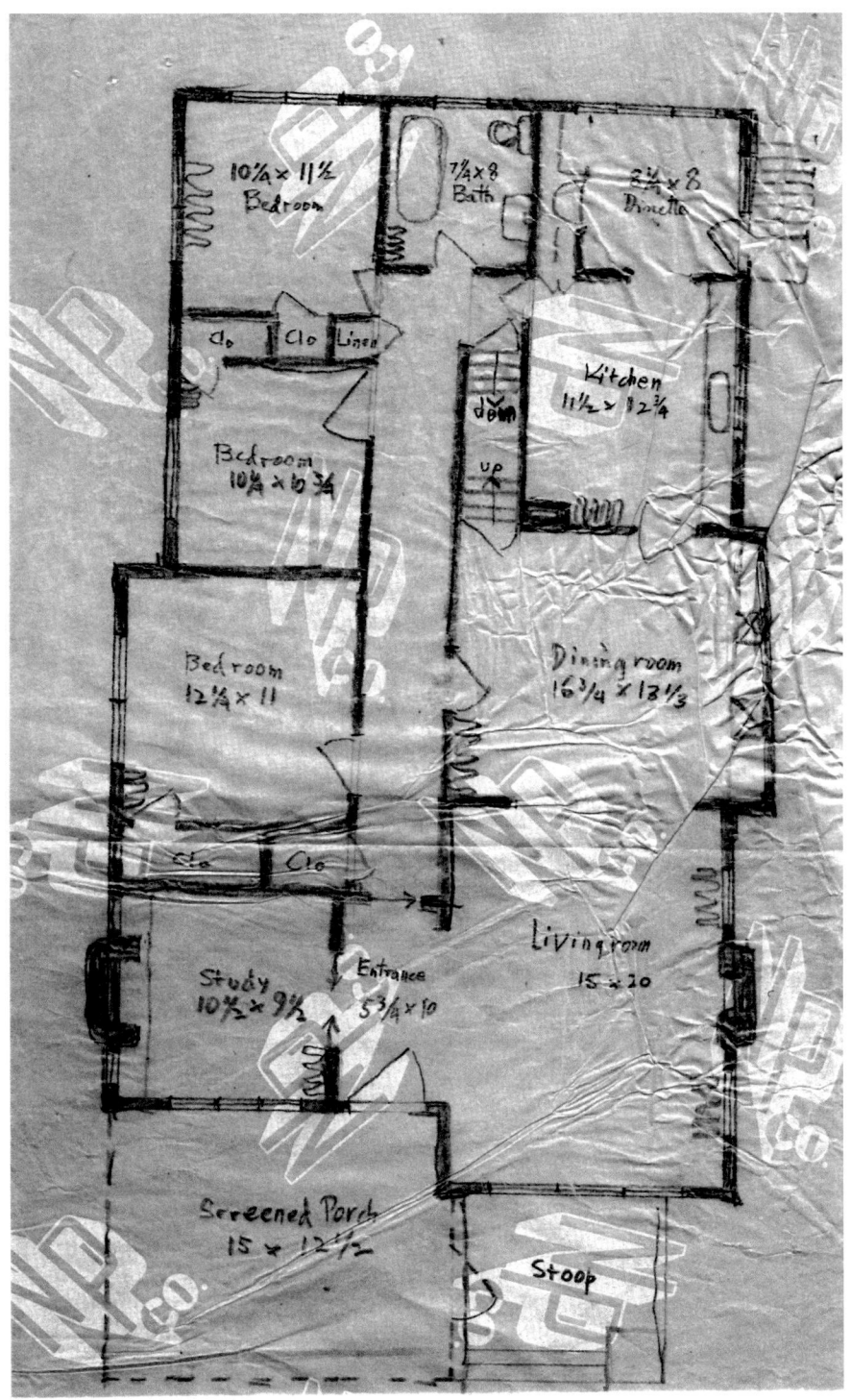

Floor plan 409 S. 13th St. Herrin Illinois. By Clara.

Kroger Grocery
Advertisement, c. 1950.

Household budget 1950.

March 1952

House	72.01
Help	72.72
Communications	165.60
Food	123.44
Clothing	54.35
Gifts	33.85
Miscellaneous	181.82
	703.79

exclusive of insurance

Herrin, Illinois. The House on 13th Street: 1947–1952

Dr. Bornstein is on a separate diet

all breakfasts for children:
    juice - dry cereal - milk

Monday lunch: vegetable soup (big can) with
    bread + butter sandwiches, apples ~~bananas~~

Monday supper: shell maccaroni (already cooked)
    with tomato sauce (can), carrots (can), corned beef
    bread + butter

Tuesday lunch: cottage cheese, bread + butter,
    bananas, soup for Mrs Jennings (can)

Tuesday supper: meat loaf (already cooked) with
    carrots ~~peas~~ (can), bread + butter, vanilla pudding
        (already cooked)

Wednesday lunch: cheese sandwiches, apples
    soup for Mrs Jennings (can)
    Supper; chili con carne (3 cans together)
    Banana jello bread + butter

Clara's handwritten menu for the babysitter, 1951.

Herrin Feb 9, 1951

Permit me please to offer these
With my sincere apologies.
For neither book nor (better) toy
Has our Southern Illinois
To offer to the one in quest
Of birthday presents of the best.
The brain is stumped, the heart is & 334,
The fingers are however busy
Forever making booties - ach -
Accompanied by Brahms and Bach
To keep the Loved One adorned.
And thus I hope they won't be scorned.
You won't be named one of the 10
Of our nation's best-dressed men,
Nor will the Bollingen Award
Come here to crown this labour hard.
Oh, but for one Redeeming feature
No consolation for this creature
And this is that I love you still,
And always did, and always will.

Clem

Philipp, Olga, Fred with sled in Herrin, Illinois c. 1948.

Clara's handwritten poem to Fritz, 1951.

Jobs for week beginning Sund████████ght Nov. 19th

Make own beds   Philipp & Olga

Dress and undress Aaron   Olga *P*

Wash dishes   Fred *P*

Dry dishes   Phil *O*

clear table   Phil *O*

set table   Olga *F*

clear kitchen and ████████ dinette   Philipp *O*

carry in milk and newspapers   Fred *F*

straighten bathroom   Olga *F*

sweep basement   *P* P██████

burn garbage   on call

make tea   Phil
dry silver close gate   Aaron

special jobs 1 Fred 2 Olga 3 Phil.

	cheerf.	eff.	pay
Phil	80%	72%	23 c,
Olga	60%	60%	18 c
Fred	70%	70%	14 c (minus 4 for gun)

*Weekly chores for the
Bornstein kids.*

Southern Illinois, Little Egypt

409 S. 13th Street
living room

The Navajo blanket from
Fred Schuster

From the Elbe to the Rio Grande

CHAPTER 13

El Paso, Texas
1952–1958

Bornstein family in El Paso. Left to right: Philipp, Olga, Aaron, Clara, Fred, Fritz, 1954.

FOR THE BORNSTEIN CHILDREN, the move from flat, verdant Illinois to El Paso in July 1952 was nearly as wrenching as Clara and Fritz's move from Germany to the United States was some twenty years before. The bare scenery of the mountainous Chihuahuan desert scared me. The land was so big and empty. Where was the grass? Where were the trees? Where were the Midwestern-style two story white wooden houses? In El Paso, the southwestern light was brighter, the sky was bluer and bigger, and the air had the scent of something like pine, but not quite. We lived at the foot of the Franklin Mountains of El Paso, where the southernmost Rocky Mountains end in the United States. The Rio Grande twists at the southern edge of the city, separating the United States from Mexico.

*El Paso Skyline looking
into Juarez, Mexico.*

*In the living room at 1009 Park Road.
Left to right: Olga, Philipp, Fred,
Fred's first wife Dorothy, Aaron. Clara
and Fritz standing.*

Living room at 1009 Park Road.

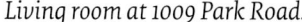

Newly constructed Providence Memorial Hospital, 1952.

We first lived in a rented house in the "Lower Valley" (the valley of the Rio Grande) southeast of downtown. We attended North Loop School in the Ysleta school district. I was no longer the only girl named Olga in my elementary school class! There were many Latina Olgas in my class. I was used to raising my arm immediately when the teacher asked for Olga to answer a question. My idea that Olga was only a Russian first name had to be abandoned.

One day we walked out our front door on La Senda Drive and found that the floodgates of the nearby irrigation ditch (with water ultimately from the Rio Grande) had been opened to soak the front lawns in our neighborhood. We had no idea that this was the Lower Valley method of lawn watering. My brothers chased horny toads, boiled June bugs, and pulled the wings off of insects. Of course, I joined in the fun!

Another day, I came home from school with news for my parents: a classmate bit my cheek while we were on the playground. Goodness! They said bites can be really dangerous and that I could become infected from the bite. I survived, but there's nothing like having a father who is a pathologist to learn about potentially scary life-threatening scenarios.

After six months living "down the valley"[1] we moved into the house at 1009 Park Road that would be the Bornstein home until 1988. We lived in Kern Place.[2] My father

[1] The terms "down the valley" (lower valley) to the east and "up the valley "(upper valley) to the west refer to the valley of the Rio Grande River.
[2] Peter E. Kern (1860–1937) was a jeweler and real-estate entrepreneur in El Paso and Skagway, Alaska. Check him out in Wikipedia. Fascinating.

now worked at Providence Memorial Hospital, a short five-minute drive from our house. To the north of us we could see the tail end of the Rocky Mountains. When we walked one block east, we could look over to Juarez, Mexico, fuzzy and grey with pollution. The Franklin Mountains were dotted with spiny cacti and painted rocks outlining the initials of the local high schools. During the fall football season, "Letter Clubs" from the local high schools climbed the mountain to light tar pots that outlined the letters. The letters glowed on football game nights for all below to see. In Juarez, on the southern side of the Rio Grande, the northernmost spur of the Sierra Nevada mountains loomed large, where rocky hills were covered with the initials of Mexican political parties. The initials P.R.I. and P.A.N. were scored into the face of the mountain.[3]

Our home, built around 1917, fit perfectly into the dominant Mexican architectural style of our neighborhood. In Illinois, homes were constructed either of brick or wood. Here stucco, mostly painted white, gave a vague nod to the pale adobe huts across the river in Mexico.

Our house usually was painted white. At some later point, our mother had the house painted a light blue.[4] She called the new color Peñíscola blue, after the seaside town she loved on Spain's Mediterranean Costa Brava. Our house was built in a U shape.[5] Along the spines of the U were four separate rooms, all of them interconnected. Some rooms had up to three doors! Privacy was minimal, and loud noise from a house full of school children usually filled the air. The empty space inside the U contained a large, enclosed patio that required a step down from all the rooms.[6] The open end of the U was closed by a long bank of glass doors.

In summer, two swamp coolers, an early air conditioner common in the dry southwest, kept the thick walls of the house pleasantly cool. When winter came, the puny heating system was barely adequate for the size of the house. A gas floor furnace was installed beneath the floor between the living room and the dining room; another gas floor furnace was located in the west-most bedroom. Barefooted guests beware! These

---

[3] P.R.I. = Institutional Revolutionary Party; P.A.N. = National Action Party.
[4] Today the house is painted a very light brown, and it looks much like many of the homes in Santa Fe, New Mexico.
[5] Visit the Magoffin House, a Texas Historical site in downtown El Paso. The floor plan is quite similar to floor plan at 1009 Park Road.
[6] Almost a hazard to the unwary. It was easy to stumble and fall when exiting the bedrooms, kitchen, dining room, and living room.

floor-level grates would leave nasty burns on the soles of many feet. Nowhere in the house was there a temperature control.

In the large, enclosed patio,[7] a small black gas furnace tried in vain to keep the large room warm. In summer we spent much of our time on the screened porch which extended along the entire front of our house. Here we visited, read, played chess, canasta, and ping pong. Summer evenings in El Paso, at an elevation of 3,740 feet, were wonderfully cool. The porch was the best place to relax at that time of year. In a corner of the long porch languished our old snow sled which we had brought with us from Illinois, never to be used again.

The biggest room in our house was the living room, measuring 20 by 30 feet, large enough for the grand piano we wanted but never had. The previous owner of the home, Mrs. Causey, had eliminated walls to create this large open space since she ran a ladies' lunch and catering event space there (of course not approved by the permiting authority).

Later the room would be filled on Saturday evenings with live string quartet concerts played by my parents' friends including the violinist Abraham Chavez.[8] All the Bornsteins were great music listeners, but not performers. That ability came with Jacob, Olga and David's son, who has great musical gifts as a jazz guitar teacher and performer.

Sometime in the mid-50s, Abraham Chavez decided to form an all-string ensemble called "The El Paso Symphonette." Each week a group of about 14 musicians would rehearse in our living room. The house was filled with music! A piece I learned to love then was Samuel Barber's *Adagio for Strings* (1936).[9] For one concert, the group prepared the *Bachianas Brasileiras #5* (1930) by Hector Villa-Lobos. This piece was written for eight cellos and a soprano. The group produced an amazing, unforgettable sound that resounded in every corner of the house. I have goose bumps even today when I even think of that music echoing throughout our house.

---

[7] We called this area the patio even though it was completely indoors. Originally the patio was open to the sky. The rest of the house surrounded the patio. After the patio was roofed (long before we moved in) we had the ceiling in various rooms collapse during the August summer monsoons, when El Paso could have up to five or ten inches of rain. Of course the roof's drainage system was completely inadequate for those huge summer rainstorms.

[8] Violinist Abraham Chavez later became the conductor of the El Paso Symphony orchestra. The symphony's current performance space is named for Abraham.

[9] Perhaps you can tell me why in recent years, this piece of music has become popular funeral music?

The house didn't have much of a yard. In the front of the house was a nice half-moon garden area. Fritz had all the bulbs pulled out and used our outings in the desert to gradually assemble a handsome cactus garden. We all laughed when mother fell into the spiny ocotillo. Later Fritz learned that an old house with large palm trees was being torn down. Without telling Clara, he purchased one of the palm trees to transplant into the front yard. What did Clara say when she saw the flatbed truck in front of the house, loaded with a huge and ancient palm tree?

When we moved from Illinois to Texas, Clara said: "Leave the piano behind. We can always find a decent used piano when we're settled in El Paso."[10] She was wrong; there were no used pianos to be had. Everyone who had moved to El Paso had left their piano behind too.[11] Eventually mother found an upright piano that had been retrofitted from a player piano. This piano was always somewhat out of tune but since my brothers and I were not going to be great pianists, that didn't bother us.[12]

 Our piano teacher Anna Gelb[13] taught one Bornstein child after the other at her house. While each of the four children awaited their turn, Mrs. Gelb let us watch television. That was a real treat because there was no TV at home. Our favorite black and white television programs were *Dragnet* and *Victory at Sea*.[14] After our lessons were completed, our parents came by. They and all the kids ate dinner with the Gelbs. I do not remember who cooked since Anna had been teaching for two hours straight. And these were not the days of take-out meals. So much for lost memories.

The doors at 1009 were always open to guests. We became accustomed to a steady stream of dinner and overnight visitors. Beyond that, large parties often took place in the living room and patio—all of Fritz's laboratory employees at Providence Hospital or our eighth grade Mesita School graduation party or weekly Cub Scout meetings[15]—you name it! Mother loved having company and always could find room for yet another visitor. Did

---

[10] Those were the days when the ability to play a piano was a required middle-class skill. That isn't true today.

[11] Of course in 1952 we were light years away from Craigslist!

[12] We certainly did not practice enough to advance our skills very far.

[13] Whose husband Joseph played second violin to Abraham Chavez during the musical evenings in the living room. Joe had attended Juilliard. He was a master sewing machine mechanic.

[14] About World War II with emphasis on naval warfare.

[15] With Clara as den mother!

her parents have a skimpy social life in Berlin? Clara only talked about visits of Westphalian relatives to Berlin, not about any family friends.

We attended Mesita Elementary School, located down the hill from our house, and about a ten-minute walk past Madeline Park.[16] Philipp and Olga were known as the serious Bornstein twins, extroverted Fred as the favorite class officer and joker.[17] Aaron? He was just our little brother and I wasn't paying attention. But was he ever cute!

We Bornstein kids did well in school and none of us was ever a problem for our teachers, except once when Philipp and Olga were in seventh grade. Our popular teacher, Miss Harvel, became gravely ill. Administrators sent our class a succession of substitute teachers, among them a detested Mrs. Wilbanks, whom the class worked hard to drive crazy. We missed our beloved Miss Harvel. No one warned any of our substitute teachers in advance that they would be teaching a class of specially selected "bright kids."[18] I remember being sent to the office of the principal, Mrs. Reed. She said to me: "Olga Bornstein! I never thought I'd see you in my office." What weird things had we done? The entire class had escaped our classroom to play hide and seek among the cars in the teachers' parking lot. We were searching for "cooties."[19] Also we had a slogan: "No more Wilbanks, no more war, we're the class of '54." So much for acting out in the 1950s!

We had excellent teachers, among them Mrs. Maloney, the wife of an army colonel stationed at Ft. Bliss. She drove a red convertible sports car and wore décolleté dresses and backless high heels. As Philipp once said: "She taught the boys to appreciate breasts." She was a demanding teacher who knew how to keep the attention of a horde of wild, smart students. The later success of her many students attests to her teaching ability. Her fame as a sixth-grade teacher lives on: Aaron's sixth grade class still holds Mrs. Maloney's class reunions every few years, usually at the same time as their high school reunions.

Our music teacher, Miss Jenkins, made us listen to recordings of famous pieces of classical music. We even had music listening contests, where we had to identify a piece

---

[16] Named for the daughter of Peter Kern, the original developer of Kern Place.

[17] He ran for class president one year with the slogan: "Use your head, Vote for Fred."

[18] I no longer know why, but sometime in sixth grade, we were all moved up half a school year. When we graduated from elementary school we were in "low eighth grade." So we could start El Paso High School as freshmen, the entire class spent the summer of 1954 attending "high eighth" at El Paso Technical School. The classes were mainly for students who had failed that part of school. We sailed through without any trouble.

[19] Cooties = headlice or other "bugs." To have "cooties" meant you weren't very clean.

of music after only hearing a few bars. Our art teacher, Mrs. Walshe, taught us to love the classics of world art. Her classroom walls were covered with colorful reproductions of works by famous artists. Mrs. Walshe[20] also gave us a special treat in seventh grade: she taught us to chip our designs onto wood boxes with an Exacto knife. At age 13 we were now considered mature enough to handle a dangerous weapon.

Many years later the federal government declared Mesita school a toxic super-fund site because of contamination from the smelter of the American Smelting and Mining Company (ASARCO) located directly on the United States/Mexico border. The smelter and the smokestacks were demolished in 1999 by order of the U.S. government.

ASARCO Smelter in El Paso. One of the smokestacks was the third highest in the U.S., 828 feet tall.

---

[20] Jane Walshe was also our neighbor and a special friend of Clara's. Mrs. Walshe gave David and Olga a wedding present: a framed colorful Mexican bark painting of a tree with birds, which still hangs in our house today.

During its 100 years of operation in El Paso, ASARCO's three furnaces smelted lead, zinc, arsenic, cadmium and copper from all over the world and poisoned generations of El Paso and Juarez citizens. Our grade school, built in the early 1950s, was demolished in the 1990s. The soil was remediated, and a new Mesita Elementary School was built on the old site. Finally it was clear why we were always coughing and gasping during recess or physical education classes outside on the playground in the 1950s. A cluster of cancer and multiple sclerosis cases found later among graduates of Mesita was perhaps attributable to the pollution from the ASARCO smokestacks. Philipp and Fred died from colon cancer, Olga survived breast cancer, and Aaron survived a melanoma on his face. Should we thank ASARCO?

Graduates of Mesita School went on to El Paso High School (EPHS), located two miles from Kern Place.[21] Still one of El Paso's architectural jewels, EPHS was designed by the well-known architectural firm of Trost and Trost and opened in 1916. When we attended EPHS, El Paso had only four high schools; in 2021 there are 14![22]

El Paso High School, 1916.

We were so excited to finally attend EPHS! We were going to be EPHS Tigers![23] But what a disappointment that turned out to be. I was bored and spent most of my time daydreaming as I stared out the large classroom windows. Our teachers were well-mean-

---

[21] We could either walk to and from school or take a city bus. No parental car delivery or pick up. No large parking lot for student vehicles.

[22] In the first decades of the 20th century it was a considerable accomplishment to graduate from high school. President Truman, served 1945–1953, was a high school graduate and no one thought less of him.

[23] The school mascot was a tiger. Enshrined in a case outside the principal's office was a genuine, stuffed tiger. By our 50th class reunion, the tiger was intact, but rather mangy.

ing but unexciting. In an English class, after I'd read *The Mill on the Floss* over and over during our "silent reading" period, the teacher, Mr. Kendall, sighed in exasperation and gave me Thackeray's *Vanity Fair* to keep me occupied. I loved the novel, even though I really didn't understand its satiric elements or its importance in the history of English literature. Philipp and I were in Mrs. Hanson's slide rule class. Native Spanish speakers were discouraged from speaking Spanish at school. Hall monitors would grab students speaking Spanish and send them to study hall as their punishment. That was a far cry from today where students are encouraged to be bilingual, and sometimes only encouraged to be English speakers by fourth grade.

Of course we attended Friday night football games, a strong Texas tradition. I loved the cheerleaders and the band music although I had no clue what was happening down on the field.[24] I even remember going on school trips to out of town football games. I traveled once through New Mexico to a football game in Dimmitt, Texas, around 400 miles away in the Texas panhandle! We packed into uncomfortable buses and were driven home to El Paso through the night.

I was the dependable go-to babysitter in our immediate neighborhood, earning 35 cents an hour! I kept quite busy on weekends. One evening I came home from a job with a five-dollar bill! I had never seen one of those before! My father doubled any money I made from my babysitting if I put it into my savings account at the bank. But not this money! Without asking permission, I took the city bus downtown to a beauty shop and had my waist-length hair chopped off. There was hell to pay when I came home. My first and almost only act of adolescent rebellion was greeted with outrage by my father. In his European mindset, all women should have long hair. How dare I have it all cut off? That wasn't something for me to decide without permission.

By 1955 I had saved enough money from my baby sitting to take a big trip. I made my first flight alone, and I flew to the east coast to stay with family friends and distant relatives in Washington, D.C., New York City, Boston, Buffalo, and Chicago. My parents thought nothing of sending me out on my own alone to faraway places. I saw the Empire State Building and Niagara Falls and more. All very exciting!

---

[24] Our parents certainly could not help us out here!

One Christmas while still in high school, I got a job working at the largest downtown department store: the venerable Popular Dry Goods Department Store.[25] I was assigned to the fragrance department, I think, because I was good at calculating the tax on items. We'd send the customer's cash through a pneumatic tube to an unknown location in the basement of the store. We didn't have to learn how to use a cash register.[26] By return tube, we received the customer's receipt and any change. Residents of Mexico were not charged any Texas state tax.

Until 1966, Texas voters were required to pay a poll tax to be registered to vote.[27] This Texas legal requirement was imposed in 1902. All voters had to pay the poll tax, but the law was intended to exclude Blacks and other minorities from voting. In those days, the poll tax cost $1.50[28] or more, a significant sum, especially for poorer people.

Clara was a member of the League of Women voters and worked as a LWV volunteer selling poll taxes around town. One of the sales booths was set up at a central location inside the Popular Dry Goods Department Store so that shoppers wouldn't have to go to a special state office to pay the required voting fee. All her life my mother was an impassioned supporter of the voting process, despite her disagreement with the poll tax laws.

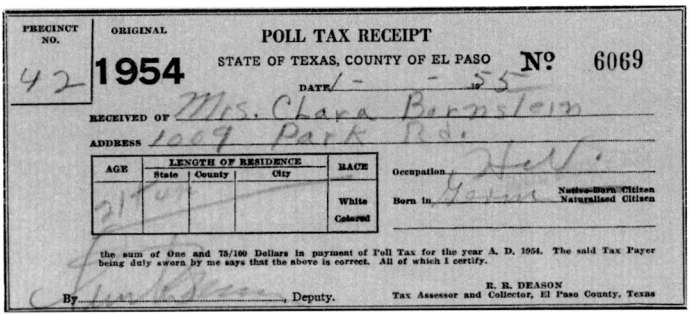

Clara's poll tax receipt, note the Occupation: HW (housewife), 1954.

---

[25] The owners started making real money during the Mexican Revolution, supplying Pancho Villa's men with clothing and other necessities.

[26] This was a system developed to deter employee theft, I think.

[27] In 1964 I voted in my first presidential election via absentee ballot since I was living in Seattle, Washington. Clara purchased my poll tax for me!

[28] A sum equivalent to $17.77 in 2021.

El Paso, Texas: 1952–1958

In May 1958, Philipp and I graduated at the age of 17 from El Paso High School. I wish I could tell you more about my brothers, Fred and Aaron during the 1950s. At this point in life, self-involvement is the most prominent adolescent emotion. I was just vaguely aware of what my younger brothers were up to.

We all learned to drive from my father. The family had a used Willys Jeep as a second car. Usually mother used it for running errands and grocery shopping. We all enjoyed trips on bumpy corduroy roads far into the desert. The Jeep also gave Fritz the opportunity to share the skills he'd learned in the army. He did not declare me fit for driving alone until I could downshift from third into second gear when stopped at an angle at the top of a hill. I'm not sure I could do that today after driving with automatic transmissions for so many years.

Sunday at the Alcazar Restaurant in Juarez, Mexico. Left to right: Olga, Philipp, Fred, Fritz, Clara, Aaron, two unknown friends, beret-wearing waiter in back.

Often on Sundays, we ate at the Alcazar Restaurant in Juarez. We'd park the car on the El Paso side of the bridge and walk across the Rio Grande to Juarez. The restaurant was located on a side street in the first block past the river. The Alcazar served the sizeable Spanish community in Juarez and featured Catalan and Basque dishes in addition to Mexican food and steaks. The waiter or owner would offer guests a drink of wine from a bota (leather) or porrón (glass) wine holder, which poured wine down the side of your nose and into your mouth![29]

In summer of 1958, both Philipp and I attended Texas Western College[30] to earn a few credits before we began full-time college in the fall. The college architecture was unusual, built in Bhutanese style. It is said that the wife of the first president of the college was inspired by photos of Bhutanese buildings in the April 1914 issue of the *National Geographic* and thought Bhutanese buildings would fit nicely into the bare, hilly El Paso campus. To this day, the campus retains a unique heritage: Bhutanese architecture in El Paso.

Texas Western College, later renamed UTEP.

At the end of the summer of 1958, the entire family piled into our station wagon for our last extended family trip together. We went to the Grand Canyon, a park with special meaning for all of us from our many trips there together. On the last night of our trip, we ate a picnic dinner at Coolidge Dam in southern Arizona. Fred was a great cornet player. After dinner he played taps on his cornet. My father said that was a special moment: the last of our times as the nuclear Bornstein family. In the next years we all would scatter in many directions.

[29] A porrón is a traditional glass wine pitcher typical of Spain, originating in Catalonia and eventually spreading to other parts of Spain. This invention allows everyone to drink from the same pitcher without touching it with their lips.
[30] Since 1968 The University of Texas at El Paso (UTEP).

In fall, 1958, Philipp started his college education at Texas Western College. As you know, I was the only girl in my family. I had been my mother's right-hand for years. Boys back then were not expected to be handy at housekeeping tasks. My father, especially, felt it was important for me to leave home and get out from out under my mother's thumb.

My father and I went out to dinner together one evening in a lovely Juarez restaurant, just the two of us, shortly before I was to leave for St. Louis and start college at Washington University. My father told me that if I were to become pregnant, I should come home immediately, have the baby,[31] leave the child with my parents and go back to college and finish my degree. His advice and assumptions totally astounded me. I'd rarely been on any dates and still had no clear idea about how babies were made. I just nodded, unable to add anything to his statement. In later years I would joke with friends that my father's admonishment was the best birth control ever.[32]

Olga and Lana take the train from El Paso to St. Louis to start their junior year. Left to right, front row: Aaron, Olga, Fred, Clara (with ever-present cigarette); back row: Cousin Bernie Asher, Olga's college roommate Lana Tevis, Fritz.

A few days later, I boarded the train for St. Louis. With me I took my father's old WWII army trunk, a portable LP player, some suitcases and a shoe box filled with mother's sandwiches and an apple. I was filled with excitement! I was seventeen years old, ready to get on with my life away from home.

---

[31] My father had a total abhorrence of abortion because he had autopsied too many women who died from bungled illegal abortions.
[32] In 1958 birth control pills were not available. In fact abstinence was the only birth control generally out there.

—»«—

KE3-7801
El Paso, Texas 1955
by Olga Wise

Remember that old black, plastic telephone
With a dial for numbers?
How is it that when I pick up the receiver, I can still
Smell my mother's breath, hear her voice?

I step outside. I see the solid mountain where we
climbed over barren rock, pinched by low-lying cacti—
now fancy houses look down upon us,
scornful of the resilient simplicity below.
We called the lower mountain Crazy Cat but now it is tamed,
the ridge line no longer bare and gleaming.

The higher Franklin mountains still carry the initials of area high schools, once white-
washed and brilliant in the sun,
now faded and crumbling on the mountainside.
We miss those giant letters encircled by
flaming tar pots celebrating Friday night football.

We knew the blue sky—so brilliant and piercing
that we could hardly believe it.
What has become of that sky now?
Now painted grey with smoke from
pollution—our own and a gift of more from Mexico.

What luck to remember the bountiful before,
filled with light and laughter and beauty.

Summer 1958
By Olga Wise

It is June 1958, 6:15am on a bright and sunny El Paso morning. The dry air at 3,740 feet is refreshing. The sun is beginning to rise. Everything smells fresh: piñon, fresh grass, and that special desert scent. The world looks new. I'm walking about a mile from my parents' home to my 6:45am Economics class at Texas Western College. Here I am, a seventeen-year-old, high school graduate for less than a month, already going to college classes at the crack of dawn. Parking on campus is a problem. Luckily, I live close enough to campus to walk there.

Why do the classes start so early? Because Texas Western has many older buildings without air conditioning. To make classes more bearable, most summer school offerings finish by 10am. The campus blends in nicely with the desert landscape—the original buildings were constructed using Bhutanese-style architecture.

I am registered for economics and logic classes. The college I will attend in the fall accepts logic as part of the mathematics requirement. Since math is not my forte, this seems to be a good choice. I find the class completely absurd—we learn about syllogisms that contain words like "My aunt knits antimacassars." Who even knows what an antimacassar is, much less has an aunt who knits them?

Economics seems to have more potential. After all, one day I hope to be self-supporting. I barely remember anything from the class except the concept of gross national product, a term which falls by the wayside in the next fifty years. At the end of summer school I have six hours of college credit but no excitement about the classes I took, just relief that I made decent grades and that I'd never have to study those topics again.

After classes are over each day, I work at the accounting office of the El Paso General Hospital, a decrepit building in east El Paso. My father, a pathologist, finds me the job, since he's there almost every day performing autopsies and running the medical laboratory. I get to see the morgue and bodies being rolled in and out.

I drive to work in a used cream-colored Studebaker Champion my dad purchases for his three driving teenagers. Most of the patients who come to the hospital cannot afford their care. We work out payments of between $1.00 and $5.00 per week or month for bills in the hundreds of dollars. I have no idea about the costs of medical care when I start work. The women in the office are very nice to me because I can spell and speak some Spanish. I get their filing caught up, evidently a first for the place.

By the time my day is over, I'm ready to relax. I hardly remember studying but I must have done that somehow in between classes and work. Before I know it, the summer has finished, and it is September. I'm on the train from El Paso to St. Louis, ready to start the next chapter of my young life.

Shopping check Fritz mailed to Susanne from El Paso.

Family at the supper table 1950s.

Ode to Summer 1958

by Olga Wise

We drive to the International Bridge

Park and lock the car, ready for anything.

We strike out for an

Evening of teen-age revelry

In Juarez, city of sin and otherness.

Revelry, really?

Is that what this is

Sitting in a smoke-filled bar,

Surrounded by the noise

And chatter of the other boozers.

Shall we have another

Shot of tequila?

Only five cents each.

No, let us move on to that

Bar with the great mariachis.

My God, they're loud.

Who cares?

Have another nickel shot.

One bartender says:

Try this tequila.

It is flavored with the body of a

Dead worm in the bottom of the bottle.

Dare we?

Only five cents a shot.

Oh my, is that a cockroach skittering across the table?

Well, what else do you expect from a bar

Called El Submarino?

We keep walking.

We've got some nickels left.
The powerful stench of
Old booze and cheap cigarettes
Follow us out of the bar
Onto the dirty sidewalk.
Wanna catch a show?
Can you believe it?
Those dancers in baby-blue tulle
And fancy high heel shoes are
Dancing the can-can?
Are they really men?
See the hair in their armpits as they twirl?
We need another shot to get past that one.
It is getting on to three a.m.
Think we can do the bridge thing?
And so we move slowly over the
Badly lit bridge into familiar territory.

Spring 2015

— Personalamt —
Ruhestandsversorgung

(24a) Hamburg 11, den 24. März 195 3
Steckelhörn 12 III

A.-Z.   B 1033/53

Es wird gebeten, bei Schreiben die
vorstehende Nummer anzugeben.

xxxx Susanne Bornstein, Jerusalem/Israel,
Frau   Montefiori Elternhaus

Auf Grund des Gesetzes über die Gewährung von Ruhegeld xxxxxxxx und Hinterbliebenen-
versorgung für hamburgische Staatsangestelle — xxxxxxxxx — in der Fassung vom 27. Juni 1927
(Hamburgisches Gesetz- und Verordnungsblatt Seite 293 ff.) ist Ihnen xxxxxxxxx

_____ zu Ihren sonstigen regelmäßigen Einkünften im — angenommenen —

Betrage von insgesamt   125   DM --   ₰ ein   Ruhegeld
von monatlich   225   DM   74   ₰, zahlbar ab   10. März 1953,

bewilligt worden. Die Zahlung erfolgt monatlich im voraus durch Postzustellung.

Den Bescheid der Landesversicherungsanstalt wollen Sie
bitte sofort nach Erhalt hier vorlegen oder einsenden.

Sie sind verpflichtet, es sofort hierher mitzuteilen, wenn Sie außer den berück-
sichtigten Bezügen noch weitere Renten oder Erhöhungen von Renten erhalten.

Falls Sie künftig noch eine Erwerbstätigkeit ausüben oder Arbeitslosenunterstützung
beziehen, müssen Sie auch hiervon Mitteilung machen.
Ihre Steuerkarte für das gegenwärtige Jahr muß hier hinterlegt werden.

Für die Berechnung des xxxxxxxxx Ruhegeldes   ist maßgebend nach den

§§ 6 und 7 des Gesetzes der Grundlohn von monatlich . . . .   DM _____
— nicht ruhelohnfähiger Teilbetrag (Senatsverf. vom 21. 12. 1931) . . . .   DM _____

nach den §§ 6 und 7 des Gesetzes eine Grundvergütung von monatlich „   429,60
+ 3% Sonderzuschlag . . . .   „   -,-
+ Wohnungsgeldzuschuß B . . . .   „   71,50
                                zusammen DM   501,10

Es werden angerechnet gemäß §§ 3 und 6
        27   Jahre = 67/100 von DM   501,10 _   335,74

Zu kürzen gemäß § 7 Abs. 2 sind
        Jahre × 1/100 = /100 von DM _____ _
                                DM _____

Hierzu tritt
der Kinderzuschlag gemäß § 6 Abs. 2 für . . . . _____
                                _____
                                zusammen DM _____

*Suse will get a monthly pension from the city of Hamburg starting on
March 10, 1953 in the monthly amount of 335.74 German marks.*

With Fritz's
Deux Chevaux Citroën

Our WWII Willys Jeep

El Paso, Mount Cristo Rey

CHAPTER 14

New Families, New Stories
1958–2021

Bornstein family reunion, 1977. Front row: Fred, Diane Bornstein, Olga with Jacob, Natalie Bornstein with Margaret, Andrea, Eric, Aaron Landon. Back row: Clara, Fritz, David, Aaron Claire, Barbara Bornstein, Philipp

CLARA LÖWENSTEIN BORNSTEIN (1909–1988)

CLARA ENROLLED AT UTEP AROUND 1958, studying geology and teaching undergraduate paleontology laboratories. She was determined that she would not be the only family member without a college degree. She succeeded and received her B.S. in Geology in May 1974. She was active in community affairs as a member of the League of Women Voters, the El Paso Archaeology Society,[1] and the National Council of Jewish Women (NCJW) where for many years she was the chair of the annual Book Fair, the main NCJW fundraising activity. Everyone who knew her was grateful for her marvelous book finds. Who else would give you a copy of *The Golden Bough, A Study in Magic and Religion?*[2] Clara was an avid rockhound, hiking eyes down to find interesting rocks and fossils. Her geology hammer was her boon companion, usually with her in her Willys four-wheel drive Jeep.

---

[1] With which we made an unforgettable trip to the Trinity Test Site in New Mexico. That's where the atom bomb was first tested in 1945. We roamed the site, picking up pieces of glass ("trinitite") that were made from sand fused by the heat of the blast.

[2] Sir James George Frazer's wide-ranging, comparative study of mythology and religion was first published in 1890.

Clara was a smoker from the age of 13 onward, or so she said. It was no surprise then that she suffered in her last years from COPD and had to have home oxygen care. She died in 1988 at the age of 79 and is buried in the same plot as our father at Ft. Bliss National Cemetery in El Paso, Texas. Clara was a wonderful wife to Fritz, and mother and grandmother to her children and grandchildren. One of the greatest pleasures of her life was to see her family increase to the next generation.

Clara and Fritz at 1009 Park Road. Franklin Mountains in the background. March 1962.

Book Fair Chairman, Jeep Familiar Sight In El Paso

By ART LEIBSON

A familiar figure on El Paso's west side these days is Mrs. Frederick Bornstein as she moves through the streets in her slightly battered jeep, accompanied by a dog that stands almost as tall as herself, collecting books from barrels placed in supermarkets and other locations.

Mrs. Bornstein, who was in her final months of training to become a dentist when Hitler's helpers convinced her the time had come to get out of Germany, is chairman of the committee in charge of the annual Book Fair to be held in the Coliseum judging barn April 6-9.

About 15,000 books of all kinds have been collected so far for the fair, sponsored by the local chapter of the National Council of Jewish Women as one of the major fund-raising projects for the chapter's civic and charity program. El Pasoans are asked to go through their libraries, cull out volumes no longer wanted, and donate them for the fair. They may be left in the barrels or, if in quantities, they will be picked up if a call is made of either cochairman Mrs. Lawrence Cole, Mrs. Siggi Schlusselberg, Mrs. Ronald Marks or Mrs. Bornstein.

The chairman had studied English for nine years in German schools before entering into the study of dentistry. When Hitler's anti-Jewish drive began, she was notified that she could no longer take part in any of the laboratory work vital to any dentist. Continuing without the laboratory study would have been useless, so Mrs. Bornstein quit.

Her father had been a doctor and after his death the office sign had been continued as one of his sons was in medical school and planned to take over the offices. When Nazis began throwing rocks at the sign, in 1935, Mrs. Bornstein left for America where her fiance, Dr. Frederick Bornstein, El Paso pathologist, was interning in Chicago, having read the political handwriting earlier than herself.

Three days later they were married and soon afterward she was working in a downtown restaurant, cleaning vegetables, fruits and shrimp.

"I scrubbed and I cleaned and I cleaned—no end of it," she recalls of those hectic but happy days when her husband was struggling to get a medical foothold in the United States. "At least we could have all we wanted to eat—but on one condition. My employer would tolerate no waste and if we left anything on our plates we had to pay for the

After more internship, Dr. Bornstein entered the Army in 1944 and served overseas in the war against his late lamented homeland. He was a third generation doctor in a family that numbered 37 medical men in four generations. It was while in the service that Dr. Bornstein met Dr. Vincent Ravel, a native of El Paso, who urged him to come to the border after the war.

They came here for a visit, in 1948, on their way to the Four Corners area where New Mexico, Colorado, Arizona and Utah join, a desert area that had become a scenic favorite of the Bornsteins. And in 1952 they came here to stay. Soon after arriving, Mrs. Bornstein began attending the University of Texas at El Paso while rearing four children. Carrying between three and six hours each semester, she figures she is halfway toward a degree, having long since been passed by two sons, Dr. Philipp E. Bornstein, and Aaron, now a senior majoring in geology. She had one class together with Aaron, in engineering drawing, in which Aaron made a B while she had to be content with a C.

Another son, Frederick Bernard Bornstein, is in the Signal Corps, heading for Vietnam next month, while a daughter, Miss Olga Jean Bornstein, is an instructor in German at the University of Kentucky. Mrs. Bornstein has switched her interests since arriving in El Paso, into geology and paleontology, having served as treasurer for many years of El Paso Archaeological Society.

"El Paso has been wonderful to us, and we have come to love El Paso and its desert surroundings," Mrs. Bornstein said. "As kids we always loved to go to the ocean on vacations. Now we find that a little ocean goes a long ways. We like the sand and the sun."

This is her eighth year of working with the Book Fair, since its beginning, largely because of her interest in books that line the walls of her home at 1009 Park and overflow into boxes. Dr. Bornstein's favorite reading is books on the Civil War. His wife has a wider range of literary interests, but between them they have read all the several thousand volumes in the home.

So if you see a bustling little woman in her jeep, along with her mixed-breed dog, Pollux, named out of Greek mythology, it's odds-on that she is at her job of rounding up books for a fair. The fair will be open at 7 p.m. on the opening Saturday night and from 9 a.m. to 9 p.m. on the remaining days.

Article in El Paso Times, March 7, 1968.

Clara Bornstein, Chair, National Council of Jewish Women, Book Fair, El Paso, March 7, 1968.

Sunday May 27, 1973,

Liebes Olgachen:

A loving note for you enclosed in the letter to David about his paper. —

We talked with Philipp a while ago — he called — and he said you meet with them and their friends and helped a lot with the painting in the Springfield house. He said you were going by way of Camp Butler. I want to tell you that I am very deeply touched by the thought of your remembrance of Hajo, and I want to thank you for being so dear. On May 24 it was 23 years since we all went to his military funeral (I'm not sure that we took ACB along). It is quite possible that you remember something about it — a sunny day, and the gun salute, and blowing taps. You children sensed something extraordinary. You were silent, and you were very good. Thinking back over my 64 years, nothing ever has been as crushing as the loss of Hajo. His death did not change our life outwardly as the death of parents of young children does. But life has never been the same again.

1972. Clara's letter to Olga about the
death of her brother Hajo in 1951. Page 1.

New Families, New Stories: 1958–2021

Grandma was courageous and beautiful

By Margaret Bornstein
9th grade, Loretto Academy

Every line on her face showed what she had endured; leaving her homeland, death, racism. Her smile showed light on everything she loved; her grandchildren, Sunday morning breakfast, geology.

From the black coals she touched, diamonds would emerge, when dark clouds filled the sky, her sparkling blue eyes drew out the sun. Her kindness touched everyone's heart.

The wrinkles that lined her face told of the harsh winds that had blown through her life. Her voice told of the winds and how she managed to calm them. Her rough hands told of how she fought them, for herself and those around her.

Her wild glasses perched on her nose, her long white hair wrapped in a bun, her hands decorated by the most beautiful jewelry. As she grew older she became more of a person, yet she grew weaker, old age enveloped her body, sickness took its final lethal grip.

Only after her death did I realize how much I had come to look up to her. I loved my grandmother when I was small, I admired her when I was young, and now I respect her as I grow. Her strength inspired me, her courage gave me hope. She was more beautiful than the prettiest model, more courageous than the most renowned war hero, she had more strength than the strongest man.

She was Clara Bornstein, she was my grandmother, she is the woman I admire most.

Newspaper article by Aaron's daughter Margaret, 1992.

EL PASO HERALD-POST
3/19/92

Clara receives an award as the geology major graduating
with the highest GPA.

Fritz and Clara in Europe c. 1955. Fritz
balances Leica on Clara's shoulder.

Pollux, Clara and Fritz's favorite dog.

Clara with one of her cats.

From the Elbe to the Rio Grande

Philipp's brief talk at Clara's funeral, July 1988

I want to talk about our mother, Clara Bornstein. She always said speak nothing of the dead but good. It is not hard to follow her advice.

She was not a "good mother" in the sense of the Good Housekeeping Seal of Approval and she would not want to be remembered that way. She was not sentimental. She was not necessarily affectionate. She had a loathing for things we call cute. She saw herself as tough and wanted the kids to be [tough too]. She was a hard core European whose reluctance to accept American childrearing and social practices was always obvious. But she was a wonderful mother. She always did what was…the best for her husband, four children, no matter what the cost to her. She always cautioned us to do right. She was painstakingly honest and thoughtful to people. When she was polite in the sense of European style or Emily Post, she meant it. Our father told me once that he married Clara because she was the most charming woman he'd ever met. I believe it, because she showed that side when she wanted to. She was the [soul] of our family, not Pop.

Clara and Fritz's gravestone. Ft. Bliss, Texas. Fritz's information is on the other site of the gravestone.

CLARA BORNSTEIN GEMS IN THREE LANGUAGES

Our mother Clara had a way with words, and not only in her native German. This is a list of characteristic utterances and phrases that my husband David and I recall. Clara grew up in Berlin in the 1920s. Berlin humor is biting and ironic.

"It's exactly what I always wanted." Clara's invariable response on receiving any gift, no matter how dreadful.

"Ye gods and little fishes." An expression of shock, amazement, or disbelief, used from the 1920s to the 1950s. Several books bearing that title appeared between 1927 and 1952.

"You ain't in Paducah yet, honey." Don't count your chickens before they're hatched; or, the outcome remains to be seen. The punch line of a vulgar joke not reproduced here.

"I hear you talking, but you're talking shit." Source unknown, the meaning self-evident.

"She was dressed up like a Polish Christmas tree." The meaning is self-evident; not helpful to German-Polish friendship.

"Letzte Grüße aus Davos." "Final greetings from Davos." Used when a person suffers a bad coughing fit. (Davos in Switzerland was known for its TB sanitariums.)

"Ein Stück Malheur." "A piece of work," in the negative sense. A bilingual construction: German Stück (piece) plus French *malheur* (misfortune).

"Knusimon." Corruption of French *a qui nous aimons* ("to those we love"), used as a toast.

"I'll tromple you in the mud." What Clara would say when she was really mad.

FREDERICK PHILIPP EMANUEL BORNSTEIN (1910–1978)

Our father worked as a pathologist in El Paso from 1952 until his death in October 1978. He also created El Paso's Office of the Medical Examiner and served as the first city and county Medical Examiner.[3] He specialized in anatomical and forensic pathology. He had a life-long habit of coming home for lunch and taking a 30-minute nap afterwards. He developed this habit during his medical training in Germany. Woe betide the person who knocked on the front door or called on the telephone during his nap! He demanded complete silence throughout the house while he rested. After he woke up, mother would make him a fresh cup of espresso or Turkish coffee. Otherwise he was a confirmed tea drinker, a habit he acquired while growing up in Hamburg.

Another rule for the children was to always answer the phone saying: "Doctor Bornstein's residence, who is it please?" We only had one telephone line (with a black rotary-dial phone, of course), which always had to be free in case he received an important medical call. As a result, I never became a long telephone conversationalist. Aaron was our champion telephone chatterbox, with Philipp and Fred not far behind.

Fritz was permanently interested in his work and came home to regale us at the dinner table with fascinating stories of detection and death. We did not find this strange at all. We were happy to share his enthusiasm and passion in trying to unravel the many ways life can be extinguished. Some evenings he would entertain us with color slide shows—photographs of some his most interesting tumor slides. We loved all the various stain colors in the slides but had no idea what the microscopic tumors represented. His devotion, energy, and continued learning gave his children a wonderful model for being true professionals.

Fritz died shortly after his diagnosis of pancreatic cancer in 1978. He is buried with Clara at Ft. Bliss National Cemetery in El Paso, Texas.

---

[3] Earlier called the Coroner's Office.

Fritz in the desert. Probably lemonade in the liquor bottle. The Bornsteins recycled.

Fritz's gravestone Ft. Bliss Texas.

Fritz & cigar.

Fritz preferred bolo
ties to bow ties.

Council Honors Medical Examiner

El Paso Times, 1977 or 1978.

The El Paso City Council honored El Paso County's medical examiner, Dr. Frederick P. Bornstein, with a certificate of appreciation during a meeting in council chambers Thursday morning.

"The certificate was given in recognition of the distinguished work he has done on the examination of rape cases for so many years," Alderwoman Polly Harris said.

Bornstein, 67, was commended for 25 years of service, three of which have been spent as medical examiner.

"The doctor has been very sympathetic toward trying to get better consideration for victims of rape cases," Mrs. Harris said. "So many times, people try to take a very prosecuting point of view, and he has made great strides toward humanizing the situation and fighting against rapes."

FREDERICK BORNSTEIN

The certificate cited Bornstein's "long years of dedicated service marked by rare professionalism that has gained him such recognition as an award from the Alliance Against Rapes in April, 1977."

It said: "Dr. Bornstein is to be commended for having been a part of a program for handling of rapes that was the first one for a major community in the United States when it began in 1952."

El Paso Times, Fritz the Medical Examiner, 1970s.

Centuries-Old Duty Of Medical Examiner: Learning Why

By GREGORY JONES

Just about every evening Dr. Frederick Bornstein sits down before the television and watches the 5:30 p.m. network news. He doesn't mind all the other times the phone rings, it's just that he doesn't like to miss the news.

But, as El Paso County medical examiner, he has had to learn to live with the telephone ringing at odd hours, whether the calls are from the police or local press.

He seems always ready to assist, however, and explain in layman's terms the technicalities of the special training required for his special work. As medical examiner, he is charged with a centuries-old duty of inquiring into a death that appears to be due to unnatural causes.

The office of coroner originated in England during medieval times of the 13th Century.

Today, in the United States, the coroner (medical examiner) is the only person who can definitely give the cause of death. The job is important. Without the office, it is often difficult to establish material evidence of a crime.

"Do we, or do we not do an autopsy?" he says, as he begins a description of his duties. That is the question to be answered first, after one of the office's three medical investigators decides a post-mortem might be necessary.

"There probably aren't any two jurisdictions in the United States with the same post-mortem policies, either," he says. "An example, is that San Francisco performs post-mortems on all its cases, but that takes a tremendous staff size and I think results in a lack of detail in the long run."

Bornstein, 66, whose parents and one grandparent were medical doctors, has performed by his own estimate about 12,000 autopsies, many of them in El Paso where he has been practicing for 25 years.

Of all the cases that he receives concerning deaths, he says, about 30 to 40 per cent of that number requires an autopsy. During 1975, he performed 635 autopsies on persons who died of natural causes, accidental deaths, suicides and homicides.

As an example of how the medical examiner fits into the system, Bornstein, in his strong German accent, describes the following scenario . . .

Someone calls the police or sheriff's department that a body has been found. Detectives are dispatched to the scene. The sheriff's dispatcher phones the medical examiner's office and reports to the medical investigators. The three investigators — Al Mestan, Manuel Diaz, and James Kingwell — are available or on call during their respective eight-hour shifts.

The investigator goes to the location of the body. He and city or county detectives check the body and surroundings. If things look suspicious, or obvious, the investigator calls Bornstein and reports.

Bornstein then directs the body to the morgue at R. E. Thomason General Hospital for a post-mortem, or to a local funeral home for embalming.

If an autopsy is performed, a copy of the findings goes to the district attorney's office. A second copy is kept at the examiner's office.

"Take the case of a man in his early 30s," Bornstein says, "who one day just falls over and dies. This is unusual, although not impossible, for a man in his late 30s."

Bornstein says he later found out the man's medical records showed him to have been in good health and a physical he took before leaving the Armed Services showed him free of any obvious disease.

"Then suddenly he collapses, and is dead upon arrival at the hospital."

Since the man was from out-of-town, Bornstein had no idea of the dead man's medical history.

"The next thing we did was open up the body, beginning with the V-shaped incision," he says.

"You can tell a lot just from looking," he adds.

"In this man's case, the only unusual finding was in the heart. What was there?" he asks. "We found extremely bad coronary arteries.

Stone hard. And blocked with calcific masses, none of which happens overnight.

A blood clot, "which only added insult to injury, probably was fatal to the heart."

Signed and sealed, Bornstein's final conclusion and opinion on the man's death would prove important to the man's widow.

"About two weeks later I got a letter from his widow who needed death certificates for mortgage payments. She also needed some information for widow's benefits."

The problem, Bornstein says, had been that the man's medical examination for the year or two

preceeding his death showed nothing wrong. By this time, the Veterans Administration had entered the picture, and requested a copy of Bornstein's report.

As Bornstein explained it, coronary disease is slow.

Bornstein says the case was closed in a few months, and ruled a routine death.

"The post-mortem turned out to be of great importance to the family and survivors."

When asked if his lifetime as a pathologist, where the dead are almost as much a part of life as the living, has caused him any philosophical changes, the native of

Hamburg, Germany, says "It hasn't really affected me that way."

Exhibiting the detachment common to persons who dedicate their lives to science, Bornstein adds, "What we're really dealing with is matter. You're only dealing with matter in this world."

Something that interests Bornstein is the natural life span for human beings.

"At the present time," he says, taking a long drag on his cigar, "we do not know what the life span of humans would be under the totally ideal condition. We do not know up to what point the length of life is

determined by genetic or extraneous factors."

"Practically every animal species has a fairly well-defined age limit. Rodents about 4 years, dogs and cats about 10 to 12, horses about 20, parrots and tortoises a couple hundred.

"Has man reached his natural life span? Who knows?"

When asked his plans for his own future, Bornstein says he'll continue in medicine until age itself restricts his abilities.

"I'm going to have my turn too, you know. But I'm in good health now. I had a heart attack eight or nine years ago, but I've had no problems since."

Has Man Reached His Natural Life Span? Who Knows?

You're Only Dealing With Matter

DR. FRED BORNSTEIN, EL PASO COUNTY MEDICAL EXAMINER
Considering Questions Of His Philosophy Of Life And Death

PHILIPP EMANUEL BORNSTEIN (1941–2006)

In May 1962 my twin brother Philipp graduated from UTEP and started medical school at Washington University in St. Louis where he would specialize in psychiatry. After he completed medical school, an internship at Strong Memorial Hospital in Rochester, N.Y., and a residency at Barnes Hospital in St. Louis,[4] Philipp served in the U.S. Army (1970–1973). His final assignment was as the stockade psychiatrist at Ft. Hood, Texas. Philipp practiced in Springfield, Illinois at the Vine Street Clinic. He was one of the first board-certified geriatric psychiatrists in the U.S. He worked with a group of Washington University trained psychiatrists at Springfield's Vine Street Clinic until his death in 2006. Like our brother Fred, he died from colon cancer.

Over the years, Philipp and I grew closer and closer. As children we often conflicted. He was always there for me when I needed to talk over a problem. His advice was always simple and solid. We enjoyed many trips together, especially while he was ill. Our last trip together was my first cruise—to celebrate our 65th birthday. We enjoyed the Caribbean but mainly just each other's company.

Philipp was an enthusiastic world traveler. He visited Nepal and Bhutan[5] several times on trekking expeditions and even traveled to South Africa after his colon cancer was diagnosed in 2001. He was a resilient and mentally focused patient, willing to undergo aggressive treatments in order to prolong his life. Philipp died at home on August 10, 2006 and is buried at Camp Butler National Cemetery outside Springfield, Illinois. Philipp married Barbara Bayer in 1968. Barbara and Philipp divorced in 1991. Philipp did not remarry. They had two children: Andrea and Eric. Andrea now lives in San Francisco and has a daughter named Alexandra. Eric lives in Springfield, Illinois.

---

[4] Philipp's professors at Barnes Hospital in St. Louis were among the early promoters of biological psychiatry rather than (as Philipp would put it) blah-blah psychiatry. In the next decade this would become the leading trend in the treatment of mental illness.

[5] Perhaps influenced by the UTEP campus being filled with Bhutanese architecture.

Philipp's gravestone Camp Butler National Cemetery Springfield, Illinois.

Philipp in 1946.

Philipp and son Eric.

TELEPHONE (217) 528-8425

PHILIPP E. BORNSTEIN, M.D.
PRACTICE LIMITED TO PSYCHIATRY

OFFICE HOURS
BY APPOINTMENT

VINE STREET CLINIC
(AT SIXTH AND MADISON)
301 NORTH SIXTH, SUITE 220
SPRINGFIELD, ILLINOIS 62701

Philipp 1970/80s.

Andrea Bornstein Bayer and daughter Alexandra.

OLGA BORNSTEIN WISE (b. 1941)

I enrolled at Washington University in St. Louis for the fall semester of 1958. I was not especially well-prepared at El Paso High School for serious study, but I persisted and in January 1962 I graduated as a German and Spanish major. In March 1962 I made my first of many trips to Europe. When I returned in August that year, I entered Washington University's graduate program in German. Philipp and I were in St. Louis together during his first couple of years of medical school. We made many long non-stop drives together between St. Louis and El Paso in his Ford Falcon.

After receiving my MA, I worked as an instructor of German. At that time a master's degree was a sufficient credential to teach at a college.[6] I married David Wise in June 1970 while he was a student and I taught at Western Illinois University. When David graduated in 1971, I changed careers by enrolling in the Graduate School of Library Science at the University of Illinois in Urbana. David also studied in Urbana in the graduate program in Spanish, where he completed his Ph.D. in Summer 1978. I completed my MLS in Summer 1972 and worked for the next 30 years as a professional librarian and information specialist, mostly in the computer industry. David taught for four years at Texas Woman's University. He too changed careers by enrolling in law school at SMU in 1983, graduating in 1986. Our only child Jacob was born on February 14, 1977 in Urbana, Illinois. We have been living in Austin, Texas since July, 1987. Jacob also lives in Austin with his wife, Claudette Murphree.

---

[6] I had positions at Rockford College, the University of Kentucky, and Western Illinois University.

Clara holds granddaughter Margaret Bornstein; Olga holds
son Jacob Wise, Summer 1977.

Olga and David married on June
12, 1970 in Macomb, Illinois.
From left to right: Fred and son
Aaron Landon, Fritz, Adele Wise,
Oakley Wise, Dorothy Bornstein,
Bob Wise, Clara Bornstein,
Philipp Bornstein, Mary Beth
Wise, Olga Wise, David Wise.
(Aaron was in Vietnam.)

New Families, New Stories: 1958–2021

Jacob Wise and Claudette Murphree celebrate their wedding, 2018.

Olga swimming in January 2021.

Olga and David with Jacob and Claudette
on Olga's 80th birthday, 2021.

New Families, New Stories: 1958–2021

FREDERICK BERNARD BORNSTEIN (1943–1989)

After Fred graduated from El Paso High School, he attended the University of New Mexico in Albuquerque and was a theater major. During his time at UNM he was a cheerleader for the UNM athletic team, leading Fritz, in full European mode, to ask: "What are cheerleaders for?"[7] After college, he was deployed to Vietnam as a platoon commander in the Signal Corps. When he returned to the U.S. in 1969, he enrolled at the University of Colorado and obtained a master's degree in Communications. He taught Radio and Television at Grossmont Junior College in San Diego. Later he was employed by the San Diego CBS station KFMB and then by the national CBS station in Los Angeles.

Fred married Dorothy Gillespie in 1965. They had one son, Aaron Landon (born 1968). Fred later married Diane LeRoy who survives him. They had two children: Tyler and Lara. Lara and her husband Lance Healy have two daughters, Taylor and Hayden, and live south of Los Angeles. Tyler lives with his wife Jelena Jokiç in Vienna, Austria where Tyler works as an architect. They married in May 2021 and welcomed their son, Elio Frederick Bornstein, born in Vienna on June 22, 2021.

Fred was diagnosed with colon cancer in 1983 and passed away in January 1989. During his illness he and Clara spoke daily;[8] after she passed away, I spoke with him almost every day. He was a determined and courageous patient. Fred is buried at Rosecrans National Cemetery in San Diego, California.

Fred became a Methodist during his illness, which explains why his gravestone bears a cross rather than the Star of David. It is difficult to write about Fred without using superlatives. He was a terrific stage actor, the person who would light up a room with his outgoing personality, an instant lifelong friend to many, and a brother who left us way too soon and whom we still miss terribly.

---

[7] How would you answer his question?
[8] Back then there was a charge for each landline long distance phone call. No unlimited calling. No cell phones.

Fred U.S. Army officer, around 1967.

Fred U.S. Army around 1968.

Fred, 1955.

BORNSTEIN HONORED AT CBS GALA

FIRST EDITION
JULY 14, 1989

COMPUTER PRESS
SPRINGFIELD, ILLINOIS

PENGUINS STRUT!

by Philipp E. Bornstein, travelling correspondent

It was difficult to see clearly in the spotlights which outlined the massive crowd in colorful shadows. Elaborate evening dress hung fashionably from local and national celebrities as they swished into Thursday's especial festivies thrown by CBS executives to celebrate the birthday of National Sales Executive Frederick B. Bornstein.

Invitations and Tickets were in sharply increased demand, as CBS staffers vied for the opportunity to join the higher echelons at this unusual affair.

First hand reports leaked by enthusiastic staffers inidicated that the initial plan to celebrate the up and coming French Bicentennial had been scrapped in a last minute planning session by the CBS executive committee when news of Bornstein's 46th. birthday mysteriously appeared on the desks of a number of interested associates of the well-known Bornstein.

Shaking his head in utter amazement, Fred (as he is known to his co-workers and well-wishers) responded in his usual enthusiatic manner by smiling and making familiar, lewd hand and body gestures.

Well known Hollywood and network celebrities were seen competing with one another for attention of the guest of honor.

The high point of the gala evening was the presentation of a check for an as yet unnamed amount.

In his customary bold manner, Bornstein, held the check high for all to see, and yelled "pour down the champgane and bundle up the lox, ---CBS should be putting its money where it really belongs...in my pocket!.

Red-faced personnel officers indicated that the enthusiastic response of high echelon executives to this well known staffer boded well for up and coming contract negotiations with Bornstein.

Also attending the party were numerous family and friends from around the United States.

Special guest from Florida, Captain Cady (US ARMY ret.) indicated that he was not surprised to see such enthusiasm about his former Lieutenant and Bronze Star Medal winner. "I knew that f...g s.o.b. when he wss nothing! "   P.E.B..

Joke birthday card from Philipp to his brother Fred for his last birthday. Fred honored at CBS gala, article by brother Philipp, 1989.

Fred sailing—one of his favorite activities.

Fred's gravestone with his granddaughter, Hayden Marie Healey.

New Families, New Stories: 1958–2021

Aaron Landon Bornstein with
niece Taylor Healey.

Lara and Lance Healy with their
daughters Taylor and Hayden.

Tyler Bornstein and Jelena Jokiç on their wedding day, May 2021, Austria.

Tyler Bornstein, his step-dad Paul Sanders, and mother Diane Sanders.

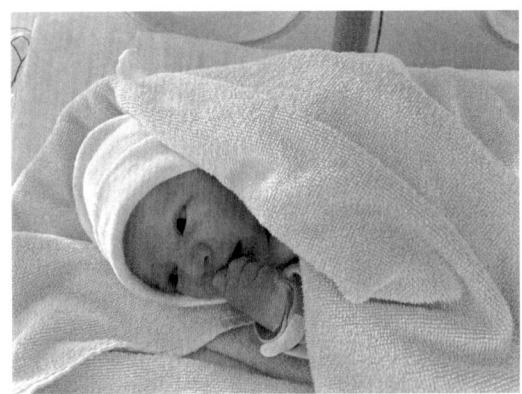

Elio Frederick Bornstein, son of Jelena Jokiç and Tyler Bornstein, on the day of his birth, 2021.

AARON CLAIRE BORNSTEIN (b. 1946)

Aaron graduated from UTEP with a major in geology in 1969. After serving in the Navy in Vietnam, he returned to UTEP and earned his MS in Zoology/Parasitology in 1974. He attended medical school at the University of Texas, San Antonio, graduating in 1981.

Aaron married his first wife, Natalie Tolbert in 1974. She also became a physician. Their daughter Margaret was born Dec. 31, 1976. Margaret lives with her husband Leslie Saulsby and their two sons Lucas and Levi in Glendale, Arizona.

Aaron married Jane Loranger in 1989. They have two daughters: Erin (b. 1991) and Rosemary (b. 1994). For many years Aaron was an avid skier and flew his own airplane with gusto. He served in the Arizona Air National Guard and was twice deployed overseas, to Uzbekistan and to the Green Zone in Baghdad, Iraq. Aaron retired from the practice of family medicine in Show Low, Arizona at the age of 73. Like his siblings, he loves travel and the outdoors.

Aaron in Vietnam.

Aaron, 1954

Aaron, 1970s.

Aaron, late 1970s.

Margaret Bornstein Saulsby with family. From left: Son Lucas, Margaret, husband Leslie, and son Levi.

Aaron Bornstein and family: Daughters Rosemary and Erin, wife Jane, and Aaron.

New Families, New Stories: 1958–2021

Olga and David marry

Philipp in medical school, Olga granted MA, Fred as cheerleader, Aaron on the phone.

Aaron in Vietnam

CLARA BORNSTEIN'S BLOCK PRINTS

EACH CHAPTER OF THIS BOOK begins with a block print by my mother, Clara Bornstein. When possible, the print corresponds to the time and place covered by that chapter. Additional block prints appear at the end of several chapters, in Additional Materials.

We can't say for sure how our mother became interested in the woodblock print art form. Fortunately for us, she honed her craft for the family holiday greeting card. Clara carved her designs into linoleum mounted on blocks of wood. Every year, the block print depicted a unique image of our family's current experience in the United States. For example, the living room of our new house, a map of southern Illinois (with pyramids for little Egypt), or a desert agave plant from El Paso.

Clara created her earliest blocks in the late 1930s and printed the images on pieces of toilet paper. The print was glued on a small, folded piece of construction paper. Clara made her "Best wishes" and "Season's Greetings" cards as a way to stay in touch with family and friends who, lucky to get out of Germany, were scattered far and wide in Chile, New Zealand, England, and so on. Clara made the cards herself to save the cost of purchasing commercial holiday greeting cards. As the years rolled on, the cards became a seasonal tradition eagerly awaited by friends. Clara ceased making cards after Fritz's death in 1978.

Woodblock or block printing has a long tradition in Japan, Korea, and Europe. The form became popular in the 1920s in Germany perhaps thanks to a renewed interest in Japanese artwork and the Arts and Crafts movement, which valued handcrafted decorative design over industrialized products. The woodcut craft requires only a plank of wood, a few gouges and cutting tools, ink, and paper. The use of linoleum adds ease to the process.

FURTHER READING

Bonner, Thomas N. "Pioneering in Women's Medical Education in the Swiss Universities 1864–1914." Gesnerus (Swiss Journal of the History of Medicine and Science) Vol. 45 (1988), pp. 461–74. Fascinating study in history of medical education: explores the role of Swiss medical schools in training European women as physicians.

Efron, John M. *Medicine and the German Jews: A History.* New Haven, CT: Yale University Press, 2001. What attracted Jews to medicine in pre-1933 Germany? Why did they specialize? Chapter 7 (pp. 234–64) covers Jewish doctors in the Empire and the Weimar Republic and provides some answers. Defect: not much statistical information.

Elon, Amos. *The Pity of it All: A Portrait of the German Jewish Epoch, 1743–1933.* New York: Picador, 2002. Despite its title, this book is not weepy. A classic study of the Jews in Germany over two centuries, it does not neglect the Jews of Germany's countryside and small towns for those of its big cities. (Available from Amazon and other vendors.)

Faesecke, Karl-Peter. *Arbeit im Überdruck: Die medizinischen Forschungsarbeiten von Arthur und Adele Bornstein beim Bau des ersten Hamburger Elbtunnels 1909–1910.* (Working Under High Pressure: The Medical Research of Arthur and Adele Bornstein during Construction of the first Hamburg Elbe Tunnel 1909–1910.) Ph.D. diss. Univ. Hamburg 1997. Definitive medical-historical study of bariatric research done by Arthur and Adele Bornstein during massive tunnel project under the Elbe River. German only.

Kaplan, Marion, ed. *Jewish Daily Life in Germany 1618–1945.* New York: Oxford University Press, 2005. Solid scholarly work by four authors, based on letters, memoirs and other original documents. See especially Part III, Kaplan's "As Germans and Jews in Imperial Germany" (pp. 173–252).

Kaplan, Marion. *The Making of the Jewish Middle Class: Women, Family and Identity in Imperial Germany.* New York: Oxford University Press, 1991. The best history of German-Jewish women, families, and households during the Kaiserzeit (1871–1914). Meticulously researched and readable. Covers domestic life, marriage strategies, education, women's associations and organizations, early feminism. Recommended: Chapter 1, "Cultivating Respectability: A Family Enterprise" (pp. 25–63).

Stern, Fritz. *Einstein's German World.* Princeton, NJ: Princeton University Press, 1999. Essays by academic historian on Jewish-German figures and themes in the 20th Century. Chapters 1–3 cover four giant figures in research and science (Einstein, Ehrlich, Haber, Planck). All males. Reader alert: if you picked up this book hoping to learn about notable Jewish-German women, you can put it back down. You won't find anything here.

Wise, Olga B. and David O., eds. *A Jewish Girlhood in Berlin, 1859–1879: A Memoir* by Jenny Barth Bornstein. Lulu Press, 2010. A lively memoir of childhood and adolescence by Jenny Barth Bornstein, who became one of Germany's earliest women physicians. Valuable introduction and epilogue. (Available from Lulu Press and Amazon.)

—» «—

ACKNOWLEDGEMENTS

My deepest gratitude goes to my mother, Clara Bornstein and my great-grandmother, Jenny Barth Bornstein. These two women saved a wealth of family documents, photographs, stories, and other materials. Thanks to them, we have much of the information that forms the basis of this family history.

My profound thanks to:

My husband David who said: "Finish this history already. You've been at it for over ten years! Put it to bed." Great advice. His editorial efforts were exceptional.

My "outside project manager" Betsy Pfeil didn't let my manuscript go astray and was a fantastic shepherd of the entire publication process. I thank my graphic artist, Sara Rubinett, for her excellent design.

My friends and family who didn't tell me to shut up when I went on and on about this project.

My dear departed friends Alix Magnus for her transcription of Emmy's baby diary and Uli Ness who navigated the German bureaucracy for me so I could find original birth and death certificates for family members.

Dr. Karl-Peter Faesecke and Dr. Anna von Villiez for providing me with official documents from Hamburg.

And you, dear readers, for reading what I wrote and David improved.

—»«—

A NOTE TO FUTURE FAMILY HISTORIANS

Have (paper) prints made of all documents you want to preserve. Use high-quality paper so the prints will last. Do not trash original documents or the prints you make of them. Be judicious in making and keeping electronic records, because 100, 50 or even 20 years later there may be no device or technology that can retrieve electronic records you create now. In the case of photographs, identify the people shown, the place and the year the photograph was taken, and if possible, the occasion at or for which the photograph was made. If you preserve letters and postcards, be aware that envelopes, return addresses, stamps and postmarks convey important information. Do not keep a letter and discard its envelope.

I also hope that the Bornstein-Löwenstein "archive" I have organized will remain intact and be donated at a proper time to the Leo Baeck Institute for the Study of German-Jewish History and Culture in New York City.

ABOUT THE AUTHOR

Olga Wise combined her German language skills (BA 1962, MA 1964, Washington University) and research and information skills (MLS 1972, University of Illinois) to create this history of her Bornstein family. She and her husband David also translated her great-grandmother's memoir from handwritten German. The memoir *A Jewish Girlhood in Berlin: 1859–1879*, was published in 2010 and is available from amazon.com.

Back cover: Bornstein siblings: Olga, Aaron, Fred, Philipp, 1952. Photo by Bernard Asher.